Sunderland afc
CULT HEROES

Sunderland afc
CULT HEROES

ROB MASON

breedon **books**
PUBLISHING

First published in Great Britain in 2008 by
The Breedon Books Publishing Company Limited
Breedon House, 3 The Parker Centre
Derby, DE21 4SZ

Dedication

To Ian and Philip Mason:
two of Sunderland's most ardent supporters.

ISBN: 978-1-85983-650-7

Printed and bound by TJ International Ltd, Padstow, Cornwall.

CONTENTS

ACKNOWLEDGEMENTS

Thanks to Jim Jeffrey for researching Dick Malone's career in Scottish football, Spencer Vignes for permission to use two quotes and photographs from his excellent book on L.R. Roose, Jeremy Robinson for being a sounding board for the book, Mike Gibson for help with checking facts, Barry Emmerson for the use of his front room to interview the one and only Vic Halom, Tania Henzel for transcribing, Barbara Mason for transcribing and assistance with picture research and to Paul Briggs of Twocan Design for assistance with photographs.

Thanks also to staunch Sunderland supporters: Tom Lynn, Mike Love, Keith Chapman, Andrew Smithson, Ken Hall, Doris Turner, Barbara Cromar, Wayne Talbot and Dave Smith for their stories about Sunderland's cult heroes, and of course to all of the players interviewed in this collection.

INTRODUCTION

It must have been my apprenticeship as a Sunderland supporter – 16 years as a Roker Ender from 1967–1983 when I migrated into the Main Stand paddock because that was a bit of the ground you could buy a standing season ticket for – that I learned that Sunderland supporters always seem to have a cult hero. Such a figure often is not the best player in the team, but once he has got the crowd on his side he can do no wrong.

Staff at the Stadium of Light used to joke that Julio Arca would always win the Man of the Match vote – even if he was not playing – while John Kay says that his popularity reached such a point that it 'got to the stage where the lads used to want to run out beside me because I was the only one getting a cheer.'

There is a counter-balance to the cult hero, and that is the scapegoat, the player who, no matter how hard he tries or how well he does, there will be some who just never rate the guy. Take former England international right-back Steve Whitworth for instance, ever present in the 1980 promotion team but a dead loss in many of the fans' eyes. More recently, Kevin Kilbane just could not get the crowd on his side. As nice a guy as you could wish to meet and popular with managers and teammates, Kevin just could not win the fans over. Gareth Hall, Rod Belfitt, Brett Angell, Steve Berry, Steve Doyle and Shaun Cunnington are just the tip of the iceberg of players who, for one reason or another, the crowd at Sunderland as a whole never took to. Like Kilbane, some of those lads lacked nothing in terms of character and commitment, but you will not find them featuring in anyone's list of favourites.

Cult Heroes, however, deals with a selection of some of the most popular players to entertain the red-and-white army. This collection of stories seeks to explore why they were popular and what they have in common. With one exception, all of the players featured have played for the Lads from the 1970s onwards, right up the present day, so many readers will recall some of the tales they have to tell, be it Vic Halom torturing some poor centre-half more used to dishing out stick than receiving it, Barry Siddall insisting he was not fat, despite one of his unfortunate nicknames, or Julio Arca explaining why it was always his destiny to play for Sunderland and why he could never celebrate scoring against the Lads.

As much as you will hopefully enjoy reading these stories, it has been a pleasure to sit down with the players and set them off reminiscing. Vic Halom is fantastic company. Strongly opinionated and as direct as he was as a player, Vic has lost none of the comic aspect of his character that so endeared him to the public. Listening to the stories of his family before they came to England, though, was an education.

Joe Bolton was never one for interviews, preferring to stay in the background and just do his job, but over a pint in Birtley he was as entertaining as Vic, and that is no mean achievement. Dick Malone leads a busy life in business and through his role with the Sunderland Former Players' Association, but he found the time to spend an afternoon chatting about how his upbringing shaped him and how he was close to chinning the referee in the Cup Final of 1973.

Goalkeeper Barry Siddall is now a Lancashire postman, with full-back Chris Makin now living not far away from 'Seedaaalll' in Manchester. Both were more than happy to explain why, of all the clubs they played for, Sunderland and their relationship with Sunderland supporters was so special.

Cult hero of the late 1980s and early 1990s John Kay was always one of the jokers in the dressing room but now has a serious line of work, assisting people trying to cope with having taken drugs. We met in Chester-le-Street civic centre, and Kaysie was as down-to-earth as the forwards he used to tackle.

You would struggle to find two players as different in style as John Kay and Kevin Arnott, the gifted and creative 1970s midfielder. Like Kaysie, Kevin has some serious work commitments nowadays, and like Joe Bolton he is not normally given to doing interviews, but again he found the time to recollect his days as a cult hero for the red and whites.

Nyron 'Nugsy' Nosworthy did not have to delve deep into his memory bank as he brings the story of Sunderland's cult heroes right up to date, having been Player of the Year in 2007 and a key part of Sunderland staying up in Roy Keane's opening season as a top-flight manager. The one player featured who no one reading this book will have seen play is L.R. Roose, a goalkeeper who was killed in World War One but who shows that cult heroes have been part and parcel of Wearside footballing folklore for a century or more.

About the Author

Rob Mason works full-time at Sunderland AFC. He is the editor of the club's match programme *Red and White*, official club magazine *Legion of Light* and junior supporters' magazine *24–7*. This is his 12th book on the club, and previous titles include *Sunderland: The Complete Record* (with Mike Gibson and Barry Jackson), *Match of My Life*, *The Sunderland Story*, *Sunderland's Number Ones* and *The DVD Book of Sunderland*.

Now in his fifth decade of attending matches, he assures readers that he definitely did not see L.R. Roose play.

FOREWORD

by Niall Quinn, chairman of Sunderland AFC

You need to be a special kind of player to do well at Sunderland. You might play for 10 clubs in your career, but when you come to this club you quickly realise that things are different. Football isn't a part of life to Sunderland supporters, it is integral to everything they do. Work, weddings and holidays are arranged according to the fixture list, and everyone has an opinion on everything that moves at the club.

I got booed when I came on as a sub against Nottingham Forest over a year after I'd come to the club. At that point I'd barely played because of injury problems, we'd been relegated since my arrival and I had a lot to prove to Sunderland supporters. When that happens to a player there are two ways of responding, you can either blame everyone else and feel sorry for yourself or you can get stuck in and win people over. When you do get people on your side the feeling you get is one of elation. Not long after, I chipped the 'keeper to score one of the best goals I ever managed, and that seemed to seal my relationship with the crowd. Knowing I'd had to win people over had taken me out of the comfort zone, and I became a far better player for coming through the experience.

I was learning, and I kept learning. Sunderland supporters will let you know if they don't think you're up to the job. I also came to realise that if they do think you're up to the job they'll be just as quick to tell you, and you'll know it is a genuine compliment. Once you have the crowd on your side at Sunderland, they can make you feel you are a better player. If you understand that when you pull a Sunderland shirt on you're climbing under the skin of the people who are the lifeblood of the club, you start to realise that the connection between players and supporters at Sunderland can be enormously powerful.

The players featured in this book of Sunderland cult heroes all had that understanding. I played with a couple of them, I've seen others and I've heard plenty of tales of all of them. What they have in common is they all developed a deep affinity with the club and the supporters. Reading the stories in this book, you'll see that time after time these players have had a different – deeper – rapport with the red-and-white army than any other set of fans they've played for. What's more, you'll realise that it's not simply a case of players being hero worshipped by supporters, but that these players thought just as much of the people who backed them.

I know how immense the power of the crowd can be at Sunderland. It's why I'm so proud to be chairman of the club. I hope that in reading the stories of these players you'll see the lifetime connection there is between everyone who has Sunderland at heart.

SO WHAT IS A CULT HERO?

Every player featured in this book is a Sunderland cult hero. There is something special about a player considered a cult hero. To be afforded the description, a player has to have endeared himself to the crowd in more than one way. Simply to be a great player does not make a player a cult hero, neither does fantastic commitment earn the accolade if there is not much else to go with it. Cult heroes possess a combination of attributes.

None of our cult heroes showed anything other than 100 per cent commitment in a Sunderland shirt, so clearly that is an essential factor in becoming a cult hero. However, commitment alone does not bring such cult-hero status – Jeff Whitley and Kelvin Davis are just two examples of players whose commitment could never be faulted, but the crowd never took to them. Whitley was effort personified, and he did not lack bottle, as his failed penalty shoot-out attempt against Crystal Palace in 2004 illustrated, while goalkeeper Davis endured a torrid time, having been one of Sunderland's major signings following promotion in 2005. Davis was arguably the poorest goalkeeper Sunderland have had in half a century. 'What's it like to see a save?' the crowd chanted at him as Darren Ward saved well at the other end when Davis returned to the Stadium of Light with Southampton in 2006. However, credit where it is due, Davis never once shirked his responsibilities, was always available for selection, never invented or exaggerated an injury to take him out of the firing line and was one of a highly select group of goalkeepers who played 30 or more games and never conceded more than four in a match. Cult hero though? No chance, the fans did not rate him and did not like him, attributing many a goal to his mistakes. So commitment is a prerequisite of being a cult hero, but in no way does it alone give a player such status.

What about sheer talent? Of course supporters want to see players with ability. Good money is not paid in the hope of watching 'nuggets', although the loyalty of Sunderland fans is such that many have stayed with them over the years when the necessary ability to be successful was painfully but undeniably missing. Sunderland, though, is the club for which the expression 'The Team of All the Talents' was first spawned. Sunderland supporters appreciate skill and ability as much as any fans in the world. Players blessed with such gifts can be vital, but Jim Baxter in the 1960s had talent in abundance but not much else. When he was on song he was admired by the fans and indeed his teammates, but loved as a hero by fans en masse? Definitely not.

Sunderland have had no finer post-war goalscorer than Kevin Phillips. After beating Brian Clough's post-war seasonal goals tally, 'SuperKev' went on to become the only Englishman to win the European Golden Shoe for being the continent's top scorer. A fantastic 30 goals in 36 Premiership appearances earned Phillips that award, and the fans obviously loved seeing the net bulge time after time when Phillips got the ball. He was brilliant and never anything but hugely popular with the fans, but loved? Did he have that special relationship with the crowd that the cult heroes featured in this book have? Football is a game of opinions, and yours might be different, but *Sunderland Cult Heroes* argues that, while SuperKev was a 'superhero', he was not a 'cult hero'. Indeed, the man playing alongside Phillips in his best years, Niall Quinn, could lay more claim to that title. Certainly, Chris Makin from the same 105-point side of 1999 does fit the bill and is included here.

What all of the cult heroes featured in this book have in common is that they were all lovable. The crowd adored them. They all possessed unstinting commitment, and they all possessed a fair degree of skill…but, crucially, in some cases that ability revealed itself in unorthodox fashion. Take Dick Malone and Nyron Nosworthy for example. Both were right-backs until Nyron's successful conversion to centre-back. It is noticeable that a high percentage of cult heroes are full-backs.

Malone and Nosworthy are the quintessential Sunderland cult heroes. At first glance, neither are great players. Both could look awkward and unorthodox. Sometimes people would watch them and think, 'What on earth are they doing or trying to do?' Either of them in possession could worry even optimists that something was about to go horribly wrong, because they often would not look to have the ball or the situation under control.

Looks, however, can be deceiving. Bob Lee, when he arrived in 1976 as a club record signing, had the physique and appearance of a superstar in the making; he was not. Tore Andre Flo, another club record signing in 2002 looked like an experienced and talented striker who would score the goals that would help make Sunderland great again; he did not, and Brazilian World Cup star Ronaldo is not the only person to have been taken in by an apparently beautiful woman who turned out not even to be a woman at all!

In the cases of Malone and Nosworthy, Sunderland unearthed two people who have the respect, admiration, gratitude and enduring love of Sunderland supporters. Sunderland is a city built on solid foundations. Once the biggest ship-building port in the world, the club's badge for many years featured a ship typical of dozens built and launched on the Wear. The club's present ground, the Stadium of Light, stands on the site of what was once the biggest pit in the Durham coalfield, and the miners' wheel outside the stadium and on the club's modern badge pays tribute to that. Sunderland is a city where you are expected to earn your keep, do your bit and come up with the goods.

Dick Malone, a 1973 FA Cup winner, serves as an example of someone who earned respect. Unlike Nosworthy, the crowd did not take to the Scottish signing straight away. Injured on his debut, Malone did not get off to an auspicious start. He came into a struggling side at a time when crowds were low and spirits even lower. He explains in his chapter in this book that when he first played for Sunderland he would be looking to play short passes and attractive football only to discover his teammates were running away from him, expecting him to do what the crowd demanded and hoof it, 'Get the ball up the pitch Malone' he remembers the crowd advising him. A tall, seemingly uncoordinated player, Malone would attempt to dribble down the right flank, sometimes seeming to head up more cul-de-sacs and dead-ends than even Washington New Town has to offer.

Dick descended on Wearside in 1970, the year of decimalisation, and eventually the penny began to drop with people that although this lad at right-back might look like he was always going to lose the ball he would invariably still have it. He could play, and he was trying his heart out to play the sort of football Sunderland at times looked as if they had forgotten how to. His day would come of course at Wembley when – in the days when teams could substitute just one player – the man who pundits had predicted would win the game for Leeds by getting the better of Malone was taken off.

In his early days at Sunderland, Nosworthy bore certain similarities to Malone, operating in the same position and looking equally gangly and unorthodox, yet the crowd immediately took him under their collective wing as if to protect and nurture him. Here was a player who at first looked completely out of his depth. Supporters had been looking for the club to prepare for their return to the top flight, two years after an ignominious relegation with a record low number of points, by signing proven players. Here was a debutant signed on a free transfer from a club relegated from the division Sunderland had just won. Introduced as substitute, Nosworthy's his first touch was not a touch at all, a simple pass to him being allowed to roll under his foot and out of play. It was a start that confirmed the worst fears of those who had been underwhelmed by his acquisition.

Here, though, was a lad from the other end of the country, plucked from a small club into an arena where 40,000 crowds are not even unusual if the team are bottom of the League. It was as if the crowd collectively thought 'This lad needs all the help he can get.' Seconds later, faced with a tricky situation, Nosworthy extricated himself deftly with a self-assuredness that had people thinking 'Did he really do that?' closely followed by 'Did he mean it?' Immediately a new cult hero was born.

For the rest of his time at right-back Nosworthy remained a player capable of moments of magic and madness. Built like a brick out-house, he showed he had stacks of strength. He could shift as well. Speed merchants met their match in Nyron, who could glide through the gears, but once he had the ball no one was ever quite sure if they were about to see an *A Question of Sport* style 'What Happened Next?' contender.

While not everyone's cup of tea because of this, Nyron nonetheless had significant parts of the crowd behind him, not least the most vocal areas of the ground. Roy Keane's transformation of him into a central-defender, where those ball-winning attributes came to the fore while the potentially ball-losing times in possession were minimised, proved to be a master stroke, while the longer Londoner Nosworthy has been at the club the more the fans have sensed how much Sunderland means to him, and thus his cult hero status is ever more cemented.

There is a difference then between a cult hero and a hero. This book does not include some players who were undoubtedly crowd favourites and great players. Kevin Phillips is a good recent example. This can become an exceptionally cloudy grey area. No doubt many would name people such as Kevin Ball and Niall Quinn as players who should be included in this book. Both Ball and Quinn are right up there in the highest bracket of Sunderland heroes. They were great players, are great blokes and have great relationships with the crowd built over many years service as dedicated players and latterly off the pitch as well. Whether either can be classed as cult heroes, though, is a matter of debate.

Perhaps Jimmy Montgomery, Len Shackleton, Len Ashurst, Gary Bennett or Gary Rowell, to name a further quintet, are people who should have been featured in this collection of Sunderland cult heroes. This is not a book of the greatest players or biggest crowd favourites. It is an attempt to focus on some of those players whose greatness was not always as obvious as that of some of those just mentioned. Messrs Quinn, Ball, Montgomery, Ashurst, Bennett and Rowell are included in a previous book by Rob Mason, *Sunderland: Match of My Life*. The players included in this collection under the heading *Sunderland Cult Heroes* are all players whom the crowd have taken to for a variety of reasons.

Sometimes, as in the case of Nyron Nosworthy, players become instant cult heroes. At times, such as with Dick Malone, such status is acquired gradually. In other cases a player can become a cult hero having once been relatively unpopular. This was the case with Richard Ord.

Ord got off to a fabulous start, debuting as a 17-year-old on a night Sunderland wracked up their biggest win for over 30 years. He continued to do well for a while but took the rap for a heavy home defeat to Ipswich in the opening home game of the season a year and a half after his debut. Ord was still a teenager then and took some time to recover and fully establish himself, but he eventually did so to such an extent that a group of supporters even released a CD in his honour with the refrain *Who Needs Cantona When We've Got Dickie Ord?*

Ord, like Dick Malone, was a tall and unlikely looking player to be so skilful on the ball, but the fondness fans had for full-backs Joe Bolton, John Kay and Chris Makin was essentially based on a much simpler attribute: violence. From Joe Bolton's debut in April 1971 until Chris Makin bowed out almost 30 years later, these defenders endeared themselves to the red-and-white army by taking no prisoners and each being as tough as boots.

Bolton played in an era when defenders could still dump wingers on the cinder track around the pitch and not expect too much more from the ref than a talking to unless they did it once too often. Joe took full advantage. His game was a simple one: stop the other guy playing, and if you get forward crack in a shot as meaty as your tackles, and woe betide anyone who gets in the way.

The crowd lapped up Bolton's 'don't mess with us' approach to the game, and in the dark days of the Third Division right-back John Kay provided a similar role in the minds of the supporters. Before long, new arrival Marco Gabbiadini became the fans' favourite, ripping defences to shreds and scoring a boatload of exciting goals. Simultaneously though, 'Kaysie' was putting paid to the goalscoring ambitions of any opponents and, as always at Sunderland, the fans were just as keen to see someone 'getting stuck in' as they were to see a front-man rattling goals in at the other end. It is a bit like music aficionados appreciating the creative genius of Lennon and McCartney, Townsend & Daltry or Jagger and Richards, but at the back providing a solid base to build on would be Ringo, Keith Moon or Charlie Watts. You can almost think of Bolton, Kay and Makin as drummers, but ones whose steady beat would occasionally be accompanied by a crashing of cymbals representing another winger sent spinning to the ground.

Add to the mix Joe Bolton's wrecking of the training ground pitch by driving his car over it – revealed in his chapter here – John Kay's tackles being so agricultural that Leeds manager Howard Wilkinson said one of his players looked like he had been run over by a tractor and Chris Makin's alleged rendezvous with some bint from a Boddington's advert, and the appeal of this trio was further enhanced in the eyes of those who made them cult heroes. When John Kay broke his leg on his 199th and final League appearance but bade his farewell by sitting up on his stretcher and 'rowing his boat' off the pitch, it simply sealed his place in Sunderland folklore.

Being able to see the funny side of every situation is something which several cult heroes have in common. None more so than 1973 Cup-winning centre-forward Vic Halom. He was as tough as any of the aforementioned full-backs, often 'getting his retaliation in first' and never batting an eyelid at completely ignoring the laws of the game and sorting out any defenders before they could get on top of him. No matter what mischief he was up to, Vic would play up to the crowd on the blind side of the referee. It is a good job there were not the innumerable cameras watching his every move that there are for players now. Indeed, in Halom's heyday many games had no TV cameras present at all, and it is probably just as well in that he got away with such a lot that only the supporters saw, although it would be great to be able to compile a selection of Halom's Greatest 'Hits'.

Halom was carrying on a tradition of aggressive, rough play from the days when football was not the subject of ridicule from rugby followers appalled at the sight of footballers diving and rolling around in agony when no one has touched them. A century ago, Welsh goalkeeper L.R. Roose was as tough as anyone, dishing out the most robust physical challenges in an age where goalkeepers were afforded none of the protection they have expected in recent decades.

Roose was undoubtedly a cult hero from before World War One, a war he gave his life to. Perhaps the first playboy the game of football knew, Roose was renowned for having a string of women all over the country, and he was a huge practical joker who liked to talk to the crowd while play was at the other end. He was also responsible for the rules of the game being changed. Until 1912 goalkeepers could handle the ball up to the halfway line, but while most 'keepers would not venture far from goal Roose would regularly bounce the ball halfway up the pitch before launching it towards his forwards. Sunderland supporters thought so much of him they raised the money to provide him with a beautifully crafted 'Illuminated Address' spelling out how highly they thought of his efforts on behalf of the club.

A more recent goalkeeper, Barry Siddall, was on a hiding to nothing when he was bought in 1976. Quite apart from the fact the lads were adrift at the foot of the table and that Bob Stokoe, who signed him, resigned after Barry's debut, Siddall was taking over from the club's all-time record appearance maker and producer of the greatest save ever witnessed at Wembley as the FA Cup was won three years earlier, Jimmy Montgomery. Siddall, though, did so well that having lost his place the legendary Monty never got it back. The new acquisition was a very different 'keeper to 'The Mighty Jim'. Whereas Monty was lithe and acrobatic, the finest reflex 'keeper of his generation regardless of London media claims for Chelsea's 'cat' Peter Bonetti, Siddall was thick set, so much so that some thought when he was between the sticks there was not much left to shoot at.

Siddall spawned a steady stream of nicknames: 'The Flying Pig', 'Basil' – after the TV character Basil Fawlty, the TV character whose moustache some said resembled the 'keeper's, and 'Soddall'. None of these seem terms of endearment, and yet there was an underlying affection, and whenever Barry came steaming off his line clearing all in his path to take a cross his gathering of the ball would be accompanied by a slow, deep chorus of 'Seedaaalll' from behind the goal.

Most of Sunderland's cult heroes have featured as much strength as skill, but two of the cult heroes we celebrate here were all about grace under pressure. 1970s midfielder Kevin Arnott and everyone's favourite Argentinian from the Stadium of Light years, Julio Arca, were both blessed with an abundance of ability on the ball. Both were teenagers when introduced into Sunderland's midfield, and both got the crowd behind them by virtue of their ability on the ball. Arnott put down a marker on the centre circle. From there he dictated games, spraying the ball around in the style of the classical Italian 'fantasista'. Unlike so many of the cult heroes, aggression was not key to Arnott's game, but the way he could dictate play, combined with his youthful exuberance, gave him status as a cult hero that even now he is spoken of in wistful terms by those who long for Sunderland to have a modern equivalent in their midst.

Julio Arca was born and bred in Argentina but grew up on Wearside. Arriving as a teenager, a world away from home, Arca was 'adopted' by the crowd as Nyron Nosworthy was a few years later. Julio's skill on the ball was fabulous, his control instant. What made the crowd take to Arca was the fact that he would stick to the task as closely as he could make the ball stick to him. He would harry opponents like a limpet, displaying an appetite for endeavour not usually associated with players who knew they could do much more with the ball than most of their teammates. Watching Arca was a bit like watching the lead violinist with the London Philharmonic give a hand with carrying the grand piano. Too many times in the past Sunderland supporters have watched players who should be 'carrying the grand piano' playing lead violin.

Any list of players, be it the best ever, worst ever or indeed those who are the cult heroes, will never get everyone to agree, and you may well have chosen players other than the ones featured here. Arguably what matters most is not which players we have as cult heroes, but that we have cult heroes at all. Their very existence is evidence of the link between supporter and player. When Niall Quinn came back to Sunderland and spoke about the need for there to be interaction between supporters and supported once again it was born of an understanding that football clubs are based on passion, and that at Sunderland passion takes second place to no club.

LA-LA, LA-LA, LA-LA

VIC HALOM

Centre-forward
1973 FA Cup winner with Sunderland.

Born:	3 October 1948, Burton upon Trent.
Signed for Sunderland:	7 February 1973 from Luton Town £35,000
Transferred:	10 July 1976 to Oldham Athletic £25,000

Charlton Athletic:	Apprentice March 1964, 9+3 League apps, 0 goals
Orient:	August 1967, 53 League apps, 12 goals
Fulham:	November 1968, 66+6 League apps, 22 goals
Luton Town:	September 1971, 57+2 League apps, 17 goals
Sunderland:	7 February 1973, 110+3 League apps, 35 goals
	134+5 total apps, 42 total goals
Oldham Athletic:	10 July 1976, 121+2 League apps, 43 goals
Arcadia Shepherds (S. Africa):	8 apps, 4 goals
Rotherham United:	February 1980, player-coach, 19+1 League apps, 2 goals
Frederikstad (Norway):	1982, coach
Barrow:	1983, manager (Northern Premier League champions)
Rochdale:	May 1984–December 1986, manager
Burton Albion:	September and October 1987, manager
North Shields:	1992, manager/commercial manager

A combination of Marston's Pedigree, an injury to an international centre-forward on his only SAFC appearance and Everton not wanting him Cup-tied all had a role in Vic Halom becoming one of the greatest of all Sunderland's cult heroes. Halom's popularity was based on goals, laughs and bravery…with the bravery often being a euphemism for violence! Nonetheless, Vic was also a man of principles. In 1986 he vowed to give up professional football and did so after his distasteful experiences as manager of Rochdale, while his beliefs also saw him stand as a Liberal Democrat candidate for Sunderland North in the 1992 General Election.

'Lots of fans wished that they could have had the opportunity to go and do the things I used to do on the pitch. Basically there were two elements to that: score goals and knock people out!' says Vic laughing, but it is not the sort of laugh that indicates he is joking. It is a laugh of reminiscence as he recalls flattening some opponent or other.

Vic Halom in 2005.

'It didn't matter which way round I did it, the fans loved seeing me score. and they loved seeing me dish some stick out just as much. I watched a modern game on Sky, and loads of fans were saying things like "whack him" or "go and sort him out". In the game now of course they can't do it, but when I played that was exactly the way I played! I enjoyed doing it. Don't get me wrong, I never felt guilty. If I smacked you round the head, or put my elbow down your throat, or cut your eye, or hurt you, then it didn't bother me one little bit. I think the fans enjoyed that, especially as I smiled when I did it! I had a good time. I enjoyed what I did.'

Sunderland supporter Barry Emmerson sums up why the fans adored the centre-forward for whom the description 'barrel chested' has never been more appropriate: 'The fans can associate with it because Vic was out there wearing the strip that we'd all love to wear and putting himself about for the team, giving 100 per cent for the cause and enjoying it and putting the ball in the back of the net to go with it.'

Vic used to get stuck in. He'd dish it out, and a lot of defenders who could give it out didn't like getting tackled. I remember once in a match against him at Oldham I went up with him for a ball and he split my eye open, and I had to have stitches. He was a smashing bloke, though with a great laugh. I was just a bairn when I played with him at Sunderland, I was just like the 'gopher' really, but I think he liked me as well, and we all got on great.
* Joe Bolton, Sunderland, 1970–81.

Vic Halom was on a football pitch to enjoy himself. In the era that he played the game was riddled with hatchet men such as Tommy Smith, Ron 'Chopper' Harris, Peter Storey or anyone wearing a Leeds shirt. You had to be tough to survive as a forward, and Halom was no shrinking violet. As the centre-forward who led the line against Leeds as Sunderland famously caused one of the biggest FA Cup Final upsets of all time at Wembley in 1973, Halom might have been forgiven for taking it easy in the lead up to the game, but nothing could be further from the truth.

'I wish you hadn't asked me that!' he says when reminded: 'It was a memorable experience in the sense that we played Orient on the Monday before the Final. The game included one of the worst tackles I ever saw – and the worst thing was that I did it. Some of the lads we were playing against had been my apprentices when I'd been there five years earlier. I was saying to them "Look lads – don't come whacking us, we're playing at Wembley on Saturday and we don't want to get injured."

Halom fires in a shot.

A couple of minutes in, their centre-half Paul Went whacks me – and I said "Look, if you do it again, I'm going to hurt you." He came across again, and little Terry Brisley came in – and I have to admit I got him with one of the worst tackles I've seen. I went right over the top and laid him out. I said "I told you", and he nearly hit the floodlights. He'd been winding me up so I smacked him – I nearly broke him in half. I splattered him. I went right over the top because I was about to get minced. I

apologised afterwards and picked him up. I said "Look, I'm sorry, but I've a Cup Final to play, I'm not getting t*****d by you two." He was alright. He was my apprentice when I was at Orient. I got away with it. How the hell I never got sent off I'll never know. That would have been terrible, even worse.'

The modern game, however, leaves Halom as cold as he left some of the defenders who used to challenge him: 'These days, though, I've never seen so many Jessies in all my life. Football has moved on in terms of fitness levels and height, but have you seen these big lads of 6' 3" getting blown over by the wind and diving

Vic airborne without heed to the possible consequences for Manchester United 'keeper Alex Stepney.

in the box? There was the odd one in my day such as Franny Lee, but now it's wholesale cowardice. I don't like it. You get people like Vieira when he was at Arsenal, 6ft plus, built like a brick s**thouse and if somebody just touches him he's on the floor. You just think "Stand up man!" I would have been ashamed to do that. You don't let a member of the opposition know that he's hurt you…you might put him in the black book though! To let somebody know that they'd hurt me, it just didn't happen. You look at Arthur Cox [coach of Halom's 1973 FA Cup winning side]. When Arthur was a young pro somebody broke his leg and he got up and stamped it. It ruined his career.'

Vic was not just about violence though. There have been similarly brutal centre-forwards at Sunderland since that the fans did not take to, such as Billy Whitehurst or local lad Mick Harford. Halom knew where the back of the net was – he averaged almost a goal every three games at Sunderland, as he did throughout his career – but his terrific relationship with the crowd was based on the fact that he was always full of mischief and always looked like he was having a good time.

'There was a classic one when we played Luton at Roker Park. There was Keith Barber, the Luton goalkeeper, and myself – head to head. He had the ball in his hands about to clear it but I had my back to the ref and my hand on top of the ball. The fans behind the goal can see, but the ref can't, and I'm laughing at him, saying "What're you going to do now Keith?" He went to go left, then tried to kick it but stepped outside the box and we got a free-kick. He called me a few choice words I can tell you, but I was pissing myself.' It is typical of Halom that he often relates such tales in the present tense, the memories being as fresh in his mind as they are in the minds of those who simply loved to see him in red and white.

There was one more key factor in Vic Halom cementing his place in the hearts of Sunderland supporters right from the off. A goal in a 4–0 win over Middlesbrough on his home debut did no harm, but on just his second outing at home he scored a goal that is still regarded by many as unsurpassed since, and it came in the match voted Roker Park's greatest-ever game when the ground closed a quarter of a century later. It came in an FA Cup fifth-round replay. Over 50,000 crammed into Roker Park for the match with Cup favourites Manchester City. The Brazil side that had won the 1970 World Cup are still considered as arguably the greatest world champions of all time. The pick of their four goals in the 1970 World Cup Final was similar to Halom's goal against Man City, except that Halom's strike at the culmination of a series of slick short passes along the edge of the box was, if anything, more spectacular than Carlos Alberto's low flying rocket against the Italians in Mexico! 'When that one went in, it just lifted. I'd really tonked it' says Vic. 'Hughsey will tell you it was meant as a cross, but it wasn't. Joe Corrigan was in goal for Man City, and to this day if I ever see him he always greets me with "Not you again!"'

His superb strike against Manchester City during the 1973 FA Cup run would be enough to guarantee his cult status, however his place in the hearts of Sunderland fans goes much deeper. The bulging chest, the toothless grin, the fearless spirit and the wink of satisfaction as he takes the ball and the Derby full-back into the net on his way to completing a hat-trick, are etched in the memory. At Sunderland he found HIS stage and HIS audience, and how we loved him!

Mike Love,
South East Nothumberland Sunderland Supporters' Association (SENSSA).

Vic slides in.

Every Sunderland supporter old enough to have seen that goal will never forget it, yet Vic insists it was not the best of his career: 'I've scored better. I was a natural goalscorer. Even if I played centre-half, I'd always be looking to score. I remember playing against Derby, where I scored an overhead kick from the edge of the 18-yard box. I smacked it past Les Green right into the bottom corner. There was another that sticks in my mind at West Ham from the halfway line. Scoring good goals wasn't a problem. That one at Roker was special because Man City were a fabulous team, and the importance of that game with it being a big FA Cup tie makes it even more important.'

If Halom was a forward with the knack of being in the right place at the right time, that did not just extend to what he did on the pitch at Sunderland. Football managers and supporters so often talk about needing to add just the final piece to the 'jigsaw' that is their team, the fantasy player who will make all the difference. The trouble is that so many players bought to be this missing piece are indeed too much like a jigsaw: they go to pieces in the box.

In Vic's case, though, he was indeed the player who made everything happen at Sunderland. Arriving between the third and fourth rounds of the glorious 1973 Cup run, the last of the team to be signed, he became the fulcrum of the attack, and crucially his presence allowed erstwhile centre-forward Dave Watson to remain at centre-half, where he was brilliant.

'I suppose the difference is that the nucleus of the squad I signed for were very, very good players, who were just looking for the final piece of the jigsaw. I probably happened to be that final piece. Bob Stokoe had already signed Ron Guthrie and David Young. Dave Watson no longer being centre-forward allowed a more natural leader, and everything dropped into place. We never looked back from there. That side was capable. The side was ready – well schooled, trained and well worked. The club had everything it needed to have to be a successful First Division [now Premier League] side, let alone Second Division side, so when we beat clubs like Arsenal and Man City it was no surprise to us. It wasn't fluky, it wasn't luck. We were a better team, we were better than them.'

Sunderland may have been the most unlikely of underdogs for the '73 Cup Final in the eyes of the rest of the country, but on Wearside they were the favourites. Supporters who had seen 'Stokoe's Stars' knock out City and the Gunners knew that Sunderland were irresistible. 'Sunderland were complete,' presses Halom. 'We didn't just beat Man City or Arsenal – we took them apart. They were fabulous sides, and we dismantled them. I certainly knew that we would lift the Cup. It's that little thing that you never say – but it was in there. Once we'd beaten City in the replay, the rest was a formality. Some will say it was written, but there's a long way from it being written, to actually getting there. There's a lot of hard work and sweat that still needs to go into it. We really did take Arsenal apart, which was no mean feat with the players they had.

'At Hillsbrough in the semi-final we should have been three or four up at half-time. I had two cleared off the line. We "marmalised" them, it was no fluke. When Arsenal were a goal down at half-time they were probably saying to themselves that we hadn't taken our chances. They thought we wouldn't have another half like that, but we did. There was a genuine belief that we could take the big side apart. I don't know whether they'd underestimated us, but we knew.'

Halom had opened the scoring in front of the giant Hillsbrough Kop end filled with Wearsiders: 'Mickey Horswill lifted the ball on – I just chased it down.

'Arsenal's centre-half Jeff Blockley got murdered unfairly afterwards. He tried a back-pass to Bob Wilson in goal, and I just latched onto it and knocked it in. The thing is it bobbled as I hit it and it went in off my ankle bone. For a moment I thought I'd missed it!'

It was a magical time to be a Sunderland supporter, and the fairytale swept up the whole footballing world. Just a few months before Halom's arrival the club had been at one of its lowest-ever ebbs, but Bob Stokoe's arrival ignited Wearside: 'Crowds went from 11,000 just before he took over to just under 40,000 for a routine League game with Oxford and over 50,000 in the Cup games.'

Halom at full stretch.

Vic flattening the Forest 'keeper.

Vic had first-hand knowledge of the pre-Stokoe Sunderland. In the month before Stokoe took over Halom had scored as Luton comfortably won 2–0 at Roker. 'I remember playing against Sunderland for Luton and Jim Montgomery pulling off this wonder save. I could have smacked him, I'm not kidding, I'm never one for pulling out! The goalie's job was to come out to collect the ball, my job was to go in. I'd spun off to get into the box and knocked this ball down, and Jim had the audacity to put his hand on it and stop it. I went in, and he nearly lost his head, I nearly put it in the back of the net. I stepped up and over him and ended up in the back of the net myself. From

that little bit of information, though, I knew that he was an exceptional goalkeeper, and when I came I realised Sunderland had some terrific players who had been given what they needed – confidence.'

Luton played at Sunderland twice in the 1972–73 season. Almost exactly five months after their 2–0 League win they lost by the same scoreline in the quarter-final of the Cup, with Halom by now an integral member of the home side.

That side was far from orthodox in their approach to the Cup Final. 'We went to the Sports Writers' dinner on the Thursday and gate-crashed a wedding on the Friday at the hotel, so the night before the Cup Final we were out and had a few beers. I don't know what the wedding guests thought, but we had a good time. Billy Elliott and Bob

Halom beats two Forest defenders.

Stokoe didn't put pressure on anyone, they took it away. They were good at that. They didn't put pressure on us, they put it on referees. Bob handled that well.

'What that side was very good at was having a laugh and not being uptight. In order to laugh and to earn the right to have a laugh and relax, we put the hard work in first. That side used to work really hard. I used to train and run alongside Ian Porterfield, who was as strong as a horse. You'd never want to run alongside Hughesy or be in the gym with him if he'd had a few beers the night before – his breath was ridiculous. The biggest thing in that period was the team spirit. That was there long before I ever got there. It was part of that growing up process, because the nucleus of the team had been together for years. Several of the lads had come through as apprentices, and they knew each other inside out. It was easy for newcomers such as me to slot in though. On the first day, my trousers went missing. Hughesy had stuck them up some poxy pipe at the training ground at Washington, and I couldn't be bothered with going to fetch them, so I just put my tracksuit on and got a lift back to the ground with the physio Johnny Watters. There was always someone taking the p***. God forbid if it was your birthday, there was Vaseline and boot polish and goodness knows what. The lads certainly liked a laugh! Everyone knows about Billy Hughes and his laughing box on Cup Final day, but that was just typical of how relaxed we were.

'We weren't allowed to do anything though. I got banned from going out when we were in London in the week of the Final. Stokoe wouldn't even let me go out to the bank. He lent me some money because my mum and dad were in London for the week, staying at my sister's. The owners of the hotel had a Rolls-Royce, and I hired it for my parents. It picked them up in the morning, took

Vic (second from the right) with his teammates from 1973 at a tribute to Cup Final goalscorer Ian Porterfield after Ian's death in September 2007.

them for lunch and I'd ordered some champagne so it was a very special day for them. My mum said she felt like the Queen of England driving down Wembley Way with a great big red-and-white rosette on the Rolls. Stokoe said "No you're not going out, but I'll help you arrange that." The rest of the time I was confined to quarters. Bob had a point – I used to go straight from wherever I'd been the night before to training.'

Sometimes Cup runs damage League form, but, having been fifth from bottom when Stokoe took over, Sunderland ended up in what would have been a Play-off place (had Play-offs existed then), despite the fixture congestion of a Cup run that began with replays in the first three ties. Had the Play-offs been in operation then, maybe Sunderland would have had cause for a double celebration, and the Cup team may not have broken up so quickly.

'We went on an incredible run of wins in the League. We believed there was a very good team there; a team that was ready, it was their time. We didn't fear Man City, or anybody, or Arsenal, and we had absolutely no fear of Leeds going into the Final. Everyone played their part. Dick Malone was a real p***-taker, Dave Watson, Jim Montgomery and Bobby Kerr and the rest of the lads were superb. Then you'd have the idiots: Hughsy and me. We shared a room. It was always us that were in trouble. I still ring Billy from time to time and see him at former players do's.'

Perhaps fate has a lot to do with football. Halom and Hughes became known as 'The H-bombers', and both scored in the famed wins over Arsenal and Manchester City, yet Halom was only signed after an injury to Billy's brother John. Known as 'Yogi', John Hughes had been a terrific striker for Celtic, but his career was ended through an injury picked up on his Sunderland debut, and Halom was signed in time for the next home League fixture.

Signing photographs of his brilliant goal from the FA Cup tie with Manchester City in 1973.

Had those events not taken place, perhaps Sunderland's Cup run would have been nipped in the bud, and Vic's wonder goal against City in the fifth round might never have happened. As it was, Halom was there to give Leeds a tough time beneath the twin towers of Wembley. His presence disturbed United's defence, and it was Vic who knocked the ball down for Porterfield to score the only goal of the game. Halom had the ball in the net himself later, only for it to be disallowed as he had blatantly barged Leeds 'keeper David Harvey over the line.

With characteristic honesty, Vic does not think he played well in the Final: 'I've played better. I didn't like the conditions, it had rained and I'd made a wrong choice of studs. I was up on my toes for the whole 90 minutes, hoping that I'd get a bit of a better grip, but all I got was cramp. But in saying that, it was against a super, super team with a lot of class players. As a striker you have to do a lot of chasing just to try and close them down. You have to do that. Somebody has to do it in the team – the dirty, heavy stuff that takes people away and creates openings for other players. I take a little bit of satisfaction from that, but in terms of a footballing performance I was crap. I've played a lot better.

'We were under the cosh for long periods of time, but the nice thing about being a centre-forward is you're the only player everyone else looks at. You can see all the work, and the work the others put in was far greater than mine because they were more involved. You know that when somebody whacks a ball out to clear it there's nothing worse than when it comes straight back down your throat, so my job was to stop that as much as I could. To have had a hand – or a foot – in the goal was OK, but it was a day I felt I could and should have done better.

'It's a question of balance. You think "yes, the most important thing is that the club won." The secondary reaction is "what was your individual contribution – what could you have done better?" That's something you need to do. From that perspective you have self-criticism. The Cup Final was one of those occasions in life when I wish things had gone better, and that's all, no more than that.'

From a supporter's perspective, what I always remember about Vic Halom was that he always played the game with a huge smile on his face. The barrel-chested target man was one of the main catalysts behind the 1973 FA Cup run, and his defining SAFC moment was that thunderous goal he struck against Manchester City at Roker Park, in a 3–1 mauling of one of England's finest post-war football teams that included the likes of Colin Bell, Franny Lee and Mike Summerbee. Before his arrival, Sunderland were distinctly lightweight up front, but Bob Stokoe's outrageously shrewd £35,000 capture saw him arrive from Luton in the February of '73, and his physical presence gave the lads a real cutting edge up front and allowed the likes of Billy Hughes and Bobby Kerr the freedom to utilise their natural ball skills to great effect. Vic was no world beater, but what you knew with him was that you would always get 110 per cent commitment in each and every game. 'Vic Halom, Vic Halom, Vic Halom, la-la, la-la, la-la!' was sung exceptionally loudly after he scored the opener against Arsenal at Hillsborough in the 1973 FA Cup semi-final, another all-time classic Sunderland encounter, and no one should ever underestimate Vic's role in that amazing ride to Wembley.
Tom Lynn, Sunderland supporter.

Within 48 hours of the Final, Halom found the net in a re-arranged game that was drawn at Cardiff, one of two remaining League fixtures played in the first three days of the week the Cup was won. In between, the team brought the Cup home amid scenes of unbridled joy. If there was ever a case of Cup fever, Sunderland had a huge dose of it in 1973.

'That evening was an incredible experience simply because of the amount of people and the diversity. We were going past nurseries and hospitals with children and patients brought outside, bedecked in red and white. There were fields with horses having their tails done in red and white. We got an inkling of what was about to happen because we'd changed coaches at the Ramside at Durham. People were following in their cars and flashing their lights. It was over 10 miles up to Sunderland, and the crowds were building up. Coming onto the main streets, there was what seemed like millions of people, it was incredible. For all of us it was the first time we'd experienced such success. We were a bunch of players that enjoyed those things and enjoyed being together as players. We worked very hard together, played very hard together and enjoyed that day. The magnitude of feeling generated after we'd won important games and won at Wembley was simply fantastic, but I don't think the power of that size of reception can ever be matched.

'We went to Spain after the Cup Final. Word got round that Bob had won a golf tournament. This was years and years before mobile phones remember, and we were all out in different bars, but we all got there to see the trophy presented. Now you feel the same way, any member of that squad – we'd stick together. The team spirit was the most important thing. There is a bond between us – more than a football bond.

'That's what I want to get across. They were powerful things that for some reason happened at the right time, and it was that power that drove the thing on. When we look back, it was there right at the start. To be the centre-forward of that team was a great honour and a great privilege. There's a kind of feeling you get when you lead the line, and the time that I led that line was very special because, as a centre-forward, you're about the only player that faces the rest of the team. You have your back to goal for a large percentage of the time. Bob Stokoe used to say "You lead, you set the tempo. If they see you working, they'll work, they'll follow you. You chase the lost causes, they will too." It was a super feeling, because in that period you had the massive support of the team, you could have a laugh as well as it being a bloody serious business. That was one of the most important things – the ability to enjoy what I did.

'When you look back and you have the likes of Guth [Ron Guthrie], Ritchie – what happened to Ritchie was tragic [Ritchie Pitt's career was ended through injury early the next season] – and so on, we had some bloody wonderful players. When we were training at the gym, Hughsey would stay back and strike balls until nine out of 10 went into the top corner. That kind of dedication, that willingness to sacrifice until you get it right, that is instilled in you at 14, 15, 16 years old. So you had Billy's pace, Dennis' trickery and Ian's left foot, with Bobby Kerr swatting flies in midfield and Mick Horswill stopping the opposition midfield from playing. The balance was right.

'You look at the England side now, and it isn't balanced. I would certainly have hurt a few people if I was playing football today, and some of them might have been in my own team. When you see people get to the by-line and check back and not cross the ball, as a centre-forward, you might as well sit in the stands. You've made your run, but the winger turns back on himself and crosses with his other foot and it always goes wide. It's frustrating as hell.

'One of the things that disappointed me was the break-up of the side. It really didn't have to happen. We lost Ritchie Pitt through injury. Then we lost Dennis [Tueart] and Micky Horswill who were next out. They went to Man City and were followed by Dave Watson. Dave was a good lad –

a very difficult customer to handle, his ability in the air was awesome. I mean he had everything. Dennis too – they all could have done what they wanted.

'Dave Watson could go back to centre-half because he'd been playing up front. Everybody knows he's a natural centre-half and a lot better in that position. In our training games he was a big sod. I whacked Watto a few times. I remember one training session in particular. Dave and Rod Belfitt were going to play twin centre-halves and we were doing a session on crossing with the reserve 'keeper Trevor Swinburne, who was a very big lad. I'd whacked them all a few times and Arthur Cox had a word with Trev. The next time he came out for a cross he absolutely splattered me in the six yard box. It was a lively session! Arthur Cox turned round to David, put his arm around him and said "Don't worry David, it won't be as bad as that in the game."

'The routine stuff in training was mostly done by Arthur. Bob sometimes joined in and whacked you, but Billy [Elliott] didn't say too much – I didn't know him too well.

'Arthur was like Bob Stokoe in many ways – an honest man. Very straight, direct, knew the business. And you knew where you stood with Arthur, he was OK.'

Sunderland's FA Cup triumph brought European football to Wearside, and the draw for the first tie against Vasas of Budapest was especially significant for Vic. Born of a Hungarian father, the game gave him the opportunity to meet some of his family for the very first time. 'It was nice because my dad is from Budapest, and my uncles too. I met my aunties there for the first time. The problem was that a few days before, we'd played at Oxford and I'd t*****d the centre-half – both of them I think – and the right-back, left-back and the goalkeeper by half-time. Somebody must have said something in their dressing room, so as we kicked-off the second half I knocked the ball, went up the park, turned round and somebody tapped me on the shoulder. As I turned around, someone smacked me right in the mouth and I lost all my front teeth. I had to go to Vasas with no front teeth; there was no time to get anything done about them. So I met my Aunty Elizabeth at the NEP stadium. She said "Which one's Vic Halom?" And when she saw me with no front teeth she nearly passed out. She must have been thinking "What an ugly kid he is".'

> *I remember when we were playing in the Cup-Winners' Cup. Vic Halom was an absolute card when we were about to play Vasas Budapest. Vic had some Hungarian blood, and he was going to fix us up with friends over there. He always had a smile and a quip, you'd certainly get a laugh from Vic.*
> * Keith Collings, Sunderland chairman 1971–80, director 1965–83.

'My parents' story is fascinating, although I don't bloody well know what my dad Louis did. I know that his best friend was captured and hung. My aunts (who are still alive in Budapest) didn't do anything. They were imprisoned and tortured for six months. My dad got out and came to England in early 1948 – he probably left Hungary around 1946–47. The family was in concentration camps in Austria during the war. My dad played football for the Austrian police. That's how he met my mum. Mum was a nurse – he got hurt playing football, and she treated him.

'My mum was from Savastopol in Russia. I'm led to believe my grandfather was a Cossack who was killed by the Communists in the 1930s when my mum was a very small girl of about five, six or seven years old.

'I intend to go there and explore that, and document the truths. Hungarian football was actually fundamental to my game. First of all you enjoy playing football, you don't play if you don't enjoy it.

The European Cup-Winners' Cup games with Vasas Budapest in 1973 gave Vic the chance to meet some of his Hungarian family for the first time. Here he strikes a shot in the second leg at Roker Park.

They had certain rules that absolutely wouldn't apply today. You never pass backwards – always look to go forwards. In English football that doesn't apply now, because if you can play square you can still be playing when you are 40 years old. That wouldn't happen 20 years ago – you wouldn't have a 40-year-old footballer as long as you've got a hole in your backside, it just wouldn't happen. Those were ideas in father's head and he taught me. I could make the ball talk if I wanted to, but that gets knocked out of you in professional football. My love came from my father's love of football and the way that he'd been taught. The rest of it was discipline.'

News of Halom's Hungarian parentage sparked rumours of an international call-up by Hungary as Sunderland began their European adventure: 'That's true, I received a phone call from a journalist based in London, a Hungarian. It was up for discussion – he'd been asked to contact me for my reaction. I always wanted to play for England – I never got opportunity. I got injured at England

In possession.

schoolboys, for England Youth, and when I was recommended for the Under-23s. Peter Reeves, who took my place at Charlton Athletic and captained England Youth, took my place because I was injured. That's the luck of the game. Some full-blown mature players that were fabulous never made it because they never had a career. I made it and had a career without any major accidents, which was great, but nothing further came of the possibility of playing for Hungary.'

Halom's appearance in the land of his father was a success though: 'We played really well and won both legs against Vasas, but in the next round against Sporting Lisbon we were a little naïve – just a little – which eventually cost us the game.'

Inevitably, as FA Cup holders, Sunderland were a big scalp in the Second Division the following season and never quite got into the promotion places, eventually finishing sixth: 'The following season I felt players didn't deliver what they were expected to. It often happens that when you have a major success, the following season it is very difficult to maintain that expectancy level. You see it now with rugby; England were a major success in the World Cup, but for the next four years were garbage. There was an element of that with us.

'There was also an element of the players wanting more money for what they did, and I think that was a valid point. In 1973–74 there was a freeze on pay. The Labour government had a three-day week. They made a rule in Sunderland to say you can't have a pay rise. Fine, you've won the FA Cup but on £50 – or in Ritchie Pitt's case (I'm sure he won't mind me saying) – on £25 a week. There were two or more players in the Wembley side on £25 a week. The nature of the profession shouldn't have allowed that – it's a very short career, as Ritchie Pitt found out when his career was ended half a dozen games into the following season. The majority of players were on £50 a week but wanted to share in the success of the club financially. The club wasn't allowed to give them that, or so they said. The problem for me was that it broke the side up. Instead of encouraging people to stay – I'm talking of Dennis Tueart, Dave Watson, Mickey Horswill – the side broke up unnecessarily. You see a repetition in history that certain clubs get to a certain stage, but then pull back. They take a different tack and bring in second-rate players compared to the current squad, instead of adding to what they already have. Sunderland should have gone and got more internationals while they had a big reputation and fan base. Players would have begged to play in Sunderland. Alright, we got promoted three years afterwards, but I think with players who didn't have the ability that the original squad had.'

Halom top scored with 21 goals the season after the Cup was won. Included in that haul was a hat-trick that helped teammate Dave Watson towards his England debut. Watson was pushing hard for a cap but was unable to dislodge regular choice Roy McFarland of League Cup opponents Derby. The Rams were a powerful side who were champions twice in four seasons during that era, but after two pulsating draws Sunderland wiped the floor with them, Vic grabbing all three goals in a 3–0 win: 'Roy McFarland was the centre-half – we've never really got on very well. Actually we did our coaching badges together. I know the badge system's different now, but it was very difficult then. I did it with Roy and Denis Smith who was at Stoke too. They kicked bloody lumps out of me on the training ground because they couldn't do it on the pitch. I still see them from time to time,' says Halom with a knowing glint in his eye. Demolishing McFarland with his hat-trick while Watson was elementary at the other end helped to illustrate who was the better defender, and Watson began his England career two internationals later.

> *Of course the goals against Man City and Arsenal in the '73 Cup run spring to mind, but I recall two goals against Millwall in 1973–74 that were a springboard to an uplift in form which nearly resulted in promotion. That year Halom produced his Cup run form for the whole season, this could not be said of all the Cup-winners.*
> Ken Hall, Sunderland supporter, Newcastle.

The goals did not come so freely for Halom a year later when promotion was narrowly missed, and by the time it was finally won in 1976 he had lost his place, eventually moving on to Oldham – who he had played his final game against.

Hanging around and being a bit part player was never going to satisfy Vic: 'Now, you look at squad players. What does that mean? Something like you might play once a month. I wanted to play all of the time. If I wasn't playing I wanted to leave. Mel Holden had been bought and Bob also signed Rod Belfitt from Everton – he didn't do anything God bless him. You could see it was turning then because they weren't getting top-class players, and the players they were signing weren't going to take the club on to the next giant leap into the First Division and onto European success. At that point Sunderland were ripe for it, they were set up, and everything was in place to go and take the next steps.'

Someone who knew Halom's value to a side was Billy Bremner, Leeds' captain in the 1973 Cup Final and by now player-coach at Hull City: 'Billy Bremner wanted me to go to Hull. I needn't have gone anywhere as I had a contract at Sunderland, but I'd had words

Another defender hits the deck.

with Bob Stokoe and I wasn't happy. I wasn't one to sit and moan, I always think I might as well get up, get out and see what's what. I ended up going to Oldham Athletic – I had a few good years, and I think Sunderland tried to sign me back at one point. I'd scored a lot of goals – there were rumours that they wanted me back. Nothing ever came of it. It was all rumour – a lot of football is. I was happy at Oldham – they brought in a young lad called Allan Young, so I was allowed to drop back into midfield and given the run of the park. I scored a lot of goals.'

Oldham was Vic's sixth club. It was a happy time for him following on from his halcyon days at Roker Park. Halom was only 27 when he was allowed to leave Sunderland. Like Jimmy Montgomery, who despite making the last of a record 627 SAFC appearances left at the ridiculously young age (for a goalkeeper) of 33, Halom was allowed to leave Wearside too early, and yet Vic insists 'Stokoe did it right – I had a six-year contract, but he knew me better than any man. He'd signed me pro at 17 – he had ripped up my apprenticeship and signed me professionally. He knew what made me tick.'

Halom spent three and a half years at Oldham, scoring 43 goals in 123 games despite mainly playing in midfield: 'I always enjoyed scoring goals and always did score goals. I often thought that I was a better midfielder than striker because I didn't have any natural pace, but I could read things and get in there, especially at Roker Park. I was never as popular with the supporters at any club as I was at Sunderland, but Oldham came nearest. I still meet people who are Oldham supporters and who felt the same way about me as they did at Sunderland.'

While Vic was at Boundary Park he missed out on the chance to play in America, and his Oldham clubmate Dave Irving, a former Everton forward, went to the States instead, where he teamed up with George Best and forged a lasting career in US soccer. Irving played against Sunderland for Fort Lauderdale Strikers in 1980 and in 2004 managed a North Carolina side, Wilmington Hammerheads, in a friendly against the Lads. 'A few years later I was on holiday in Florida and drove past Fort Lauderdale, and I thought "you swine", but Dave Irving was a good player and we had a good time together at Oldham. I'd been offered a job in Detroit many years earlier when I was at Orient as an 18-year-old lad recovering from a cartilage operation, but they wouldn't let me go. When I got a second offer from Miami [Fort Lauderdale] I'd just signed a new contract at Oldham and Jimmy Frizzell wouldn't let me go. None too happily I thought "you can stick that", so when a chap called Kai Johansson came from Rangers and asked if he could take me over to South Africa where he was working, I went for it. I played there for eight weeks and scored a few goals for a team called Arcadia Shepherds, but because it was outside of FIFA I wasn't in breach of contract.

'I suppose you look back with different views. I've always been a bloody tramp at heart – there's certainly gypsy blood in me. I left home at 15 to go and play football in London, and I was encouraged to do that. Not because I wasn't very good at school – I'd done quite well at school and was about to take my 'O' levels [GCSEs], and the headmaster wasn't very happy. I suppose my parents had decided that I would not be allowed to go and join Derby – there'd been a contract on offer since I was 12 years old. Sheffield Wednesday, Wolves, virtually any reasonably local club had been in touch, but I was sent as far away from home as they could have possibly sent me – but to a club with a good reputation. Simply because of Marston Pedigree. There were some very good footballers from the area where I lived who'd gone to local clubs, and they'd be drinking the old Pedigree and they put weight on and never made it. So I got sent down to London.

'I'd always been taught well, and I could play. So football was the least of my worries, it was always attitude and desire more than anything. I found football an easy game – I didn't always take it seriously – that was my fault. I have letters since my father passed away, from Arsenal, West Ham and Leeds trying to buy me.

'It was Charlton I signed for as a young lad. Frank Hill signed me. I was the captain of Derbyshire schoolboys, had played for England schoolboys and so on. I went down with a lad called Dennis Boothe, who's now coaching Carlisle, lovely lad. We played a game against Hertfordshire on the Saturday, we beat them and were taken to Charlton on the Sunday. They'd arranged a game against their apprentices, and we stuffed them by about seven. Dennis scored about four and I scored three in the first half, so he took me off at half-time. God knows what they'd been doing on the Saturday night! They offered me a contract there and then, but I had been offered one by Wolves and Derby who were on the doorstep to Burton upon Trent. I'd been offered apprenticeships with Rolls-Royce and at Arsenal, Leicester and Leeds who were all interested, but it was Charlton I signed for.

'In those days they had people like Mike Bailey who had played for England, Frank Haydock, ex-Manchester United and Colin Appleton. They were senior players who knew their business, and they came to Eltham on Saturday mornings to watch the apprentices play, and then they'd talk to you after the game. They'd tell you if you did this well, or that wrong. Then we used to train together. If you did something wrong, you paid for it…and you paid in pain. They hurt you. You very quickly learned to look after yourself – if you didn't, your career was over. There was no let-up just because you were only 15, it didn't work like that. There were some very good apprentices there. Billy Bonds was there, although he was a couple of years older than our crop, and we had a midfield player called Alan Campbell who went up to Birmingham and ended up playing around 500 League games. We had some very good players.

'I tore my cartilage and was sent to Orient to get fit. I'd started the 1966–67 season. I played against Derby and Luton against that prat Bruce Rioch. I wasn't fit. Bob Stokoe was our manager at Charlton and gave me my break, but unfortunately Bob got the sack while I was there and Eddie Firmani took over. I was earning £15 per week as a pro at Charlton, but Orient were paying £35 per week. I said to Eddie "You can't expect me to come back for £15 a week, £2 a draw and £4 a win," which were the only bonuses they had. He went to see the chairman and they made me an offer, but I said no and they let me go to Orient for £5,000.

'I got fit there and moved up front from centre-half, where I'd been playing, and started to score goals. I started enjoying my football more and knowing more about the game. I always had the physical presence to sort out whoever needed sorting out. Bobby Robson was at Fulham and he came over to sign me. At about the same time Cloughie and Peter Taylor phoned my dad and said "We've got him a house in Derby, tell your Vic to hang on," to which he said "Tell him yourself, I'm not your messenger boy and I'm not getting involved." I didn't know until I'd got to the ground to sign. Bobby Robson was there and I duly signed for Fulham. Cloughie walked through the door and, typically of Cloughie, he gave me a bollocking for signing for Fulham!

'Actually, it was a big mistake. Bobby probably paid the price ultimately, because he'd spent a lot of money signing me and I wasn't fit – he got the sack. Bobby Robson's plan was to play me and Malcolm McDonald up front together as the strike partnership for the next 10 years. We were both 20 years old, I could lead the line and Malcolm was as quick as anything you'd ever seen. I often wished that had happened, but it didn't. Malcolm wasn't that good a footballer, but he was dynamite quick, and with that kind of pace all you've got to do is hit the target, which he did regularly. Once he got in front of the goalie he would finish it off.

'Johnny Haynes took over and we had George Cohen, who later won a World Cup winner's medal, in the side as well. Haynes sold Malcolm to Luton and I followed him again. I'd had my injury problems at Fulham and was told I had to retire. I was only about 20 or 21. They said my career was over because of a knee injury. I went to see a specialist, and he said to "tell them to get stuffed," and added "if you want to play footy, play footy." So I moved on again. Bobby Robson had paid 30 grand for me. He said to me not so long ago "You bloody got me the sack," but thankfully his career took off after that.

'Malcolm McDonald went on to Newcastle, so I never really got to play much with him even though I'd followed him to Luton. It was there that I dropped into midfield, started scoring goals again and began to attract interest from bigger clubs. Everton put in a bid of £100,000 for me and asked for me not to be Cup tied, so I was left out of the side and was waiting to move to Everton.

'Luton came up to the North East in the Cup to play Newcastle. I met Bob Stokoe while I was up in the North East and he asked, "What are you doing?" I said I wasn't very happy at the moment. I was the top scorer and playing in midfield at the time. I think I'd scored 10–12 goals already that season from midfield. Bob would have always known me either as a defender or a centre-forward.'

Having asked for Halom not to be Cup-tied, Everton lost to Millwall in the fourth round while Luton won at Newcastle, and Sunderland drew with Reading, enabling Vic to meet up with Stokoe again.

'Very quickly after our meeting Bob made an offer to Luton, and they agreed that I could speak to Sunderland. I met him at Reading football ground immediately after the replay in the Cup. Basically, Bob's pitch was that they were sixth off bottom in the League but had signed a few players and were still in the Cup. I drove up the next morning – I remember I stopped a copper on Scotch Corner and said "Can you tell me how far bloody Sunderland is from here?" I bombed up the motorway, and managed to get there and signed just before the deadline which was 5pm.

'I remember driving into Sunderland and coming onto this red road and thinking "Jesus, what a place this is." Having come up from London with all the smoke and traffic it was great to come up to this beautiful shoreline.' Vic is sat chatting overlooking Seaburn beach, on one of those too rare days where Sunderland seems aptly named.

'I was a footballer – I didn't think much in those days – I don't think much now, but if something feels right I do it, and it just felt right at the time. I found I had the likes of Ian Porterfield and Bobby Kerr with me and that quality made my job a lot easier. Add to that Dennis and the pace of Hughesy, and you could see we had a lot going for us. There was a lot of work in going to Sunderland for the likes of myself and Ron Guthrie, who had just arrived. We had this crop of players that weren't big names, all in their 20s, and were fabulous footballers – all the ingredients of an extremely good team.

'I was so fortunate to have played in teams with good players all my life. At Charlton we had Lenny Glover and Mick Kennedy – two of the quickest wingers you've ever seen. They could cross balls in and you'd live on them. Then I went to Orient, and there was a little Scottish winger there that could drop a ball right in front of me. Then I went to Fulham and we had Jimmy Conway, he was superb.'

Vic always appreciated the qualities that made a successful team. Surrounded at Sunderland by players whose time had come, he jettisoned himself into supporters' affections for a lifetime, and it was a friendship formed on Wearside that later led to him moving into coaching when he teamed up with Ian Porterfield who was in his first managerial job at Rotherham.

'I'd done some coaching at Oldham. Ian wanted me more as a player than a coach. It was while I was player-coach there that the actual ideas began to formulate. You do as you're told by and large when you play, you add your own ability but play within instructions. I always believed you play to people's strengths and devise a system to suit those strengths, because that's how to get the best out of players.

'I went to Rotherham and slipped going up a bank – my knee went backwards. I had to retire from playing. There was no coaching job there for me at Rotherham once the playing side had finished. I left Rotherham, who had got promoted as champions that year, and and went to work in Norway.

'I got my full badge, which was no mean feat in those days as less than 10 per cent of seasoned pros passed it. After that you have to go and ply your trade. I had two seasons in Norway working in amateur football. I learned a lot about people and their motivations because they weren't being paid. I made enormous mistakes, but I learned. Two years of doing nothing but train meant my knee recovered.

'I came back to England when I got the player-manager's job at Barrow. Apart from Sunderland, that was the best football team I've ever had the privilege of working with – we'd won the League by Christmas, it was dynamite. We had three or four systems that we used and could roll from one to the other to suit different problems – sometimes solutions but mainly problems. I always played with three systems all at once, there was never only one. I don't believe in just playing 4–4–2, you must have the ability to change. We would go from 4–4–2 to 4–3–3 to a rolling system. It made life difficult for the opposition. As a team you have to search out the different keys that open the doors.

'It was superb at Barrow, I couldn't have asked for any more, but then like an idiot I moved to Rochdale after speaking to Bob [Stokoe]. I was there for four years: made them a lot of money, took them to the top of the League and brought some good players in for nothing because there was no money to spend. Eventually, though, I got the sack, because the board didn't want promotion. I was instructed to sell all the players. I got Ronnie Moore for nothing and sold him to Tranmere, I got Stevie Taylor who had been at Oldham with me for nothing and sold him to Preston for about £30,000, and I had good players like Joe Cooke, a big centre-half from Bradford, John Seasman, Tony Towner and Peter Reid's brother Shaun. Having lost good players I was playing apprentices and amateurs. We needed one point to avoid re-election, but no one put their head above the parapet and said "it wasn't the manager's fault, he was told to do that." They were quite happy to take the money and get their ground back from the council. I was so disgusted that I vowed I'd never work in professional football again – and I haven't.

'It's a principle that I don't like working for people who profess to have ambition for the community or the club, when the truth is the exact opposite. I've got three children, and I wasn't on the kind of money that you could put thousands by, we were just working men. I had a brief spell with Burton Albion and took a job with Ferrodo, starting off on the factory floor and then was shift manager before I came back to the North East.

'It was the most expensive time of my life. I got sucked in and spat out, and it cost me a lot of money. You learn lessons in life. They can be very painful lessons. I think the least said the better about that because it is still very, very painful.

'A friend of mine was the groundsman at Oldham. We'd always got on and I'd never been one to be stuck up, I was just a working lad who always remembered where I came from, which was a pit village in south Derbyshire, so I was always comfortable with anybody. Jim Wibbley started this business called New Earth Water Services. He won a contract with North West Water to solve some of their problems. He phoned me up and said "Look Vic, we need someone who can talk to people, understand problems and resolve those problems. Would you be interested in doing the job?" I did that for 23 years, and during the course of that I spent two years in Mexico. That was fabulous but really hard work. I then moved to Aden to huge problems. Basically I just rode shotgun, but I really enjoyed it.'

In 1992 Sunderland reached the FA Cup Final for the first time since Vic's era. Halom was back on Wearside that year, astonishingly seeking election to Parliament as the General Election candidate for the Liberal Democrat Party. Halom has since lost faith in politicians but still has clear political views: 'I think the thing is to be honest. At that time I was swayed by the arguments. They are basic arguments. If you want to live in a good country – invest in it. Don't think you can live in this country, take out and not pay taxes, not do this and not do that. It doesn't work. It doesn't work in a company and it doesn't work as a nation. We have become a nation that wants everything for nothing. We can't do it. If you want a good health service – invest in it! They were honest answers. I was asked to do it. I was sick of the toing and froing with strikes for this and strikes for that, and that see-saw political system between Labour and Conservatives that wasn't doing the country any good at all. I fought the seat not with any real expectation of succeeding, but to highlight other Liberal Democrat campaigns in the area. I was happy to do that, but had I wanted a career in politics – and there are times when I wish I bloody did! – I wouldn't have stood as a Liberal in Sunderland North! I think some people thought "if all the fans of Sunderland vote for him he'll waltz in!"'

The prospect of Halom in the House of Commons would have been one to relish. If Chief Whips thought they could dish out aggro, what would the high and mighty have made of Vic? As for an enraged Michael Heseltine swinging the mace, how would he have reacted if Vic decided to take charge with one of his 'tackles'? The Parliament Channel would have been required viewing!

Perhaps if he had become an MP, Vic might have concerned himself with industrial injuries, because essentially that is what he now suffers from himself: 'I've just had the results of a back scan' he said in 2007. 'I need a fairly major operation to three discs and some other bits and pieces. I find a warmer climate makes me feel better, it takes some of the pain away. The plan is

Vic Halom's election leaflet.

Election Communication
Liberal Democrats **SUNDERLAND NORTH**

Photo courtesy of Northern Echo

VIC HALOM

Vic in November 2006.

to have the operations, although one surgeon has turned it down and says it's too late – we'll see! I've been having treatment of one form or another for a long time, but sadly none of it has been successful. There's no cure as such, it just makes you feel better. I know if I don't get something done I might struggle in later life.'

The consequences of a career spent as the most physical of centre-forwards is now taking its toll, but the reward for that is that Vic Halom's name will be revered by Sunderland supporters for decades to come. His part in the Cup run of '73, his classic goal against Manchester City and most of all the spirit with which he played: rough, aggressive, effective and always with the smile of a victor, all contributed to Halom being the darling of the fans without being a classic hero, in the manner of a Raich Carter or a Charlie Hurley. In the pantheon of Sunderland cult heroes, Halom must be top of the tree.

The affection Sunderland supporters feel for the Derbyshire-born son of a Hungarian father and Russian mother is mutual: 'We're sitting here over 30 years later, and I'm thinking, "I wish I hadn't left Sunderland." I used to go and talk to supporters in the crowd when the match was on. I thought Roker Park was brilliant, and when it was full to the rafters the atmosphere was electric. I feel at home here, and it's the only club that I return to. There's no other club in world I'd call home, but Sunderland actually feels like home whenever I come back. Sunderland is home to me. I try and keep in touch with people. I always see Mickey Horswill, and I always go and see little Bobby Kerr, Jim Montgomery, Ron Guthrie, Ritchie Pitt, Dick Malone – the ones that are around. I try and keep in touch, and the Former Players' Association helps a lot with that.

'I don't watch British football, although some people can't believe that. The only time I go is if I come back to Sunderland as a guest. I'm not particularly interested or enamoured. I think the standard of the game in general is bordering on pathetic, and it needs to do an awful lot in entertainment value to attract me back.

'I still appreciate the Sunderland supporters, and the whole club. They deserve the truth. Not to have chunks missed out and this and that. This is an opportunity to tell it how it was. It's not about peripheral things, there was a team here at Sunderland that at the time were second to no team in England. We believed that we were second to no team in England, and we beat the best teams comfortably.'

ALWAYS BELIEVE IN YOUR SOUL

JULIO ARCA

Midfielder
2005 Championship winner with Sunderland.

Born:	31 January 1981, Quilmes Bernal, Argentina.
Signed for Sunderland:	25 July 2000 from Argentinos Juniors, £3.5 million
Transferred:	26 July 2006 to Middlesbrough £1.75 million
Argentinos Juniors:	1 August 1998, 18+1 League apps, 0 goals
Sunderland:	25 July 2000, 145+12 League apps, 17 goals
	165+12 total apps, 23 goals
Middlesbrough:	26 July 2006, 41+4 League apps, 4 goals (to end of 2007–08 season)

'It was my mum that realised. I got the shirt when I was 11. It was my first trip to Europe with Argentinos Juniors, we went to a place near Rome. We were in a street market that had shirts all over the place. I remember getting this shirt thinking it was a Sweden shirt because it was the same colours: yellow and blue. I never understood – honestly – the badge, other than the team name started with an "S". I wore it a lot of times to play in when I was young. I was lucky because my mum never throws anything of mine out. She gives things away to friends or to charity, but she has always kept all of my football shirts.

'It was maybe two years after I signed for Sunderland that she said to me on the phone "I have a Sunderland shirt for you." I thought "So what, I've sent lots of Sunderland shirts home", but she said "It's a yellow one." I said "No, that's impossible, we've never played in a yellow shirt."

'When I went back home in the summer she showed me the shirt and it was just unbelievable. I'd never realised I'd worn a Sunderland shirt for all of those years when I was a boy, and when I held it in my hands it was a treasure

Julio with the Sunderland shirt he bought as a boy on a trip to Italy.

to me and it still is. To think I was playing for a club whose shirt I had been wearing from the age of 11 was unbelievable. It was something that I think was destiny, and I can't complain about it because I was very happy to play for Sunderland.'

Julio Arca's tale of how as a boy from Quilmes, Argentina, he had unknowingly spent his formative years developing his skills on the other side of the world wearing a Sunderland shirt, seems straight from the pages of a comic strip. As he says: 'It was destiny.'

Having made his name with his hero Diego Maradona's first club Argentinos Juniors, Julio made the move across the Atlantic, and from the southern hemisphere to Europe in the north. Sunderland was a very different place for a lad who was just 19 when he left home, and yet there were enough similarities between Julio's old home and his new one to help him settle: 'Quilmes is a big town on the coast. It is a big port but not a holiday place and most people do not have much money.'

Argentina were reigning world champions when Arca was born in 1981. Julio's countrymen had claimed the crown less than three years earlier in nearby Buenos Aires. He was five when Maradona, with or without 'The Hand of God', won the World Cup again for Argentina. Just two years before Julio's trip to Italy as an 11-year-old for that moment of destiny in his unwitting decision to pick out a Sunderland shirt from the dozens on offer, Argentina had contested another Final in Rome, losing to a late German penalty.

When Peter Reid paid £3.5 million to add Arca to the increasing number of overseas players arriving in the Premiership, Sunderland fans were keen to see the highly rated youngster – but miracles were not being expected by the Wearside public. After all, the only previous Argentinian to play for the club had been Claudio Marangoni, a midfielder who had been trumpeted as a club-record signing almost 20 years earlier but who had flopped badly. Displaying none of the silky skills associated with South Americans, Marangoni played a mere 22 games before Sunderland cut their losses and sent him back home, whereupon to everyone's absolute astonishment he became South American Player of the Year a season later!

There was to be no anticlimax with Arca. Twenty-five minutes into his debut he headed home a goal, but it was not just being a debutant goalscorer that got Julio into the crowd's good books, after all Andy Gray, Anthony le Tallec and Tore Andre Flo are among those who can claim membership of the SAFC debutant scorers club. On a night when Arca joined record signing Emerson Thome and midfielder Don Hutchison in being part of £10 million worth of talent Sunderland fans were seeing at the Stadium of Light for the first time, the 5ft 10in Argentinian teenager was an instant hit. Evidently possessing the touch of a magician, Julio spelled out that there was magic in store. Sunderland fans craved a star, someone who could do what they could not, someone who looked like he could

A young Julio with his big pal, Brazilian Emerson Thome, at Sunderland's former training ground, 'The Charlie Hurley Centre'.

make the ball talk if he wanted it to. The Black Cats had a decent team already with Kevin Phillips and Niall Quinn immense as a front two, but Julio was something different, something special. What sealed Julio's place in supporters' affections was that along with the instant control and clever touches came the willingness to 'get stuck in' – it seemed Reidy had unearthed a diamond.

It was the start of a two-way love affair as Arca took to the red-and-white army as quickly as they took to him: 'For my first game I played left wing. It was a nervous game – I was only 18 or 19. I remember scoring that goal from a Kevin Kilbane cross. It was a header – I never scored with headers. I played against players I never thought I was going to play against. West Ham had stars like Davor Suker, Paulo Di Canio and young players such as Frank Lampard, Joe Cole and Michael Carrick. It was a shock. It was such an exciting game – especially because I scored.

'It was exciting to see so many people, I had never played in front of so many people in a stadium before – I think there were 46,000 people there. At Argentinos Juniors there would sometimes be just 1,000 of our fans in the ground, and from there I went to 46,000. I'd never had that before and I could feel a bit of pressure there. Peter Reid gave me a chance, especially at that age. It was a bit scary, but I managed to stay cool and we managed to get a point. It was a good start.'

It was the first of 177 games Arca would play in a real Sunderland shirt as opposed to a childhood replica. During his six years at the club Julio deeply endeared himself to the supporters, earning cult hero status not least through his decision not to leave a sinking ship when the other big names of the day could not wait to leave, after a Sunderland side that had been good enough to finish seventh in the top flight in two of the previous three seasons suddenly registered a record Premiership low of 19 points, and with it an ignominious relegation.

> *A virtual unknown to British fans before his move to Sunderland, Julio quickly became a crowd favourite as he dovetailed his silky South American skills with a great work ethic and a fiercely competitive nature. His low centre of gravity and crouched style would have the crowd purring in admiration as he jinked his way out of a potential cul-de-sac and started yet another attack. His link up with Michael Gray provided a unique combination of defensive stability and lightning counter-attacks which was a joy to behold.*
> Mike Love, SENSSA.

Arca helped Sunderland back into the top flight, but when the Wearsiders dismally beat their own record low points tally with a feeble 15 in 2006 Julio decided to move for the sake of his own career. Almost always a player will look after number one in those situations, with no concern over anything but his deal, but while Julio had decided he had to move on there was something he could not do, because he knew it would ruin his relationship with the red-and-white army: 'I couldn't sign for Newcastle,' he admits. 'Football is football, but I thought staying in the North East was going to be miles better for me than moving away. Newcastle was all rumour, but Middlesbrough were the ones who put in a strong offer. The rivalry between Sunderland and Middlesbrough is nowhere near the rivalry between Sunderland and Newcastle, so that's why I think people at Sunderland still like me! If I'd signed for Newcastle I think it would have been different. I hope I made a decision everyone could understand. Obviously some people weren't happy about it, but most the fans who saw me play understood why I had to move. I know the fans would have been hurt if I'd signed for Newcastle, and that's why I didn't want to go there.'

At home in Washington, 2008.

There have been many big-name moves between Sunderland and their great North East rivals but, in the modern era especially, changing the colour of your stripes can leave your former fans feeling like a husband whose wife leaves him for the next door neighbour. It can be difficult to deal with, ask Lee Clark!

In reaching the stage where the Argentinian was acutely aware of how his departure would wound Sunderland fans if he joined their arch rivals, Arca had been on a journey that had seen him fulfil fantasies as a footballer and mature as a man.

Newcastle had long fancied Arca. The Magpies were interested in Julio before he even signed for Sunderland. It was at Fulham's Craven Cottage that Julio persuaded Sunderland manager Peter Reid to make a move. Playing for Argentina Under-21s, Julio shone against England Under-21s, and Reid decided to add Arca to a squad that had impressed in its first year after promotion. 'I heard from my agent' explains Julio. 'Sunderland were number one in the list. Apparently Newcastle and West Ham were interested in me, but to me they were just rumours. Sunderland were the strongest ones. They showed so strongly that they wanted to have me. I decided to go for it. I didn't know much about Sunderland. The season before I came they finished seventh, just a couple of points short of qualifying for the UEFA Cup. It was exciting to come to the UK, but it was scary because it was different food and a different country, so I didn't know what to expect.'

Given the number-33 shirt he would become synonymous with, Julio quickly established himself as a regular member of the side despite his tender age. Four days after his debut he played his first away game at Old Trafford. It would be one of only three defeats Sunderland would suffer in Julio's opening 16 games, which included a renowned 2–1 win at St James' and back-to-back 4–1 victories in his final two appearances, before returning to his homeland for the Under-20 World Cup in January for which he signed off with his third Sunderland goal, a sumptuous New Year's Day free-kick against Ipswich.

Of those who witnessed it, who can ever forget the sight of Julio Arca serving drinks in Idols with his big mate Emerson Thome, after Sunderland beat the Mags 2–1 at St Hotch Potch Park in November 2000 as hundreds of ecstatically inebriated Mackems chanted 'Julio, Julio, Julio' time and time again? It was a priceless moment and seeing the joy of players and fans together was a sight to behold. Arca has a magical left foot and won his way into the hearts of the supporters for three big reasons. Firstly, he played his game with a pride in our shirt which he still respects to this day, despite being a Boro player.

Secondly, he had an ability that supporters appreciate seeing and will pay to watch. Thirdly, he showed Sunderland loyalty after relegation and never said anything negative about the club. That is why he is still welcomed at SAFC by staff and fans alike. The fact that he still lives and socialises on Wearside cements what will be a lifelong relationship.

Tom Lynn, Sunderland supporter, Sunderland.

Julio had an Under-20 World Cup-winner's medal to his name by the time he returned to Sunderland after a six week absence. Carrying an injury, Arca was eased into action from the bench in group game hammerings of Egypt and Jamaica but became an influential figure as China, France and Paraguay were cast aside before Ghana were beaten 3–0 in the Final.

It was a massive achievement and indicative of the level Arca was at, but injury had cost Julio the captaincy of his country: 'I was a captain in the qualification games, but because I was injured and missed games I wasn't in the side at the start of the tournament. It happened away against Everton – I pulled a muscle. I was going to be out, but the manager decided to pick me for the squad even though I missed three or four games. I was lucky to be there – I always appreciate what the manager had done because not many managers will give you that chance. I consider myself lucky to have won the World Cup.'

With Argentina, Arca played as a left-back, the position he had always seen as his own, but it is a role Julio has rarely been seen in in England for either Sunderland or Middlesbrough: 'I was looking forward to playing left-back when I came over, but obviously Micky Gray was there and he was doing well. Peter Reid tried to play me left-wing, and honestly I don't think I played more than 20 games as a left-back at Sunderland because I think the only one who played me for more than the occasional game at left-back was Mick McCarthy when he became manager, and used me there when George McCartney was injured. Left-back is a position I like, but obviously I haven't been playing there for a while now. If I went back to left-back I don't know how well I could do because that position is not natural to me any more. I played mainly on the left of midfield for Sunderland, but at Middlesbrough I've played more in the centre of midfield. I'm playing in the position because I get a lot of the ball, so I have no complaints.'

There were no complaints either at the end of Arca's first season, as the Sunderland Supporters' Association named Julio as their Young Player of the Year after he had helped the lads to a second successive seventh-placed top-flight finish. Sunderland went into the final game of Julio's first season still in with a chance of earning a first ever UEFA Cup place: 'That was a good year. I remember playing for Sunderland. We finished seventh in the League here, I played in the qualification matches and then afterwards played in the Under-20 World Cup. I think that was my best year, because it was my first year at Sunderland, and I'd played quite well, and then going back to Argentina and winning the World Cup, that's even better.'

Unfortunately, Arca's second season proved to be much tougher. It began brightly enough, with the team going into a mid-October match with Manchester United in fifth place, with Arca a fixture in a side that included Stefan Schwarz and come the end of the season would draw on other established international stars such as Claudio Reyna and Patrick Mboma. However, the tide that had swept Sunderland along for Julio's first year at the club began to turn. Results ebbed away, with only three Premiership wins after Boxing Day. Indeed, a point was needed from the final game to be certain of staying up.

In an effort to arrest the decline, Sunderland dusted off the cheque book during the summer. Protracted but ultimately doomed attempts to capture Robbie Keane backed Peter Reid into a corner. With the transfer window about to close he took the plunge and invested a club-record fee in a deal said to be worth £8 million to sign Tore Andre Flo. With Marcus Stewart, Stephen Wright, Thomas Myhre, Phil Babb and Matt Piper also added to the squad, the club had invested around £20 million. This was much more than ever before, but the season was to be a complete disaster, with three different managers and a record low Premier points tally.

It was a spending spree not seen on Wearside since the 'Bank of England' days of the 1950s. However, as happened in those immediate post-war years big money only equalled big disappointment and in the end relegation. The fact that Flo was soon nicknamed Tore Andre Four because that was how many marks he regularly got out of 10 in newspaper merit marks, and the joke around Sunderland became that the club shop had run out of the letter 'p' as people bought them to add to his name they'd had printed on their shirts, indicates how, in contrast to the adoration heaped on Arca and other favourites, if the crowd did not like a player, they would certainly let him know.

Woeful performances in dismal defeats at the hands of Middlesbrough, Fulham and the old enemy Newcastle dumped Sunderland in the relegation zone at a time when Julio was out of the side through injury. Arca came back and scored in a best away win in 95 years (7–0 at Cambridge in the League Cup) and played in a Premier League win over Villa, but it was not enough to save Peter Reid who was sacked after a 3–1 defeat at Arsenal brought his seven-and-a-half-year reign to an end.

'Peter was the one to give me a chance to come to Europe,' says a grateful Julio. 'He was a nice guy. I couldn't really get in touch with him because I couldn't really speak the language when I first came to the club, so it was hard. But you could see how good he was – especially the way he treated me. Bobby Saxton and all the staff – gave me a chance to play, with me being so young.'

For an Argentinian whose only experience of an English manager was Peter Reid who had persuaded him to come to Sunderland and had brought the best out of him, Reidy's successor Howard Wilkinson must have been something of a culture shock: 'Under Howard Wilkinson I never really had a chance. I was speaking English by then, but I never really talked to him. I don't know why, I just never played much,' says Julio regretfully.

Gradually eased back into action at the start of 2003 as his injury problems cleared up, Julio never played more than three successive League games for Wilkinson before the former Leeds boss was dismissed with Sunderland rooted to the foot of the table, where they remained as all nine remaining games were lost under Mick McCarthy as Sunderland were relegated with barely a whimper.

Players were queuing up to leave Sunderland as the ship went down. Some thought one or two had been mentally boarding the lifeboats before the sinking actually took place. Players who had been involved in Sunderland's best two League placings in half a century only a couple of years earlier were now bailing out as supporters – who do not do transfers – were left to survey the wreckage.

Kevin Phillips, Thomas Sorensen, Gavin McCann and Jody Craddock led the exodus of 23 professionals from the 2002–03 season who left before the closure of the transfer window. The Premier League is seen as the only place to play, and it was no surprise that top players wanted to stay at the highest level and seek moves away from Sunderland. Always a class act, Arca could have sought the same escape route from Wearside, so why did he choose to remain with the red and whites?

'There were a couple of factors. I wasn't playing in the team before we were relegated. Mick came and started to change things around, and I wanted to stay and play. I thought we could do really well, we had a new manager with new ideas. I felt sure that if I played well he would play me. I decided to have a go. I think fans respected that.'

Not only did the fans respect Arca, they adored him for it. Here was a player for whom the shirt meant something, a player who if he 'kissed the badge' did not make supporters sick at the shallowness of the gesture. Julio was already long established as a fans' favourite, but his decision to stay with the club gave the survivors something to cling to.

Laying off a pass.

> *Julio will always have a place in the hearts of Sunderland fans and is a wonderful person for those fortunate enough to meet him. It wasn't just his talent that earned Julio Arca the respect of the supporters, Julio showed the club incredible loyalty through the dark days of the 19-point season in 2003. When Julio scored for Middlesbrough against us at the Riverside back in September 2007, he didn't celebrate and looked almost genuinely disappointed to have scored against a club that means so much to him. On his return to the Stadium of Light for Middlesbrough Arca deservedly received a standing ovation from Sunderland fans. That says it all.*
> Keith Chapman, Sunderland supporter, Jarrow.

Looking back, the player feels his decision was vindicated: 'I think it was the right decision to stay because we got to the semi-final of the FA Cup and nearly got promotion, so that was a good season, and the second season was even better because we won the League. I couldn't ask for better than that.'

To the credit of the former Republic of Ireland manager Mick McCarthy, he turned things round in his first full season on Wearside. Losing the opening two games meant he had overseen a run of 11 defeats as part of a club-record run of 17 losses on the bounce. One more and the worst-ever run in English football would have been equalled. Long-forgotten Football League club Darwen had lost 18 in a row way back in 1898–99. Things were so bad that their modern counterparts turned up at Deepdale to watch Sunderland equal the record should they lose to Preston live on TV.

Ruled out of the first two matches, Arca returned at Preston and helped make a difference as goals from Sean Thornton and Marcus Stewart signalled that 'Sunderland were back', and the nation's comics could begin looking for a new target for their football jokes. With the weight lifted from their collective shoulders, Sunderland started to recover. The next game on 25 August saw home fans celebrate their first win since before Christmas.

Now rampant, the Black Cats walloped Bradford 4–0 on their own patch, with Arca scoring his best goal for Sunderland and one of the best any player has ever scored for the club: 'I think I'll never forget the first one I scored as it was my debut, but this one was special because of the way I scored the goal – I got the ball in our box, ran all the way – no one was running behind me! I got to the 18-yard box and thought I'd try a chip. We played so well I think we won three or four nil, it was a fantastic game and exciting to score a goal like that,' remembers Julio. It was a goal that could only be scored by a player of the highest calibre. Storming out of defence, leaving a trail of defenders in his wake, the truly fantastic thing about this goal was the finish. Reaching the edge of the box with no one up in support the Argentinian showed composure, inventiveness and technique to deliver the most sublime of finishes. 'Keeper Mark Paston was a towering 6ft 5in but could only watch and wonder as this marauding left-back, looking ever so slightly bedraggled as he often did like some Dickensian urchin, lifted the ball over him and into the net.

This was perhaps the most iconic moment of Julio's time at the club. It summed up everything there was to admire about him: commitment and class. Quite often Sunderland supporters have seen players with one of those qualities without the other, Julio was the complete package. For those that were there to see it, it will be a goal they will still recall when they are too old and infirm to go the match anymore. For those brought up hearing tales of Shack and Charlie Hurley, Julio and this magical goal in particular will be one of the Sunderland stories grandchildren of the future will be told about.

Perhaps those grandchildren of the 2040s and beyond will be serenaded with the chant that received its first airing in that game at Bradford. To the tune of the Spandau Ballet hit *Gold* the red-and-white army declared their belief in Julio thus:

'JuliO
Always believe in your soul.
Always believe in yourself,
You're indestructible,
Always believe in, JuliO!'

'It's really good that they sing about me. I really appreciate it when the fans say my name,' Julio told the match programme *Red and White* at the time: 'It is great for me that the people like me when I've come to a different country, especially as last season I didn't play too much. I'm very happy that the people remember me all the time.'

It was only Arca's sixth League start in 18 months, but the return of a fully fit and in-form Julio coincided with the upturn of Sunderland's fortunes.

Arca had a welcome habit of coming up with good goals, and they were often important ones. Altogether he notched 23 goals for the club, including one in a League Cup win over Manchester United, an equaliser at West Ham on the night the 2005 Championship was clinched, winners in the opening two ties of the run to the semi-final of the FA Cup in 2004, and a couple of superb free-kicks.

Missing out on the FA Cup Final and a guaranteed UEFA Cup place for the finalists that year due to opponents Manchester United's Champions League qualification remains one of Julio's biggest regrets: 'It was such a disappointment. To see so many people there and for everyone to be let down was sad. I remember me and some of the other players sitting there after the game and thinking about how close we were to getting into UEFA, because to win that game we would have qualified to UEFA, which would have been massive for the club. We were so close, and that's what was so disappointing. I can't remember seeing so many scarves and flags in the crowd for Sunderland. Something you try not to think about too much because you try to remember the good stuff, but it's hard to forget.'

Over the years Sunderland have served up more than a fair share of misery for their supporters, and as if one semi-final disappointment was not bad enough there was another even more important one in store later the same season. Having climbed from one off the bottom of the table prior to that turning point at Preston, the Lads had risen to third and a place in the Play-offs. Leading 4–3 on aggregate against Crystal Palace with a minute to go in the second leg, they were undone by a most controversial last-minute equaliser. If Sunderland 'do' misery they certainly do not 'do' penalties! 'I remember that game. The second goal they scored was a foul on Mart Poom – a shocking foul. Then we went to penalties and we took some bad penalties.'

Previous Play-off experiences included, of course, losing a Play-off Final to Charlton on spot-kicks despite scoring all of their first six! On this occasion, despite goalkeeper Mart Poom's heroics, Sunderland contrived to miss their last two and lose, Jeff Whitley's 'twinkletoes' run-up still haunting those of a red-and-white persuasion almost as much as Michael Gray's 1998 Wembley attempt.

Julio scores for Sunderland at Brighton's Withdean Stadium in 2005.

Like every other Sunderland supporter, Julio watched the Palace penalty shoot-out from the stands, injury having eliminated him from the final few fixtures. 'Fortunes always hiding' as his debut opponents like to sing, but success was waiting for Julio a year later in the shape of a Championship-winning season and a medal for Julio to have as a memento of his time at Sunderland. Before he could embark on that promotion-winning campaign, though, Julio collected another souvenir of his time on Wearside, one he would rather not have had, a jellyfish sting, inflicted by what was believed to be a 'Portuguese Man-o-war' suffered while on a training run with the first-team squad along the North Sea coast. It was enough to hospitalise Julio, make him the butt of an endless stream of jokes about the incident, and bizarrely add to his cult-hero status.

When the competition consists of Claudio Marangoni and Nicolas Medina, being considered the club's best ever Argentinian is hardly the highest accolade you can bestow on Julio Arca. Consider the facts that he scored on his debut, had jaw dropping ball control and even postponed his international aspirations after relegation, though, and you realise why we loved him. He even took a jellyfish sting for his troubles.
Andrew Smithson, Sunderland supporter.

A meagre five points from the first six games of 2004–05 did not augur well for a season Sunderland needed to engineer their escape from the Championship or face a third year out of the big League, and with it the resultant loss of parachute payments. Fifteenth in mid-September, they clicked into gear with a Marcus Stewart hat-trick inspiring a 4–0 win at Gillingham. Julio got on the score sheet himself next time out as a four-game winning run catapulted the Black Cats towards the front runners.

Julio videoed every moment of the promotion parade in 2005.

Come the end of the season the League had been claimed, with runners-up Wigan all of seven points behind. Only the front two of Stewart and Kevin Kyle exceeded Julio's tally of nine goals from midfield, or, in some games, full-back.

Although Sunderland would decline the offer of an open-topped bus parade through the city when the Championship was won under Roy Keane in 2007, in 2005 the players lapped it up. Julio was one of many players who never let go of his camcorder throughout the journey: 'Yeah – I recorded all 45–50 minutes, and I showed it to everyone at home. It was fantastic. When we were in the Civic Centre at the start there were people in there, but not many, but when we went out it was unbelievable! How many people were there I don't know. People had just left work and left everything that they had to do to come and see us. It was fantastic the reception, people singing and shouting.'

McCarthy had bought well in the Championship-winning season, plucking players from the lower divisions and moulding them into a title-winning team. 'I think he surprised everyone when he brought players from lower divisions and everyone was thinking "What's going to happen now?" but I think he did well' says Julio, 'He got Deano [Dean Whitehead], Liam Lawrence, Neill Collins, Andy Welsh – all young players coming from nowhere – they were fantastic – they did very well. I think we played very well that season, everyone pulled their weight, but I thought Mick would buy some new players to help us in the Premier League.'

Having registered a record low 19 points in the Premiership just two years earlier, Sunderland knew how tough the top flight could be. McCarthy had been thwarted in his attempts to sign Jon Stead from Huddersfield Town, Premier League Blackburn outbidding him and reaping the rewards

At a dinner with former Sunderland defender Neill Collins.

as Stead's scoring streak of six goals in 13 top-flight games, including four winning goals, had kept Blackburn up in the season Sunderland succumbed to Palace in the Play-offs. A fee of £1.8 million was invested in signing Stead from Rovers, with the bulk of the rest of his budget going on seven figure sums for striker Andy Gray and goalkeeper Kelvin Davis.

Other newcomers included Daryl Murphy for £100,000 from Waterford and Nyron Nosworthy on a free transfer from Gillingham. Also arriving on frees were experienced ex-Everton stopper Alan Stubbs, North East born Tommy Miller who had scored freely from midfield with Ipswich and youngster Martin Woods. French striker Anthony le Tallec was acquired on a season-long loan from Liverpool, while other new faces to arrive during the season were full-back Justin Hoyte on loan from Arsenal, utility man Rory Delap whom McCarthy knew from his time with Ireland, and French midfielder Christian Bassila who looked a world beater on his debut at Chelsea, before looking like the rest of the world would beat him for the rest of the season.

This was a big season for Sunderland and an equally important one for Arca. Having stayed when other star names left two years earlier, Julio knew he was coming into his best years as he was by now in his mid-20s. Had Sunderland stayed up that season rather than failing to even match the record low number of points they had gathered last time, Arca would probably have been happy to stay. Maybe he would have become that rarity of the modern game, a player who qualifies for a testimonial after 10 years service.

Sunderland, though, were never at the races that season. Kicking-off with a home game against Charlton who had won one of their last 14 games the previous season, there was optimism that an all important good start might be managed. No chance. One nil down in 10 minutes when debutant goalkeeper Kelvin got his angles all wrong, Sunderland ended up losing 3–1 despite the visitors being reduced to 10 men. What is more, the Lads looked way off the pace of the opposition. The bright spot was a debut goal by new striker Gray…it would also be his last goal for the club. Stead waited until April Fool's

Playing cricket on a pre-season tour of Canada.

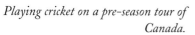

Signing autographs.

Day for his solitary goal of the season. Fortunately, one game was abandoned with the Lads trailing 1–0. It was fortunate, in that when it was replayed as the last home game of the season Sunderland finally registered their only home League win of the campaign.

These were dark days. Had the 15 and 19 points gained from the last two Premiership seasons been added together the total still would not have been sufficient for survival. Mick McCarthy had been sacked with 10 games to go. Julio was sorry to see him go: 'When Mick came everything was different. He was an honest guy, I think everyone liked him. He gave a chance to everyone, and he did as well as he could. I had some good times when he was there, I think we enjoyed some good times. We keep in touch because I think he's a really nice guy.'

Installed in the managerial hot seat on a caretaker basis was club legend Kevin Ball. Popular with the fans because of his heart on the sleeve, blood on the boots approach during his decade as a player, Bally lifted the team to put in some creditable performances, but it was far too little far too late. While the squad contained some players who evidently lacked the appetite for a battle, the players who played week in week out were in no way deserving of the tag of 'worst team ever' which their record bestowed them with. They were not much good – 15 points makes that undeniable, but being beaten week after week would knock the stuffing out of most players, and these lads never ever gave up. No one ever beat them by more than three goals, and yet they had a fraction of the ability of the '19-point team'.

For Julio, though, it was the end of the road. He had stayed when Sunderland had been relegated before and helped them back into the big time. This time, though, he could not see how Sunderland would get back to the top flight, let alone seek to make an impression on it. He stayed during the close season and went on a pre-season training camp at Bath.

The club had been in a state of flux all summer as long serving chairman Bob Murray sold the club to the Drumaville Consortium led by Julio's former teammate Niall Quinn. Niall of course was trying everything to turn around a vessel bigger than the *Titanic*, but one that had hit the iceberg some time ago. During that week in Bath, Julio confided, 'I can have the chance to go. I would love to stay at Sunderland, but it is probably best that I leave and have a fresh challenge.'

Ironically, Arca's very last game for Sunderland was the very first the club played in the Drumaville era. It was a pre-season friendly at non-League Forest Green Rovers. At that point Sunderland were yet to appoint a manager and the week's training had been supervised by a combination of coach Kevin Richardson, goalkeeper coach Tim Carter and medical man Pete Friar.

Posing with a young supporter who had painted his portrait.

Niall Quinn had been at the training camp for a day or two, but he was yet to appoint himself manager and was obviously trying to deal with a million and one things as the club was in the process of changing hands.

Looking back at his departure from the club he had grown to love, Julio reflects: 'We got to that point. After we were relegated I went home, came back and we'd parted with the manager. Niall Quinn was taking over the place, but there was no manager. Everything seemed to be going in the wrong direction. When I left the club it looked like falling apart, and before long Sunderland were one off the bottom of Championship. Things changed from one week to another, and then Roy Keane came to the club, bought some good players, won the League and then got some different players to keep the team in the Premier League, so I think Sunderland won't have this up and down habit they had before.

'Of course, when I left all that was in the future and things had been bad. When Middlesbrough came in I wasn't sure, because when you're comfortable in a place you don't really want to leave it. But because things weren't going our way, I thought maybe it was time for me to put my hands up and say "thanks very much for everything, but I think its time for me to go and find a new challenge." I couldn't have gone to Newcastle who were supposed to be interested in me, but that was never to be for me, but signing for Middlesbrough meant I could stay where I was happy living without deeply upsetting Sunderland supporters.

'Two or three weeks after I left everything changed at Sunderland, but you don't have much time to make these decisions, especially in the close-season window. I made that decision, and now I'm doing as well as I can for Middlesbrough. It was a decision that was made for me. There was no one else involved – no pressure from anyone else but, maybe the way the club was run made my decision.'

Middlesbrough have a recent tradition of signing top stars: Juninho, Ravanelli, Boksic, Mendietta and Yakubu are just some of the 'Marquee' players to have starred at the Riverside in its short history. Consequently Julio's arrival was warmly welcomed by Boro fans, who clearly were delighted at having signed their near neighbours' most popular player. Julio's relationship with Teesside supporters would be different to that at Sunderland, although the player rationalises: 'It could be because I spent such a long time at Sunderland and the Middlesbrough fans haven't got to know me as well yet. I don't know what will happen in the future. I play as well as I can for Middlesbrough, and I think that as long as fans see you working your socks off then they like you. Middlesbrough's are a different kind of fans to Sunderland's maybe, but they are good.'

Boro finished 12th in Julio's first season with them, during which he played 18 times, while Sunderland were busy storming to the Championship title at the first time of asking under the guidance of Roy Keane, who had taken over the managerial reigns from chairman Quinn less than a month into the season. Sunderland's instant promotion meant Julio would face his old club quicker than many had expected.

Just a month into the season, Arca lined up against Sunderland for the first time. Prior to the game at Boro he had made it clear that should he score he would not celebrate a goal against Sunderland, and he was true to his word. Julio was certainly at the centre of the action and not just because of the central midfield role he occupied for Boro in contrast to the wide left berth Wearsiders were more used to seeing him operate in. Just two minutes into the game he uncharacteristically gave the ball away and, as had happened so many times before, Sunderland scored after Julio had been in possession.

Arca quickly made amends for his new fans equalising just 11 minutes later at the end where the Sunderland supporters were housed. Especially as he was atoning for his earlier error Julio could have been forgiven for celebrating the goal – Sunderland fans would forgive him almost anything, except, as he rightly says, signing for Newcastle – but he steadfastly refused to do so, instead simply running back to his own half ready for the re-start. Ten minutes later he was stretchered off after a collision with Dwight Yorke. Warmly applauded by all sides of the ground as he was carried off, there was one section of the ground on their feet giving Julio a standing ovation...the Sunderland section!

Asked if he would celebrate a goal against Sunderland in a future match, perhaps considering that having refused to celebrate his first goal against Sunderland as a mark of respect there would

On his first return to the Stadium of Light with Boro, here Julio cannot stop Danny Higginbotham scoring for Sunderland.

be no problem with celebrating a future goal, Arca had no hesitation in declaring: 'I would do the same thing. I don't think it's right to celebrate against people that I'm still in touch with and still like. That's my point of view. It's nice to give that kind of respect because I left the club in a good way. And you never know if you one day have to go back, if I go back I obviously hope to have a good relationship still.'

Clearly understanding Sunderland fans' admiration of him, would Arca accept that he was idolised by the red-and-white army? 'I wouldn't say I was aware of that, but when you give a little bit of respect no matter how good or bad you are – and if you give everything for the team, I think people respect that. I think the kind of personality that you have matters. I never had a problem with the fans, no matter how good or bad the position of the team, that's why even now if I go somewhere or if I go to the stadium, people come and talk to me in a nice way.

'I think that when I moved I moved in a good way. Football has to bring you new challenges, and I saw a new challenge for me. But I never forgot why I went to Sunderland or how the people treated me there, that's why I still keep in touch and why it's nice always to go back. I have no complaints about how Sunderland and the fans there treated me, they helped me lot.'

Rumours abounded that Sunderland wanted to re-sign Arca once they returned to the Premier League in 2007, and no doubt those rumours will continue to surface from time to time. Obviously Arca as a model professional will always give his best for Middlesbrough, but nonetheless he was touched by the rumours: 'It's nice to be wanted. At the end of my first year at Middlesbrough there were rumours that Sunderland wanted to sign me again, and that made me glad even though nothing happened, because it made me think I did well there because they wanted me to go back. That made me really glad. I didn't show it outwardly, but knowing I'd be welcomed back at Sunderland where I played for so long made me one of the happiest guys in the world. If at whatever point in my future career something happened and I had the chance to play for Sunderland again then you never know. Obviously I'm under contract to Middlesbrough, and I'll always do my best for them until the day comes when I leave. Anything can happen in football, and as I say it's always nice to be wanted, especially by the club I used to play for.'

The kind of affection Arca has for Sunderland is normally the preserve of a local lad, someone who has grown up steeped in a red-and-white environment, being brought up in a red-and-white family and surrounded by Sunderland-supporting friends. The likes of Grant Leadbitter, Martin Smith, Gary Rowell or, back in the foggy mists of time, someone like Bobby Gurney all grew up in that scenario. There are, though, many players from outside the area who develop a deep love of SAFC and the passion its supporters have for it. Niall Quinn is a prime example of that, as is Kevin Ball or Len Ashurst. That trio hail from Dublin, Hastings and Liverpool, but Arca is not even from the northern hemisphere, yet he caught the bug.

'I think it's because people saw me growing up at the club. I was just a young boy when I first came to Sunderland. I was still a teenager then, but I was 25 when I left. The fans saw me changing over the years, and I grew to love the club in the way that Kevin did and Niall did before me. I think that no matter where you are from, people respect you if you do your best for the club. You get some foreign players who don't do as well for clubs as people expect them to, but I was lucky to be one of the people who did well. I was trying to do everything as good as I could at Sunderland, and that helped me to gain people's respect.'

When Boro are not playing and Sunderland are live on TV it is not unusual for Julio to be spotted about town cheering the lads on, and when he has had the chance he has taken up the opportunity to come along and see games at the Stadium of Light: 'The first year after I left I went a couple of times and I've been again since. It's always nice to go back and see people, and I like to see the team even if I hardly know any of the players because the players I knew have moved on. I like to go and see football, and I always like to see Sunderland. I normally don't like to show myself much but of course people spot me and always talk to me in a nice way, as I do to them. People always make me very welcome at Sunderland, and that is very nice.'

Julio Arca was a huge cult hero at Sunderland, one of the biggest ever. For fans starved of 'stars' Arca was someone who shone. For Sunderland supporters he was a tremendously skilful player but also a real grafter. Top that off with the fact that whenever any supporter met him Julio was invariably friendly, polite, modest and genuinely touched to be the subject of such adoration, and the bar-room stories about what a canny lad he was only served to further enhance his already glowing reputation. Whether he ever dons the red-and-white stripes again is a matter you would need a crystal ball to answer, but whatever Arca achieves in the remainder of his career his memories of playing for the red-and-white army will remain as important to him as they are for those who watched him.

'The things I got from the club – like the Player of the Year award and the Championship medal – they're things you keep in a security box. I don't want to show anyone in case I lose them. I'll remember that Championship season forever, because I'd won something for Sunderland, which is all I ever wanted to do.'

JOHNNY KAY'S RED-AND-WHITE TRACTOR

JOHN KAY

Right-back

1988 Third Division Championship winner with Sunderland.
1990 promotion winner to top flight with Sunderland.

Born:	29 January 1964, Sunderland General Hospital. Raised in Lumley, County Durham.
Signed for Sunderland:	22 July 1987 from Wimbledon £22,500
Transferred:	August 1996 to Preston North End, free
Arsenal:	Associated schoolboy, 1979
	Apprentice 1980
	Professional August 1981, 13+1 League apps, 0 goals
Wimbledon:	July 1984, 63 League apps, 2 goals
Middlesbrough:	(Loan) January 1985, 8 League apps, 0 goals
Sunderland:	22 July 1987, 196+3 League apps, 0 goals
	236+3 total apps, 0 goals
Shrewsbury Town:	(Loan) 28 March 1996, 7 League apps, 0 goals
Preston North End:	(Non-contract) 23 August 1996, 7 League apps, 0 goals
Scarborough:	September 1996, 98 League apps, 0 goals
Workington:	September 1999

Of all the stories about John Kay, the one every supporter is likely to recall first is the occasion when 'Kaysie' sat up and paddled his 'boat' off the pitch while he was being stretchered off. Plenty of players have been capable of a bit of 'Halomesque' playing to the gallery, especially if as so often happens these days seconds after the injured player has been removed from the pitch he is bouncing up and down on the touchline signalling to the referee that he is ready to come back on, having made a Lazarus like recovery. In Kay's case, though, he had just broken his leg, he was aware he had broken his leg and carried off on this, his 199th League appearance, he would never play for Sunderland again. It was a farewell that will never be forgotten.

'What a day!' says John, 'I don't know what it was that made me do it. I knew when it happened that it was serious. The physio Steve Smelt came on and tried to take my boot off. I was saying "Smelty, my leg's snapped, just leave it." Trying to take my boot off didn't help to be fair!

'Prior to the game I'd played in a reserve match when Shaun Cunnington had been stretchered off and I remember thinking, "They'll not stretcher me off." I wasn't even supposed to be playing. I'd been ruled out for eight to 10 weeks after breaking my cheek-bone, and this was about seven weeks later. I'd done well in a reserve game at Newcastle, so when [manager] Terry Butcher asked me to play I just said "Yes, no bother." But I went and broke my leg, and that proved to be my last game for Sunderland.'

Kaysie had long been a cult hero of those keeping the faith as Sunderland sunk to their lowest ever ebb with relegation to the old Third Division, with Johns Kay and MacPhail each brought in for modest fees of around £20,000 each, and Sunderland's only other summer acquisition being a loanee goalkeeper in Steve Hardwick who, when given the chance to sign permanently after a good start to the season, declined the offer reportedly because he did not want to face the possibility of taking the sort of stick he had suffered at Newcastle, when Magpie fans had apparently turned on him. John Kay, on the other hand, was up for any fights going, and if anyone wanted to turn on him he would be there in a flash.

Like Joe Bolton before him, Kay did not do '50–50' tackles. Even '90–10' tackles with the odds against him were there to be won as far as Kay was concerned, so inevitably with such an attitude John rapidly earned a cult hero status that never waned. At this time in their history Sunderland needed fighters. New manager Denis Smith had been a similar kind of 'never-say-die' character in his playing days at Stoke, and he knew that Kay had the character Sunderland needed. The fact that it was known John was popular in the dressing room and was as up for a laugh as he was for a tackle added to his popularity. Throw in the fact that as a rugged defender he would belt down the wing, often looking like he would score but never quite managing to – a bit like Tom never quite getting Jerry – and you had the identikit Sunderland cult hero.

A classic case of Kaysie doing his bit to lock down his side of the defence, and give the fans something to laugh about as well, came in the 1990 Play-off semi-final second leg away to Newcastle. Being a local lad, John knew that this was a game that needed to be won and never mind how…what was that about '90–10' tackles?

'It was an incredible game,' he says. 'I was up against a lad called Billy Askew who was from Lumley like me. He was a couple of years older than me, but we'd

John Kay arrived at a time when Sunderland needed fighters.

grown up playing on the same pitches. All of a sudden in the biggest game Sunderland and Newcastle had had for years there were two Lumley lads up against each other. No one picked up on it, and I was surprised the press never mentioned it. He was their left-winger, so he was directly up against me, but he got dragged off and subbed. I'd put him in the stand once and that helped!

'In the close season we played together up at Lumley with the lads. Billy had loads of ability. He was like Stan Cummins in that he was small and had all the touches. I'd played against him a few times, so I knew how to deal with him in the derby. In the Newcastle game I whacked him after about 10 minutes right on the touchline, and some of the Newcastle supporters came out of the paddock onto the side of the pitch to have a go with me, but I was like, "Get back." This was not some invitation to a karaoke Paul McCartney evening but basically all 5ft 10in of Sunderland's right-back saying to the Mags, 'Come and have a go if you think you're hard enough.' Later on, of course, they had a try, invading the pitch in an attempt to get the game abandoned, but by then Sunderland had it wrapped up and Kaysie's man was already in the stand long before the rest of the teams were taken off for an extended break while order was restored.

Three years earlier a contingent of black and whites had all 'laffed' at 'Sun'lund' in the Clock Stand Paddocks of Roker Park as the Lads sunk to that relegation to the Third Division, but this was the red and whites' night, and as ever Kaysie was in the thick of it.

Without winning another game – thanks to Play-off 'victors' Swindon being punished for financial misdemeanours – Sunderland were back in the top flight. It had been some turnaround from the point where John came into the Sunderland story: 'When I signed for Sunderland they'd just been relegated to the Third Division, but that didn't come into it – I just wanted to come back home from London. I'd got married to my girlfriend by then, and she was from the North East as well. It wasn't as if the football side didn't interest me, it did, but I'd have signed anyway just to come back to the North East. It was a great move for me at the time, even though Sunderland had just gone down because obviously I knew it was a big club with great potential. Financially I wasn't any better off, but I was just pleased to move.'

Like his County Durham born compatriot Joe Bolton, Great Lumley lad Kaysie was naturally hard and didn't have to work on an act to emphasise it! Renowned for the day he got injured against Birmingham and then sat up on the stretcher rowing an imaginary canoe, John also gained notoriety when Leeds manager Howard Wilkinson described a tackle on his player, Peter Haddock, an ex-Mag, as being comparable to Haddock being 'run over by a tractor,' Thus the famous 'Red-and-White Tractor' T-shirts that rose to prominence in the wake of Wilko's outburst. Kay was a key figure in Sunderland's Third Division Championship success of 1988 and although known for his eccentricities he was a pretty steady full-back whose cult status is fully deserved. Again, like Joe Bolton, it shouldn't cloud over the fact that the ex-Arsenal man was a decent player and one who is still revered by the generation who grew up watching him play.
Tom Lynn, Sunderland supporter, Sunderland.

'We won the League in my first season, but we had the best side on paper. We signed a couple of good players and had a couple of lads up front who could score goals, so to be honest that season

In full stride in front of the Clock Stand at Roker Park.

was pretty much a piece of p***' is John's succinct version of Sunderland's solitary season in what is now classed as League One. Forty-six games, 93 points, new men Kay and MacPhail the two ever presents and the Gabbiadini–Gates 'G-Force' conquering all before them. Job done.

While John's first season could not have gone much better, his second season could not have been much worse from an injury point of view. Sunderland did perfectly okay, a season of consolidation, building on promotion and establishing a base for the second promotion that would follow a year later. On a personal level, though, a run of 58 consecutive League and Cup appearances from his debut came to a grinding halt with just four late-season games being added to the tally he had reached by September. 'When I first joined Sunderland I did really well injury-wise. Even though I played every game, my performances died down in the second half of my first season, and then in my second season I struggled a bit with injuries. I had a couple of hamstrings, my Achilles played up again and I had a couple of back injuries plus a couple of suspensions, so I ended up playing just about 11 games.'

The first part of the 1989–90 campaign was not much better, but having got back into the team at the start of December John never missed a game as promotion was won with Newcastle left in the Lads' wake in the Play-offs. While John was holding down the right-back berth, his counterpart on the left was Paul Hardyman, who had cause to remember the Play-offs for the wrong reasons.

With the first leg at Roker poised at 0–0, Hardyman stepped up to take a last-minute penalty. Newcastle 'keeper John Burridge saved it, with Hardyman sent off in the aftermath for following up and seemingly trying to force the ball, the goalkeeper, the peanut seller and anything else he could find into the back of the net. 'We were gutted for Paul because he'd miss the second leg,' notes John, who still had high hopes of progress. 'We were the underdogs because they'd finished six points ahead of us. On the other hand, we'd done well towards the end of the season and had a good away record especially late in the season.' Indeed, Sunderland had won six of their previous seven away games, and although all three derbies had been drawn Sunderland had bossed them all, particularly at St James' in February, where the Magpies were grateful for a strong wind that acted as a leveller.

'I can remember going to the game at St James' thinking we had a great chance of winning because Newcastle were terrified. It was an even bigger game for them than it was for us because we had nothing to lose in a sense, because they'd finished above us and had been to our place and got a draw, so there was a lot of expectation on them. The way we'd played in the first leg gave us confidence because we knew we were capable of going there and winning.'

An early Eric Gates goal began with John's throw, and Sunderland never looked like relinquishing control. Sometimes teams just know it is their night, in the way Dick Malone, for instance, talks about the 1973 Cup replay with Manchester City. This was such a night. Newcastle could have played until midnight and not scored. In fact they nearly did have to play until midnight. Once Marco Gabbiadini had doubled the visitors' lead, thousands of the home fans disgraced the many fine Newcastle supporters who witnessed their team losing one of the most important derbies of all time without resorting to a pitch invasion. To the red-and-white army though, the spectacle only added to the unbridled joy of the evening.

As always Kaysie saw the funny side: 'All the fans came on, and we all ran for it, but Benno being Benno thought he'd walk off looking cool, only someone kicked him up the backside!' he laughs. 'George Courtney [the referee] came into our dressing room and said "Look lads, if we're here until midnight we'll get the last four minutes played." It's easier playing than watching because when you're playing you can affect the game, and you have a feeling about which way the game is going to go. We were basically a young team who'd grown up together. When we walked into the dressing rooms we had the music on and were quite relaxed, but it was clear they were a bundle of nerves. We saw Jim Smith and Bobby Saxton [the Magpies manager and assistant], and they were obviously on edge as well.'

The season had begun with a 2–0 away win at Swindon, who now stood between Sunderland and the top flight. Rumours were rife that the Wiltshire club were guilty of a long list of financial wrongdoings and would be punished for it. There were more rumours at Roker Park than a Fleetwood Mac convention, but Kay confirms the players were oblivious to such stories: 'No one mentioned it at all. Denis Smith took us away to Menorca for five days. There was no training, just a few drinks and a bit of relaxing to conserve energy. In the game itself we were awful. We did okay for about 10 minutes and then got battered even though the final score was only 1–0. Tony Norman had a good game and so did Gary Owers, but the rest of us were poor, and if we'd lost by five we couldn't have complained, but Tony kept us in it. The Newcastle game had been such a big game for us. It was a game we had to win, so much so that I think it took a lot out of us mentally and physically.'

Defeat at Wembley far more comprehensive than the 1–0 scoreline suggests left supporters at least clinging to the hope that maybe those pre-match rumours might turn out to be true, and there might be a hope of Sunderland being promoted after all. It was several weeks later when the news broke that Swindon's punishment when found guilty of financial irregularities involved Sunderland being promoted instead of them: 'Denis Smith rang us all up. I remember asking him if we still got the promotion bonus – not that it was a big deal, I think we only got a couple of hundred quid!'

Extra cash would have been useful to Kaysie, who had had his ups and downs that season, not least following a League Cup tie at the other St James' Park in Exeter. Sunderland had been there for a League Cup tie four days before John got back into action after injury. 'I'd been an unused sub. After the match Terry Cooper, who was their manager, invited us to a pub which was either his or his mate's, so we went. On the way back there were a group of us. Paul Williams was ahead of me and had jumped on top of a car. I jumped on it after him and had a little dance on the roof before sliding down the windscreen. A bloke appeared at a window and started shouting, so just to p*** him off I bent the aerial and walked off.

'Of course at the hotel later on there were police all over the place, and Denis Smith knew it was us because we'd just got back. It was one of Paul Williams's first away trips, and he was really worried, so I told him to keep quiet and said I'd take the rap, so it all came back to me and I got hammered.'

Behind Kaysie in goal for much of John's time at Sunderland was Tony Norman: 'John Kay was a fairly quiet lad until he'd had a drink, and then he wasn't!' remembers Tony. 'When you met him for the first time he was a lovely lad, but if you tried to run rings round him on a football pitch, he'd kick you. We used to call him 'Tut' because on the pitch he'd tut. Anything goes wrong and he tuts…years later we met up for a Masters six a side tournament. Our first game comes along, and we go out. Within 30 seconds Kaysie gets in a tussle, and he lands somebody on the floor after having a quiet dig in their ribs. The referee spots him and comes over and he tuts. Priceless!

'He was great. I had a lot of respect for him. We really got on; he was great to have in the dressing room. He was as daft as a brush. He wasn't bothered. If you were out on a lads night out, he'd do something daft. We stayed over after a game once and one morning Denis [manager Denis Smith] was there. He sort of looked and must have known straight off who'd been out and had a bit too much. He said "Just had the hotel on to me saying something about plants." Straight away Kaysie jumped in saying "It wasn't me!" No one had even said anything to him! He had a habit of asking everyone: "I was alright wasn't I?" From then on it was a standing joke this story about the plants.'

Tony Norman's quote taken from *Match of My Life: Sunderland*, also by Rob Mason.

That League Cup run certainly was not without incident. The following round after Exeter were dismissed is remembered for a celebrated bout between Gary Bennett and David Speedie, a re-match from the 1985 League Cup semi-final when Speedie was with Chelsea. Bennett finished up lifting Speedie into Roker Park's Clock Stand paddock, 'For the crowd to finish him off' as he jokes, but put the incident into your search box on *YouTube*, and there will be no prizes for guessing who is first on the scene to 'assist' Benno.

> *Move aside Chris Makin; this lad was the original goal-shy hard-as-nails right-back. Every cult hero needs a good nickname, and The Red-and-White Tractor just about covered it. The crowd against Birmingham in October '93 must have been about 40,000 given the amount of people that recall seeing Kaysie rowing down the tunnel after breaking his leg, and just about every fan of a certain age will have their own special memory of him; most of which will have taken place a million miles from a football pitch.* Andrew Smithson, Sunderland supporter, Sunderland.

Sunderland's promotion was not built on, although the Lads went down fighting. Going into the final match of the season they needed a result away to Manchester City to avoid the drop: 'Peter Reid was their manager and Quinny got a couple of goals, but the main thing I remember about that game is the Sunderland supporters, who were absolutely magnificent that day. There must have been 15,000 of them there,' remembers John of a day that was in a way 'Classic' Sunderland. Glorious defeat in a five-goal thriller, where the lead changed hands three times, watched by support no other club could match – 15,000 travelling away for a relegation battle – and the fullness of time bringing the opposition manager and two goalscorers to later rejuvenate the red and whites. Sometimes away followings are exaggerated, City with nothing to play for that day had a seasonal high of 39,194 compared to 24,037 at their previous home game and a second-highest gate of 36,427 in their derby with Man Utd.

'Paul Hardyman got stretchered off, and I went to left-back,' recalls John who, in an odd – pre-squad number – numbering system used by Sunderland in the last few matches of that season, was wearing number 11. The traditional left-winger's number certainly suited Kaysie as he stormed down the left flank before firing over a fabulous cross without breaking stride for Marco Gabbiadini to bullet home with a header to level Niall Quinn's opener.

Disappointment was to haunt Sunderland the following year too, and for John it was on a personal as well as a professional level. A season of struggle saw them hover just above the drop zone back to the Third Division they had left just four years earlier, but after sacking Denis Smith at the turn of the year caretaker boss Malcolm Crosby oversaw an unexpected Cup run all the way to Wembley for the 1992 FA Cup Final against Liverpool. John played in all seven games up to the Final, indeed he did not miss a match from August until the end of April, but cruelly injury ruled him out of the Final: 'I had a calf strain. It was just wear and tear, and I'd been struggling with it in the League. We had a lot of games shortly before the Cup Final, and I tore it at Brighton.' Sunderland certainly

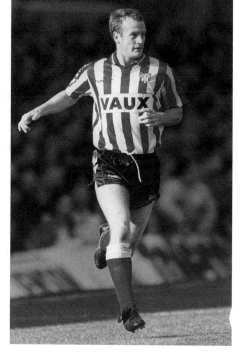

Injury ruled Kay out of the 1992 FA Cup Final.

did not have the best preparation for Wembley and beginning with a derby at Newcastle they played 12 games in 34 days leading up to Cup Final week, including the Cup semi-final, and they needed points from League games to guard against relegation.

John was a massive loss but typically did the best he could for the team and admitted he was not up to it, rather than going for personal glory and letting people down: 'We travelled to the Cup Final on the Wednesday, and Crossa gave me until the last minute. I was struggling just jogging, and while Crossa gave me every chance I knew I wasn't going to be able to play. I told him on the Friday that I had no chance of being available because I had to be fair to the other lads. It wouldn't have been fair on someone like Gary Owers if I'd turned up on the Saturday and played. I'd probably have lasted about 10 minutes then broken down, and I knew in myself that I wouldn't be able to last.'

Liverpool turned Sunderland over 2–0 in the Final and, while John was back playing another 40 games the following season, it was a joyless year featuring an even closer shave with relegation to the third tier and another managerial change, with Terry Butcher taking over as manager.

Hopes were higher going into 1992–93. Butcher had been backed by chairman Bob Murray with substantially more money than any Sunderland manager had ever had, but a terrible start to the season began with several of the new signings being injured in a road accident a few days before the start of the season, followed by the club's heaviest-ever opening day defeat, 5–0 at Derby. That was to be John's last away game. He played in a good home win over Charlton, a couple of League Cup ties and then was out for several weeks before coming back for that fateful clash with Birmingham City in October.

Remembered for his stretcher rowing as he bade farewell, Kaysie found himself up that well-known creek without a paddle when he got back to the changing room: 'The treatment was pretty primitive really. We got into the dressing room and they cut everything off. I got in the ambulance and was given morphine, but when I got to see the specialist he put this piece of wood in my mouth and then all the big lads came in. Two lads got hold of my shoulders and then the doctor took my leg, pulled it and jammed it in! That was it, he put a plaster on and sent me away.

'At the hospital what you've got to do is prove you can walk on crutches before they'll let you go. The last thing you want to do is spend another night in hospital, and I was so desperate to get out I showed I could do it, although it was a struggle. They let me go, but the thing was they sent me away without any pain killers. My leg was absolutely killing. It was like toothache multiplied by 5,000. I didn't get the painkillers until Bally brought them round a few days later, and I probably took more than I should have in one go because by then I was desperate to reduce the pain.

'I went to Lilleshall a couple of times for a change of environment. I saw a couple of lads with the same sort of breaks as me and I felt I was way back in terms of my rehabilitation so I started pushing myself harder, but all that happened was that my leg swelled up.

'I did a bit of pre-season, but it just swelled up again. Eventually I managed to get back to the stage where I could play for the reserves, but after a couple of reserve games I broke it again making a rash tackle on this lad and put myself out for another 18 months.

'When you are out for that long there are a lot of lonely days in the gym. It's just you and the gym, but it makes you a stronger person. I used to train at the gym twice a day every day including Christmas Day. The doctor had told me it was a career threatening injury, and I was determined to get back playing again. I lost loads of weight by really working hard, so when I broke it again the thought

John played 219 games for his first two Sunderland managers but none at all for his last two.

of all those lonely days in the gym was awful. It wasn't the pain again, that didn't come into it. It was the thought that I had to go through going to the gym twice a day again for another 18 months.

'What was great for me was Paul Bracewell coming back to the football club. He'd been through what I was going through so he understood, and he was a great help to me. Right towards the end of my rehabilitation my leg was still swelling up badly, and I got to the point where I said: "Look Brace, I think I'm gonna pack in." He told me to go and have a couple of weeks off to see how I felt. That was just what I needed because I never rested. I know now that rest is just as important as work, and that you need to rest to let everything heal up.

'I wasn't daft. I knew I wasn't going to play for Sunderland again. I was 33 then, and I hadn't played for three years so Reidy was obviously going to bring someone in, especially as Sunderland had just been promoted to the Premiership. There's was no chance of me playing, it was just a chance of getting fit enough to be able to play anywhere.'

Sunderland had undergone two managerial changes during John's absence through injury. Butcher had been sacked the month after John departed by boat. A home defeat at the hands of Southend United was a sixth successive defeat that dumped Sunderland in 20th place despite the money spent on the team. Sunderland born Mick Buxton replaced Butcher and enjoyed a couple of good runs that lifted the team to 12th, but he went just over a year later with the team back in 20th place to be replaced by Peter Reid.

'Mick Buxton was in charge when my dad died, and he was spot on. He couldn't have been more supportive and was absolutely great. Reidy was completely spot on as well when he took over. I think Mick had broken his leg when he was playing and of course Reidy had lots of injuries in his younger days. Denis Smith and Malcolm Crosby had been absolutely spot on as well. They were very nice characters who were very easy to work with and they were good coaches as well. They were very determined, and anyone who new Denis knew he loved the football club, and of course the same was true of Crossa who took over from him. I played alongside Terry Butcher but not much under him when he became manager. He was a great footballer, but I didn't agree with his management style. I don't want to get into slagging people off, so let's just say he wasn't my cup of tea. It wasn't so much him as a person, but the first thing he did with being ex-Rangers was to freeze out Anton Rogan who was ex-Celtic. Anton was popular in the dressing room and was a good player. Terry tried to push his way of preparing for games onto people. We all have our different methods of preparation, and if that works for someone fair enough, but he kept reminding us he was an ex-England international and insisting we should be preparing for games in a particular way, but pushing ideas like that is not necessarily the right way to go about things. Everyone is an individual, people are intelligent and could take on board what he was saying, but he would just push it and say this is the way we're going to do it.'

Having played 219 times for his first two Sunderland managers, John managed 20 under Butcher's leadership and none at all for his last two managers, but he got to the point where he could begin playing again shortly before the end of Peter Reid's first full season in charge as Sunderland were en route back to the top flight for the first time since the creation of the Premiership: 'I started playing in the March. I played a couple of reserve games around transfer deadline time. I'd played well for the reserves at Leeds, and somebody from Shrewsbury must have been there. I got the chance to go on loan and that was exactly what I needed at the time.'

Debuting for the Shrews against Hull on the day Michael Bridges famously left the Sunderland bench to score twice against Tony Norman's Huddersfield to establish a club record of successive wins, Shrewsbury gave Kay a new lease of life.

'Tommy Lynch, who used to be at Sunderland, was at Shrewsbury so I knew somebody when I got there. The lads were great, and I just enjoyed playing football again after three years. Apart from the people at Sunderland, no one had taken any notice of what I was doing for three years, so it put my face about a bit and to be fair it was great.'

An unexpected bonus – in more ways than one – having missed the 1992 FA Cup Final through injury, was a Wembley appearance. 'Shrewsbury played in the Auto Windscreens Shield Final at Wembley while I was there which was great…especially as the payment for that paid for my holidays.'

John's timing was impeccable, he ran out at Wembley just a fortnight after his debut, although such was the Shrews packed fixture list in a season where they played 17 Cup ties that was already Kaysie's fifth appearance for them. Sadly it was also his first defeat, Rotherham winning 2–1.

Having had the chance to show the tractor was back on the road, John got an offer from Preston North End, joining them on a non-contract basis at the start of the 1996–97 campaign. Past and future Sunderland players Bobby Mimms and Kevin Kilbane were playing at Deepdale at the time, as was David Moyes, but the move came about due to John's Wimbledon connections: 'They had a lad called Kevin Gage who'd been at Wimbledon when I was there and he got injured. Gary Peters was the manager, and funnily enough it was his place I'd taken when I'd signed for Wimbledon. He'd probably seen me play at Shrewsbury and he phoned me up. I was there for a couple of months and quite enjoyed it. While I was there we had a Cup run in the League Cup and played at Tottenham, I think we drew with them at home and got beat away.'

The big-time surroundings of White Hart Lane were a world away from the place where John found a home, Scarborough, still a Football League outfit back then in 1996. 'I played nearly 100 games for them and really had a great time. We played some great football down there. We played 4–3–3 under Mick Wadsworth, who is one of the best coaches I've ever played with in terms of how we played and how quick he was to change things during games if he thought they needed changing. His day-to-day work was really good as well, and players enjoyed playing for him. Harry Bassett was similar in that how you trained during the week was all geared to how you were going to play on a Saturday, whereas a lot of managers would have you playing five-a-side, doing a few stretches and that was it.'

While Wimbledon connections took John to Preston, there was no shortage of familiar Sunderland faces at the McCain Stadium: 'Gary Bennett was at Scarborough with me and we had one or two lads who'd been youngsters at Sunderland such as Stephen Brodie. Mick Wadsworth was great for me, and I was happy to stay even when Huddersfield came in for me. I spoke to Mick about it, but I wasn't fussed about moving there so I stayed at Scarborough.'

Just seven days after his final match for Preston North End, Kaysie made his Scarborough debut against a Wigan side he had helped Preston to eliminate from the League Cup to set up their Tottenham tie. The fact that Scarborough's goals came from the well-travelled Andy Ritchie and Gary Bennett illustrates that Scarborough were pushing the boat out to get promotion. Kay's introduction coincided with the beginning of a nine-game unbeaten run that took them to fourth, but that remained a seasonal high point as they fell away to finish 12th. On a personal note though, John was fit enough to end the season having made a total of just under 50 appearances for his two clubs.

The Play-offs of 1998 are etched on the memories of Sunderland supporters who watched an agonising penalty shoot-out with Charlton that Chris Makin remembers later in *Sunderland: Cult Heroes*. Kaysie only just missed out on another trip to the Twin Towers as Scarborough faltered in the Play-off semis, losing to Torquay after a terrific season for John, who had put his injury plagued years behind him by turning out 40 times in the League alone.

Sunderland's resilience, backed by their fan base, enabled them to bounce back from Play-off despair to smash all sorts of records in storming to promotion a year later, but down the east coast at Scarborough it signalled the end of their promotion challenge as they plummeted to the bottom of the table the following season, despite calling upon several well-known veterans, including ex-Everton defender Derek Mountfield and Sunderland-born former Watford midfielder Gary Porter.

By now managed by the vastly experienced Colin Addison, who had guided Hereford United to their famous FA Cup victory over Newcastle, Scarborough struggled badly. Hereford had been a non-League club when beating Newcastle, and Scarborough would be by the end of the season. When goalkeeper Jimmy Glass scored his never-to-be-forgotten last-minute goal for Carlisle to rescue their Football League status, the club falling through the trapdoor in their place were Scarborough, and with them went John Kay.

A recurrence of injury woes meant John was unable to help Scarborough in their final weeks, his 396th and final League appearance coming in a dismal 4–0 home defeat at the hands of Rotherham in March. 'I had a long hamstring injury towards the end of the season. I'd had enough by then anyway, and my mam had died by then, so it wasn't a good time and I packed in at the end of the season. I did a bit of pre-season down at Darlington, but my heart wasn't in it and I thought that was it. Trying to get back from bad injuries is hard work. On one level I was okay because I was still up with the best of them with the running, but my body was saying to me that I'd had enough.

'I called it a day when Scarborough lost their place in the Football League. I was 35 and I could have played on, but what happens is you get sick of the travelling. I'd had enough of that. We had had such a poor season and been treated so badly. We even got paid by the chairman from the takings on the bandit! Some of the lads weren't getting paid at all, and if ever a team deserved to go down it was us. They got rid of all the best players. The chairman had had a two-year plan where we had to get promoted in that time, and if we didn't well it was all going to go pear shaped. I kept at it, whereas some of the other lads moved on, and perhaps I should have, not that I had that many offers at that time, but I was just happy to be playing.'

A few months after deciding to retire from the game Kaysie changed his mind in order to have one last hurrah. Perhaps enough wingers had not had lumps knocked off them and there was still a chance to 'lift some skin' as they say in the North East. 'I went to play to play for Workington,' he explains. 'There was a lad called Tony Elliott who had played for Scarborough. He'd gone to Workington and phoned me up asking if I'd come and play. By this time I'd buried my mam and been on a couple of holidays. It was September time so I said to our lass "If they give me £100 a game I'll go and play." It turned out I was getting £400 a game so I was over there like a shot because I thought I can get a working wage playing for Workington.

'They gave me a two-year contract so I thought I was set, but unfortunately I got sent off a few times. It was a funny situation because if you get sent off in the Football League you miss three games, but at Workington if you got sent off you missed a number of days! I got sent off and then sent off again, and all of a sudden I was banned for 45 days. I played something like 20 games for them and got sent off four times, so the chairman came to see me and said "Look John, it's not working," so that was that. I'd been getting very frustrated and that was the end of things. He paid me up, and then I had a year doing gardening and stuff, but the funny thing was I still trained. I still thought I was a footballer! I'd go running all the time.'

It was a case of things coming full circle: 'At Under-15 level I'd been 200m champion for the county and came something like fourth or sixth in the North of England Championships. I used to enjoy athletics and won the decathlon at County level, and the cross country as well. My mam used to encourage me and so did my school, especially as a lot of the activities were away from the school. My schoolteachers really pushed me and were very good.'

As with a lot of young lads with sporting talent, John excelled across the board and inevitably football scouts came calling. Kay was in serious demand: 'Both of the North East clubs Sunderland and Newcastle were interested, so were Leeds, Sheffield United, Ipswich and Nottingham Forest. I nearly went to Forest, who were European champions under Brian Clough at the time, but Arsenal were the best. It was just the way they looked after you. I had a twin brother, and they looked after him as well even though he wasn't a footballer. He did play football, but he didn't take any of the trials, he just used to come down with me, he was a goalkeeper. They looked after him, for instance we were all given free football boots and they gave him a pair as well.'

Kay came through the ranks at Highbury and did well to reach their first team, breaking into the side as a replacement for John Hollins in February 1982 against West Bromwich Albion at The Hawthorns. Usually a young lad making his debut creates a bit of interest, but it was overshadowed by a landmark for an all-time great: 'It was Pat Jennings' 1,000th game. We drew, but I can remember very little about the game, which was probably pretty dour.'

John Kay is a cult hero at Sunderland partly because of all the stories about him. Rowing his 'boat' with a broken leg, running over Leeds defenders like a tractor and thinking he was some sort of monster truck when climbing over cars in Exeter are all typical Kaysie, so the following story should not surprise: 'I should have made my debut a lot earlier, but I hadn't seen my name on the team sheet because I hadn't looked as it never entered my head I'd be involved at that point. I got a phone call on a Sunday from my youth-team manager Terry Burton, who wasn't happy because he'd been pushing my case and when I got picked I didn't turn up! There was a long time between that and when I eventually got a game at West Brom because I didn't do myself any favours missing what should have been my first-team debut. There was a big fuss about it, Terry Neill was the manager and it went down like a lead balloon with Terry Burton. He's at Cardiff now, and he wasn't too happy with me, but it was just one of those things.'

If the powers that be at the marble halls of Highbury took some getting used to the lad from Lumley, the reverse was also true: 'The hardest thing wasn't the football, it was moving down there, especially with being a village lad. The village mentality I had made London a culture shock. The size of the club was the thing that struck me first and foremost, and it took some getting used to, especially when I was training with Pat Jennings, David O'Leary and the greats.' John managed seven first-team starts in the closing weeks of the season and played a further seven top-flight games as a Gunner the year after.

'The digs and the landlady I had were spot on. I lived near a park and that bit of London actually reminded me of Chester-le-Street believe it or not. I was in digs with a lad called Matty from Glasgow – that's another story as you can imagine! He was a bit of a crackerjack, but we got on really well. Homesickness was the problem. My girlfriend was at home, and obviously leaving family and mates was difficult as well.'

Someone else very dear to Sunderland hearts was also getting used to the big city with John at Arsenal at the time: 'I used to play with Quinny at Arsenal. We were pretty good mates while he was there. I'm a couple of years older than him, so I was a first-year pro when he came to the club. He was a centre-half when he came to Arsenal, and he always had this thick duffle coat on – a great 6ft 5in lad with a big duffle coat on!' It would be a few years until the Dubliner learned that wearing a coat of any kind could leave you open to ridicule in the North East!

John and Niall both had a lot of learning to do and both would play their best football after leaving Arsenal. In John's case he would move on to Wimbledon 18 months and 14 top-flight Gunners appearances after his debut.

Wimbledon were in the equivalent of the Championship at the time of John's signing: 'Wimbledon and Arsenal were as different as chalk and cheese in terms of the culture of the clubs, but I learned so much at Wimbledon about team spirit and how important it is for all 11 players to play as a team. I really enjoyed it, and it wasn't until I was older that I looked back and realised how special those days were. We did really well, I mean Wimbledon won the FA Cup the year after I left, and in my last year there we were one of the top London clubs after finishing sixth!'

A £25,000 move in the summer of 1984 took the 20-year-old Kay across London. A tractor to Plough Lane! Wimbledon had only been elected to the Football League seven years earlier. Playing alongside the likes of Dave Beasant, Nigel Winterburn, Lawrie Sanchez, future Sunderland

John was mates with the young Niall Quinn in their Arsenal days.

academy coach Carlton Fairweather and later Dennis Wise, John vied for the right-back position with Kevin Gage, playing in just under half the Dons' games. He also got a few games under his belt in the North East thanks to a loan spell with Middlesbrough early in 1985.

'At Wimbledon you don't realise how different the football is. Coming from Arsenal I struggled with the football side of things for a little bit at first because they wanted me to get it forward early and it took some adapting to after being used to playing short passes at Arsenal, so Wimbledon sent me on loan to Middlesbrough to get some games. Going there was a good opportunity for me to come back up to the north.

'I'd nearly got a move to Carlisle. Bob Stokoe was their manager, and he wanted to sign me, but they couldn't raise the fee, which was only £30,000. Harry [Wimbledon manager Dave Bassett] told me a loan move had come up at Boro and told me to get myself up there. It was only for a couple of months, but I thoroughly enjoyed it. Willie Maddren was the manager, and he said to me, "We need a player with a little bit more experience because of the situation we're in," which was fair enough, and they went and signed Brian Laws. Willie Maddren and the lads at Boro were spot on, and Steve Smelt, the physio I later had at Sunderland, was there as well. He was a good bloke and when he was at Sunderland had a column in the programme called *Felt by Smelt*.'

Returning to Wimbledon, Kaysie played his part in Wimbledon's incredible promotion to the top flight as they finished third in the last year before third place earned you a place in the Play-offs, rather than automatic promotion. For all the criticism of their long-ball style, Wimbledon under Dave 'Harry' Bassett won promotion to the highest level of English football on average gates of 4,500, marginally more than the worst-supported team, Carlisle. Meanwhile, the team with the highest average gate in the division lingered fifth from bottom, 26 points behind the Dons and only four clear of the drop. That team of course was Sunderland, who John played against twice that season, appearing at Roker Park in November and at Wimbledon's ramshackle Plough Lane five months later when a Glyn Hodges hat-trick left Sunderland 3–0 losers.

So it was that Kay's final year at Wimbledon saw him be part of a team that finished sixth in the top flight and number Manchester United, Spurs and Chelsea among the sides he collected win bonuses against. There was another against Sunderland in the FA Cup, and come the end of the season when John swapped high-flying Wimbledon to come to Sunderland he was dropping down two divisions to do so!

Time of course never stands still in football and, while since then Sunderland have built the Stadium of Light and are looking to return to former glories, Wimbledon have morphed into the MK Dons having upped sticks completely to Milton Keynes: 'MK Dons is like a different club to the one I played for,' reflects John. 'There's a new club back in Wimbledon, and I think they really are the real Wimbledon now, although to be fair MK Dons have done well, have a nice new stadium and should go on to do well.

'When I was at Wimbledon we didn't have a decent ground or much of a fan-base. If we got 10,000 it was a big crowd – we had a nice pitch and that was about it!

'I had a good rapport with the Wimbledon fans, there just weren't many of them. I played about 80 games for them, and although I wasn't one of the crowd favourites I was well up there. There was a good relationship between players and fans at Wimbledon because it was very much a community club. We'd quite often go into schools doing a bit of coaching after training. That was encouraged by Harry.'

Wimbledon may well have had fewer home fans than Sunderland regularly take away, but they did see something that Sunderland fans longed for and never got – a John Kay goal: 'I got a couple, and they were cracking goals' says John, normally naturally modest but allowing himself a little bit of glory. 'One was a half volley against Fulham and the other was a curler with the outside of my foot from the outside of the box. I just gave the 'keeper "the eyes" and he had no chance,' he laughs. Indeed, 18 months after leaving Sunderland he even scored another goal! Former teammates Shrewsbury were on the receiving end as Kaysie scored the only goal of the game for Scarborough in an FA Cup first-round meeting.

> *Johnny Kay was my first cult hero at Roker Park. An excellent right-back and a tough cookie to boot. He also added an element of banter and good humour which is rarely seen in the modern game. Never scored for us but went close on a number of occasions – including hitting a post against the Mags. Undoubtedly a tale which is fondly remembered by Sunderland supporters to this day is the game against Birmingham City in 1993, which effectively signalled the end of his Sunderland career. Kay launched himself into another typically committed challenge but came off worse and broke his leg. As he was stretchered off Kay lay upright, pretending he was rowing as he was making his way off the pitch. What are the odds you will see that in the Premier League today? No chance.*
> Keith Chapman, Sunderland supporter, Jarrow.

Although a first-team goal remained beyond him at Sunderland, Kaysie did score twice for the reserves, but it was his tackling rather than his goalscoring that he kept getting picked for. Coming from the 'get stuck in' school of defending as so many of Sunderland's full-backs have down the years, John sometimes was a bit over enthusiastic with his challenges. Since the year of John's birth – 1964 – Sunderland have had a running rivalry with Leeds United, with more than one Sunderland player suffering badly from tackles in those fixtures, so when Leeds and future Sunderland manager Howard Wilkinson complained that one of his players looked like he'd been run over by a tractor having been on the receiving end of a Kaysie tackle, it was like water off a duck's back to Sunderland supporters, especially as the poor lad who had been clattered was a former Newcastle player, Peter Haddock. Inevitably the fans came up with a chant: 'Johnny Kay's red-and-white tractor', serenading all future recipients of a Kaysie challenge as they picked themselves up.

Leeds had been the opponents on the first of two occasions Kay was sent off for Sunderland, the other coming against Charlton: 'I got sent off against Charlton because of a little winger called Colin Walsh. I nutted him, or at least pushed my face into him. It was as simple as that.

'Howard Wilkinson's comments were like water off a duck's back to me,' says John. 'I wasn't bothered about them in the slightest, but the chant that came from it was a good bit of crack. I always had a great relationship with the crowd. It got to the stage where the lads used to want to run out beside me because I was the only one getting a cheer! Some of them were getting battered, but the supporters always liked me. I don't know what it was with me because I was at Sunderland for nine seasons and only played five really. I missed three years with two broken legs, and had that season where I only played 11 games because of various injuries. We were quite successful in the years that I did play though. We got promoted twice, got to the Cup Final, and even in the year we were relegated we had a good season in a way because we took it to the last game despite not really

Still 'Kaysie' after all these years, John Kay in June 2008.

having any investment in a team that had climbed two divisions in three seasons. We were a young side that needed a little bit of money spent on some areas of the team. If we'd had that we'd have stayed up. When you think about it we were 2–0 up at Wimbledon and 2–0 up at Tottenham. If we'd had a little bit more experience in the side to keep those leads it would have made all the difference. We tried to play good football, and in the end we were unlucky to go down.'

A huge cult hero among Sunderland supporters in his playing days, John has always been an unassuming and reassuringly normal bloke. Never one for the airs and graces some footballers like to give themselves, Kaysie possesses a combination of being as down to earth as they come with the fact that he has a fascinating football career behind him. It is an ideal qualification for his second career: 'I started doing some voluntary youth work for the council, and that led into the job I have now. I work on something called the New Leaf Project. I work with lads with substance misuse problems and help them with attendance and support. The project is run by the re-generation team within the council. It's not just young lads, it is people of all ages. They're all drug addicts, heroin addicts or serious drug users who live chaotic lives.

'Some of them know I used to be a footballer, and it helps in the job. I've got a few Sunderland supporters and sometimes they say "I used to watch you play." Most lads anyway are interested in football, and even when they're young if they find out I used to play for Sunderland they go and ask their dad to tell them about what I used to be like. It gives us something to talk about because it's sometimes difficult to have a conversation with people, but once they find out you used to be a footballer they want to talk about it.

'The first thing we do is try and get them onto a methadone course. If they're homeless we try and get them into a hostel. If we can get them into council houses that's better, or if we can get them into private rented accommodation then we'll do that. We then try and support them with things like making sure their money is paid for rent, their gas bill is paid and so on, and help them to learn to budget their money. The next step is to try and get them into education and jobs.

'It can be very satisfying but equally as frustrating. We've done quite well with them though, and a lot of the lads are a lot better than when I started working with them, their lives are not as chaotic. I'm not saying none of them will ever use drugs again, that's probably not my job. There are other people there for that, what I'm doing is trying to help them to get some sort of accommodation and order in their lives.

'I go to games still. I'm a member of the Former Players' Association at Sunderland, which is brilliant especially since Niall Quinn has been back at the club. If the lads I work with are doing really well I take one of them as my guest and they love it. Some of them are on about getting season tickets now. I've got one lad in particular who used to go all the time when he was younger until he started drinking heavily and is now wanting to start going regularly again. I tell them if you're doing well I'll take you to a game, and we'll plan our routine around the match. Sunderland are doing great. It's a totally different football club to the one I used to play for.'

> *Having been brought up on a diet of tough tackling, no nonsense style full-backs, it was inevitable that 'Kaysie' would become a crowd favourite. Winning tackles that only the insane would attempt brought about a hero status reserved for kings! His canoe-paddling antics on being carried off with a broken leg added to his already kami-KAYSIE status. A tough guy on the pitch with a quiet demeanour off it (Exeter excluded), John Kay could well have been dropped by the Tardis into the wrong time period but produced a rare reminder of the 'thou shall not pass' attitude so common in the '50s and '60s.*
> Mike Love, SENSSA.

CHARLIE'S ANGEL

KEVIN ARNOTT

Central Midfield
1980 promotion winner with Sunderland.

Born:	28 September 1958.
Signed for Sunderland:	Associated schoolboy October 1973
	Professional, September 1976
Transferred:	22 May 1982, to Sheffield United, £30,000

Sunderland:	October 1973, 132+1 League appearances, 16 goals
	149+3 total appearances, 18 goals
Blackburn Rovers:	(Loan) November 1981, 17 League appearances, 2 goals
Sheffield United:	22 May 1982, 120+1 League appearances, 11 goals
Blackburn Rovers:	(Loan) November 1982, 11+1 League appearances, 1 goal
Rotherham United:	(Loan) March 1983, 9 League appearances, 2 goals
Vasalund:	June 1987
Chesterfield:	November 1987, 19 League appearances, 1 goal
Vasalund:	March 1988
Chesterfield:	August 1988, 48+4 League appearances, 3 goals
Vasalund:	June 1991
Nykarby:	1992
Gateshead	
Hebburn	
Jarrow Roofing	

Kevin Arnott is a different type of player to the other cult heroes in this collection. Unlike Joe Bolton, John Kay, Chris Makinand Vic Haloms Kevin Arnott would never win any contests when it came to selecting hard men. Arnott was not the kind of player to relish a 50–50 tackle, but boy could he play. In Italy they describe the kind of player Kevin was as a 'fantasista', a fantasy player if you like, a creative midfielder full of flair. Someone able to produce the killer pass, someone who like 'The Greatest' Muhammed Ali, could 'float like a butterfly – sting like a bee.'

'Richard Dinnis called it a fluke, but it wasn't, it was meant,' says Kevin of one of the best goals any Sunderland supporter has ever seen. It was Good Friday 1977, 18-year-old Kevin Arnott, the

Arnott's goal against the Mags on Good Friday 1977, one of the best goals any Sunderland supporter has ever seen.

youngest player on the pitch in a typically fierce Wear-Tyne derby, suddenly produced a moment of sublime skill. It had been a typical derby affair, high on graft, low on guile but four minutes before the break time stood still. It was like one of those TV dream sequences where everything stops moving except the person at the centre of the action, or one of those photographs where everything is in black and white except for one person picked out in colour.

As the ball left Arnott's boot the action froze, the ball gliding gracefully and unstoppably until it nestled in the Newcastle net, floating like a butterfly and stinging like a bee indeed. Newcastle manager Richard Dinnis was certainly stung: 'Richard Dinnis thought it was a cross didn't he?' says Arnott, still apparently bristling with indignation that such talent could be doubted. 'I beat the offside trap and was about 20 yards out to the left side of the goal. I chipped Mick Mahoney, and it went right in the far corner.'

Arnott had been in the first team for less than three months. His impact had already been phenomenal, but this sublime moment signified that Sunderland had unearthed a real talent, a player with the ability to go on and become one of the best in the game. Indeed, Kevin did go on to have a good

Kevin strikes the ball.

career both at home and abroad, but for many Sunderland supporters Kevin Arnott remains a player heralded in the North East but unknown in most of the rest of the country, a little secret we keep to ourselves, like Bamburgh beach.

> *Football now and again produces a player of such rare natural talent that reminds everyone that it is indeed a simple game. Kevin Arnott could produce moments of real magic and yet make them look fundamentally simple…a player who could 'walk with kings and yet retain the common touch'. Sadly that aura of brilliance did not translate into a long and fulfilling career, but the magical moments linger on.*
> Mike Love. SENSSA.

Sunderland had been making their supporters suffer. Prior to Arnott's introduction they were on a run of 10 League games without so much as a goal, let alone one as good as Kevin's against the Magpies. Bottom of the table and on to their third manager of the campaign, Sunderland's last goal of 1976 had come from the penalty spot in mid-November.

Manager Jimmy Adamson had taken over early in that barren run and hoped to finally get a win when the draw for the third round of the FA Cup gave Sunderland a home game with Wrexham, two divisions below them. Although his side finally scored, they had to come from behind to force a replay. Having been Footballer of the Year at Burnley during their halcyon days of the early 1960s when the Turf Moor club's success was founded on youth, Adamson decided he had seen enough. The Wrexham game marked the final appearances of 1973 hero Billy Hughes and tigerish midfielder Ray Train.

Into the side for the replay came debutant Shaun Elliott to join fellow starlet Gary Rowell, with Arnott named on the bench for the first time in the days when there was only one sub: 'I came on as a sub and got the last 20 minutes or so. It was sleeting and a horrible night,' remembers Kevin of his first-team bow that, although it was lost 1–0, signified a turning point in the season.

Three days later Arnott made his first start in a top-flight game at Leicester: 'I didn't know I was playing until just before kick-off. I suppose I had half a feeling that I might have a chance, but it still comes as a shock when you find out you are actually in the team. I'd only had few reserve-team games – I'd just really played for the youth team before then. I think Jim Holton was dropped for me.'

Former Manchester United and Scotland defender Holton was indeed the man to make way, the Wrexham replay being his Sunderland swansong, the versatile Shaun Elliott slotting into central-defence alongside Jeff Clarke who he would later form a fabulous partnership with, while Arnott was installed to dictate from the centre circle, something he was to do with great success. His ability to hit long or short beautifully weighted passes either to feet or for people to run on to transformed Sunderland from a team rooted to the foot of the table to one as good as those at the top, Sunderland taking the same number of points as eventual champions Liverpool in the final three months of the season.

Arnott's first start saw the goal famine continue, a 2–0 defeat giving little sign of the excitement to come, but after a pair of goalless draws that at least saw the points tally begin to tick over Sunderland started to click. A rare Friday night fixture brought Sunderland's first League goal in 1,020 minutes and a first win in a dozen games, and suddenly a team who had been unable to score found that they could not miss.

Sixteen goals in three games started at a time when people did not think Sunderland could score 16 times in the rest of the season. Middlesbrough were fifth from top when Graeme Souness & Co. breezed into Roker Park – they had beaten Arsenal 3–0 the week before to extend their unbeaten run to 13 games. Unlucky. Boro were blown away as, inspired by their youngsters, Sunderland won 4–0, with Kevin getting his first goal: 'It was a side-footer following up from about eight yards out. I'd just got in the side, so it was a nice one to start with.'

Shaun Elliott scored his first in the next match as West Brom were battered 6–1, and more was to follow with West Ham also being hit for six. Gary Rowell went into that trio of games with one goal to his name but scored four times to set him off towards becoming only the second man since the war to register 100 goals for the club. Rowell was joined as a scorer in all three games by both Bob Lee and Mel Holden, with Cup-winning captain Bobby Kerr also joining in the fun.

The talk, though, was of the future and in particular Arnott, Elliott and Rowell:

'That didn't really bother me too much,' remembers Kevin, 'There was a lot of publicity for the three of us because we'd all come into the team at the same time. The team had been doing badly, and things changed at the same time as we came into the side. The papers were calling us "Charlie's Angels" after the chief scout Charlie Ferguson. It got built up a bit but nothing like it would be now. There was just really *Shoot* as a local TV football programme then, but of course now football is never off the telly. The coverage we got was nice, but it was never overpowering. The three of us had no fear. We were fresh and played with no pressure on us. It was a fantastic time. We were getting big crowds, and that spell where we scored 16 goals in three games was unbelievable. The place just took off, and we were suddenly playing with so much confidence that we probably would have beaten Real Madrid.'

The Great Escape looked on as the next two home games were also won, bringing Sunderland up to an Easter programme of the sort unheard of now. In the 1970s it was normal to play on Good Friday, Easter Saturday and Easter Monday. The fixture planners of 1976–77 had given Sunderland an Easter egg that contained Newcastle at home, old rivals Leeds away and Manchester United at home.

So it was that when Arnott conjured up that great goal against the black and whites it was in the midst of a red-and-white revival. Kevin scored at the Roker End, which was where the travelling fans had been housed: 'All my mates were in the Roker End. I'm from a Newcastle-supporting family and

followed them home and away as a kid so I got a fair bit of stick from my family and friends. It still gets brought up now and then, but it's all good natured.'

Bob Lee doubled Sunderland's lead that day, only for late goals from Paul Cannell and Tommy Craig to

Arnott's first-ever goal against Middlesbrough in 1977.

Kevin in action.

force a draw with fourth-placed United. The points were shared again at Elland Road in a typically tough contest with Leeds before Kevin scored again as Manchester United were defeated 2–1: 'I can't really remember it to be honest. I think it was a right-foot shot from somewhere near the edge of the box, but I'm not sure.' Not many players can't recall with certainty a goal against the Red Devils, but that in itself indicates how hectically things were coming thick and fast at the teenager.

Four months after his debut the season boiled down to a final match away to Everton. Unbeaten in nine, one more result would save Sunderland, but it was a game too far as Everton won 2–0 on a night when the cities of Coventry and Bristol contrived to draw a game that condemned Sunderland, when a win for either would have sent the other down instead of the Wearsiders. 'Everton had nothing to play for, but they were a good side with some top players and on the night they were better than us. We didn't play as good as we had been doing before and there were no hard luck stories to tell, it was a fair result.'

Whether the result in the Coventry versus Bristol City match was a fair one rests on the conscience of those responsible for allowing one game to kick-off 15 minutes after the other and then sticking the news of Sunderland's defeat on the Highfield Road scoreboard, with the consequence that each side secured their own and their opponents safety by tamely seeing out time. 'It wouldn't happen now. The situation seems ridiculous looking back at it, some might even say criminal,' says Kevin of a scenario Barry Siddall describes in his chapter. Siddall was the goalkeeper in the Sunderland team Arnott stepped into, and was an admirer of the youngster's talents.

As an Evertonian, Kevin reminded me of Colin Harvey from Everton's 1970 title-winning side. Kevin had two good feet and was a very good passer of the ball and a great reader of the game in central-midfield. He was a decent athlete and a quiet lad off the field. I got on well with him, and we used to go racing together. He didn't drive, and I remember one day I drove him up to Ayr and we had a good day. I won about £700 and he won about £300. I remember calling into some pub in Scotland and us both having 100s of Scottish pound notes stuffed into every pocket.
Barry Siddall on Kevin Arnott.

Relegation immediately after only the second-ever promotion in Sunderland's history was a massive blow, softened only by the knowledge that the spirited and stylish showing in the second half of the season indicated that the club had some talented young players to build on. Arnott continued to be a regular member of the team until almost a year to the day of his debut when he fell out with the manager: 'Jimmy Adamson was excellent. He put me in the team and I'd only been in the reserves for what seemed like two minutes. He saw me a few times and put me straight in. He was an excellent coach who brought a new approach to the club. He had a massive reputation as a coach and was very clued up football-wise. It got to the start of 1978 though, and I just got left out. I'd had a bust up with Jimmy Adamson and got bombed out, but when he left Billy Elliott took over and he put me straight back in, and I was a regular in the team again from then on.'

Effectively it was a lost year. Having debuted in January 1977 and barely missed a game until January 1978, Kevin only played twice until January 1979. It was not as if Sunderland were blessed with an unending supply of natural talent. Kevin got back in the side just in time for Sunderland's most memorable game of the late 1970s – a 4–1 away win at Newcastle in just the fifth game after Kev's comeback.

That game is forever synonymous with Gary Rowell, who scored three and created the other. Arnott set up the pick of Rowell's hat-trick with a typically exquisite pass, although in typically modest fashion he simply says 'I just knocked a ball through for Gary and he finished it off. Gary was totally different to me. He had the knack of being in the right place at the right time, especially for a midfield player. Gary got a lot of goals at the back post coming in from the left. He was a terrific finisher.'

Rowell is more forthcoming on Kevin's contribution: 'Kevin Arnott picked me out with a great through ball for the second goal. I'd played with Kev for years and years – we played together as kids, so we had a great understanding of each other's game. I'd make runs and he'd pick me out. So Kev put the ball right in front of me. 2–0 up. Brilliant.'

Triumph on Tyneside was part of a terrific run that kept Sunderland right in the thick of a promotion race that went to the wire, a winning return to the scene of Arnott's debut at Wrexham on the final day proving not quite enough as results once against went against the lads.

There was to be better the following season, though, with Kevin a key member of a promotion-winning team. It was his best season as he played over 40 times in all competitions and kept one of his eight League goals from midfield for the night promotion was won against West Ham. 'The whole build-up was unreal,' Arnott recalls. 'We went out for something to eat in Sunderland before the match and then had to get a police escort to get the coach to the ground because, even at this time between 5 and 6 o'clock, the place was crammed and everything was blocked. We knew if we won we were up, and we certainly weren't going to get beat that night. West Ham were still partying after winning the Cup, and although we couldn't get the ball off them for the first 20 minutes we were running on so much adrenalin that we were always going to win.

'We had a good rapport with the West Ham lads. Pop [Robson] had moved backwards and forwards between the clubs, and afterwards they were as pleased for us getting promotion as we'd been for them to win the Cup.'

Nine of the Hammers players who faced Sunderland that Monday night had been on duty at Wembley just two days earlier when they beat Arsenal to lift the FA Cup, so there were a lot of happy players at Roker that evening with both sides having achieved what they wanted.

Kevin settled everyone's nerves with the opening goal in a 2–0 win shortly before half-time when he coolly slotted home a close-range chance. Arnott evidently had a taste for the capital that season,

The 1979 Daily Express *five-a-side champions.*

as that goal was the fifth of his eight to come against London clubs, and there were another six at Wembley to take into consideration!

Promotion meant a double of sorts for Sunderland because they too had been Wembley winners that season, having lifted the *Daily Express* five-a-side Championship, with Arnott scoring in every round and finishing as the tournament's top scorer.

Played at Wembley Arena with televised highlights on the BBC, the *Daily Express* five-a-side Championships were quite a big deal in the late 1970s. Manchester United, Arsenal, Chelsea, Glasgow Rangers and Spurs were among the 16 teams joining Sunderland in the competition.

Kevin started as he meant to go on, scoring both goals as 1978 FA Cup winners Ipswich were beaten 2–0. Next up were West Brom, also seen off 2–0 with Shaun Elliott joining Arnott on the score sheet. Victory

PREVIOUS WINNERS			
CHARLTON ATHLETIC	1968	ORIENT	1974
MANCHESTER CITY	1969	WOLVES	1975
MANCHESTER UNITED	1970	WOLVES	1976
SOUTHAMPTON	1971	IPSWICH	1977
TOTTENHAM HOTSPUR	1972	CRYSTAL PALACE	1978
DERBY COUNTY	1973	SUNDERLAND	1979

Picture above: Lord Matthews, Chairman of Express Newspapers presents the Fives Trophy to Sunderland's 1979 victorious team.

1979 SCORE SHEET

FIRST ROUND

Chelsea	0	Manchester Utd.	0
(Chelsea won on penalties)			
Spurs (Galvin 2)	2	Southampton (Ball)	1
Glasgow Rangers	0	Brighton (Lawrenson)	1
Coventry (Roberts)	1	Manchester City	0
Newcastle (Cassidy, Hibbitt)	2	West Ham	0
Aston Villa (Mortimer)	1	West Bromwich (Barnes 2, Robson)	3
Ipswich	0	Sunderland (Arnott 2)	2
Arsenal (Rix 2)	2	Crystal Palace (Nicholas, Cannon)	2
(Crystal Palace won on penalties)			

SECOND ROUND

Brighton (Ward, Horton)	2	Crystal Palace (Cannon)	1
Chelsea	0	Newcastle (Cassidy)	1
Coventry (English)	1	Spurs (Naylor, Beavan)	2
Sunderland (Arnott, Elliott)	2	West Bromwich	0

SEMI-FINALS

Brighton (Ward 2)	2	Spurs (Galvin)	1
Newcastle	0	Sunderland (Arnott 2, Cummings 2)	4

FINAL

Sunderland (Arnott, Buckley)	2	Brighton	0

over the Baggies set up a semi-final with Newcastle. Sunderland tortured Newcastle in 1979 scoring a total of 19 goals against them. Beginning with the Rowell inspired 4–1 at Newcastle, there had been a pair of 2–2 League Cup ties followed by a 7–6 win on penalties, followed by a 4–0 hammering at Wembley with Kevin and Stan Cummins scoring a brace each.

'The highlights were on the telly that night, so after we'd beaten Newcastle but before we played the Final I went and rang my dad to tell him if he put the telly on he'd see us playing Newcastle in the semi-final, but I didn't tell him the score!' says Kevin who proceeded to wrap things up by scoring along with Mick Buckley as Brighton were beaten 2–0 in the Final of a tournament Sunderland won, having scored 10 without 'keeper Chris Turner being beaten.

'I was the top five-a-side player in training, and it suited me down to the ground. That tournament was brilliant. We

The 1979 five-a-side winners. Back row, left to right: Peter Eustace (coach), Shaun Elliott, Chris Turner, Kevin Arnott, representative of Express Newspapers. Front row: John Cooke, Mick Buckley, Stan Cummins.

were due to play at Orient on the Saturday and travelled down in midweek. We hadn't done any training especially for it, but we thought we'll do our best but if we get knocked out in the first round at least we'll be able to go out for a few drinks in London.'

Back in the top flight Kevin played regularly, scoring in important home wins over Manchester City and Arsenal as Sunderland survived the drop after their usual last-day drama, this time an unlikely win at Anfield being required. By then, though, manager and assistant Ken Knighton and Frank Clark had been sacked, with the summer appointment of Alan Durban signalling bad news for Kevin.

'Ken Knighton and Frank Clark were great for me. They loved me to bits, and I can't speak too highly of either of them' he says. 'Alan Durban, though, simply didn't want me at all. He just didn't fancy me and must have wanted his own players in. I went from being a regular for the previous two seasons to being completely out of the picture. I was bitter about it at the time, although I realise now that football is all about opinions, and that's fair enough.'

Given just sporadic opportunities by Alan Durban, Kevin went out on loan to Blackburn in the second tier. From November to March he played 17 successive games, his away debut coming in a goalless draw at Newcastle. 'I had a great time at Blackburn. Bobby Saxton was manager and was brilliant. I was doing really well there and getting a lot of good press as Blackburn got into the top six in the division, so Alan Durban called me back as Sunderland were on the slide. I didn't really want to come back, to be honest, because of how I felt I'd been treated and the way I'd been bombed out, but I came back and played away to Manchester United, where we got a 0–0 draw.'

It was to be Arnott's penultimate match, a home defeat at the hands of Middlesbrough a week later signalling the end of a Sunderland career that, while it contained moments of magic, disappeared too soon.

> *Arnott was one of those players you look back on and think of what he should have really achieved with the ability he had. The former St Aidan's [Sunderland] schoolboy star was as stylish as they come, a genuine midfield orchestrator with fabulous feet and great vision. It is a crying shame that he never played for England as his skill levels were immense, be it from dead balls or in the thick of a midfield tussle. He should have developed into one of the SAFC's all-time greats and not many players have filled his central-midfield position since with anything like the presence he had on his day. His most famous goal was probably the one he scored in the fabulous Roker Park Monday night match in front of over 47,000 against that season's FA Cup-winners, West Ham.*
>
> *Its importance was huge on a very atmospheric, but nonetheless tense, Wearside night. Kevin Arnott, class personified.*
>
> Tom Lynn, Sunderland supporter, Sunderland.

St Aidan's school in Sunderland has produced more than its fair share of players down the years. 'Mickey Hazard [Spurs, Chelsea, Portsmouth, Swindon] and Kevin Dillon [Birmingham, Portsmouth, Newcastle, Reading] were a year or two younger than me. I knew them well through playing football over the years,' says Kevin, whose own path took him straight to Sunderland from school. 'I just got to 14 and signed for Sunderland, that was it. I never went to Newcastle or any other clubs.'

Charlie's Angels. Left to right: Kevin Arnott, Gary Rowell and Shaun Elliott.

Sunderland had won the FA Cup not long before Arnott arrived, and although he had little or nothing to do with Stokoe's stars until partnering Cup-winning captain Bobby Kerr in midfield when he first came into the team, it was another famous Cup winner who offered him a new home when he signed for Ian Porterfield at Sheffield United in the summer of 1982.

'As a trainee on schoolboy forms I trained on Tuesday and Thursday nights, and we were well away from Bob Stokoe and the first team, but we'd train during the day during school holidays so at Easter, for instance, we'd see a bit of them. I just went to Sheffield United to sign for Ian Porterfield really. He was a lovely fellow and I loved it at Sheffield United. They were a big club who shouldn't have been where they were, and I enjoyed my time at Bramall Lane.'

However, after just a handful of games for the Blades in what is now League One, Kevin went back to Blackburn on loan, playing a dozen times a division above his new club, and then in March there was another loan move when he joined Sheffield United's near neighbours Rotherham who, like Blackburn, were in the division above the Blades. Ian Porterfield was a former manager at Rotherham who had just replaced former Liverpool player Emlyn Hughes as manager, with Bobby Kerr's brother George, signing for them on the same day as another former Sunderland midfielder Bobby Mitchell. Arnott was unable to stop the Millers sliding to relegation, but he did score a couple of goals in his nine games, including one in a 1–1 draw away to Chelsea.

Having endured relegation with Rotherham, Kevin restored the balance by playing a major role in 1983–84 when he was Sheffield United's only ever present in a season where promotion was won by the narrowest of margins, the Blades edging out Hull on goals scored, having tied on points and goal difference. Kevin contributed six strikes, including vital ones against rivals Hull and a final-day goal as six were stuck past Newport County with that neck-and-neck race in mind. Former Sunderland players Joe Bolton, Mick Henderson and ex-Roker youth-team 'keeper Keith Waugh were also in that side.

Scoring a late equaliser on the opening day of the season as Sheffield came from two down to rescue a point at Wolves, Kevin went on to remain a regular in the side as United consolidated their place after promotion. Building on that, the Blades finished seventh in 1986 and ninth a year later, Kevin playing against Sunderland twice in wins at Sheffield but not featuring in the fixtures on Wearside before bringing his time at Bramall Lane to a close having made just a dozen less League appearances than he had for Sunderland.

Kevin's next stop was to be overseas: 'I went to Sweden with a team called Vasalund after I left Sheffield United. What happened was I was meant to go to America to play for Dallas in the Indoor Soccer League. The ex-Queen's Park Rangers manager Gordon Jago was there, and I'd agreed over the phone to sign for him. In the meantime, before I was due to start there I got a call from a bloke I suppose you'd call an agent now, telling me he had a team in Sweden that needed a playmaker and would I go? I agreed to go for a day or two to see what it was like. Because of the way the football season runs there they were halfway through the season, so it was sorted out that I'd play there until October and then go to play for Dallas. As it happened, something happened to Gordon Jago so I never ended up going to play for Dallas, but the football in Sweden was well paid, and I really enjoyed it. It wasn't at all pressurised, and it was a great way to earn a living.'

The summer seasons of Swedish football gave Kevin the opportunity to play again in England. 'My old teammate Mick Henderson, who I'd played with at Sunderland and Sheffield United, was captain at Chesterfield at the time. He was a lovely lad, Mick, and I went to play with him for Chesterfield through what was the winter break in Sweden, so I played for Chesterfield until April and then went back to Vasalund.'

There was an added incentive for Kevin to rush back from Sweden. Chesterfield's first fixture from the time he was available was at home to Sunderland, who by this point had sunk into the old Third Division, and they drew 1–1 at Saltergate as Arnott debuted. Kevin did not miss a game between November and March until it was time to return to Sweden.

Arnott in action.

Kevin Arnott in action.

'Vasalund were in the First Division and did quite well. Our ground was in the middle of Stockholm, near where AIK Stockholm and the national team played.' Arnott's double life continued, and he played regularly for Chesterfield throughout 1988–89 when they dropped down to the fourth tier. Remaining with Chesterfield, Arnott's 363rd and final Football League appearance came in November 1990, although he was far from hanging his boots up.

A further spell in Sweden was followed by a two-year stint with Nykarby in Finland, before a return to the North East where he wound down his playing days with Gateshead, Hebburn and Jarrow Roofing before calling it a day in 1995.

'Once I finished with football I went into the family business with my dad dealing with blockages, drainage and that sort of thing. Now I work for a firm called Artec in Washington who supply car parts to Nissan,' says Kevin, whose place in the affections of Sunderland supporters has never slipped.

In more recent years Julio Arca fulfilled a similar role in the fans' eyes in that he produced the sort of flair and class that supporters love to see, and while Julio had a number of tricks Kevin didn't, even the Argentinian could not boast the range of passing Arnott sprayed around Roker Park.

'I think the reason the supporters took to me was probably because of the way I tried to play. I had a little bit of flair and a skilful approach to the game, and it probably helped being local,' reasons Kevin. 'I had some natural ability, but I had to work at it. That's what I got paid for. Football is like any job, you have to work at it to be any good. When I first went to Sunderland I used to bend everything. Stan Ternent was coaching at the club at the time and he taught me how to strike a ball properly. He was great for me because once I'd worked with him I could bend a ball both ways or hit it true, so I had the full repertoire.'

Even Sunderland's Player of the Century Charlie Hurley jokes that even though he is now in his 70s he gets better every year. Kevin tells a similar tale: 'We all went through a bit of stick from time to time, so it wasn't always a bed of roses. I've become a better player since I've left and it's more in the past 10 to 15 years that I've realised how well thought of I was. I've always stayed in the same area I'm from so most people know who I am, although the younger generation tend not to know so much. People sometimes come up to me and say they remember the 4–1 at Newcastle, the derby goal or that spell when I was first in the team. Maybe some of those good times paper over the cracks.'

JOE, JOE, JOE BOLTON!

JOE BOLTON

Left-back
1976 Second Division Championship winner with Sunderland.

Born:	2 February 1955, Birtley.
Signed for Sunderland:	1 June 1970 professional 2 February 1972
Transferred:	14 July 1981 to Middlesbrough, £200,000

Sunderland:	264+9 League appearances, 11 goals
	315+10 total appearances, 12 goals
Middlesbrough:	59 League appearances, 1 goal
Sheffield United:	109 League appearances, 2 goals
Matlock Town:	Player-caretaker manager

'We'd been out to a pub for a basket meal, and as we were driving back I says to Sue "We'll just go past the training pitch to see if there's any hares about", so I drove onto the main training pitch at Washington. I swung round so I was facing across the pitch and put the full beam on. There was a hare sat on the field, so I set the dogs away. They eventually came back, so I checked them over and got them in the back of the car.'

Joe Bolton, one of the toughest players ever to play for Sunderland then begins making engine sounds, sounds of a car engine straining to get going. It's a bizarre moment from someone to whom the associated sounds are normally either of a bone-jarring tackle, or the chant that invariably followed it as the opposition's trainer came rushing on to administer treatment to whichever unfortunate will-o'-the-wisp winger was on the receiving end: 'Joe, Joe, Joe Bolton'.

Joe in 2005.

By now as much in his stride as when storming down Sunderland's left flank, Bolton continues his story: 'The car had got stuck in the mud. Sue couldn't drive, but she sat in the front while I got out and pushed. I said to her, "Take your time and I'll tell you when to press the accelerator", but when I shouted "Now!" she really revved the engine, the muck sprayed all over and I got completely covered in it. It was a case of, "Oh noooo!!!!" We just couldn't budge it, so I had to leave the car right in the middle of the pitch, pretty much in the left-back position in fact. We got the dogs and had to walk into Washington. I was filthy, but we got on the bus. I handed a tenner in but the bus driver said he had no change. Fortunately, a lad called Ian Diamond was sat there. He used to play for Jarrow and Felling, and he lent us some money to pay our fares.

'When we got home I said to Sue "I hope we're not training at Washington tomorrow." I rang my friend Fred Rylands, who was a milkman along Cleadon way, and asked him to try to get my car out, so he went up, but he got stuck as well. Just behind there was an equestrian centre with big Land Rovers. A farmer friend of Fred's lived there and he eventually managed to tow the car off.

'When I got into training the next morning 'Ossie' Arnott asked: "What's up? You're quiet." So I told him the story and said "I hope we're not training up there today." He tried to wind me up saying he'd already heard the manager Ken Knighton saying we were training at Washington, but luckily Knighton came in and said "Right lads, we're training at Cleadon today."

'By the time we next really did train at Washington the car had been removed, but there were two big divots where the wheels had spun getting the car out. Knighton was furious and said "Some daft b****** have been up here with their cars." They still don't know to this day that it was me!'

Joe Bolton was one of the biggest of all Sunderland cult heroes. The story above, hardly heard before, if at all, before this book will only add to the status of the Birtley lad who did things outside normal parameters! Playing in an era when 'hard men' got away with almost anything compared to the modern game, and every team had their 'hard man', Bolton was Sunderland's

designated 'assassin'. Leeds had a team of hard men of course, but Norman Hunter was probably perceived by the public as the hardest, if not the slyest. Arsenal relied on Peter Storey to 'nobble' opposition dangermen, Liverpool boasted Tommy Smith and Chelsea had 'Chopper' Harris. Sunderland had had their share of hard men through the 1960s: Jimmy McNab, 'Mac the Knife' was not shy, and if any right-wingers got past him left-back Lennie 'The Lion' Ashurst did not need asking twice to batter them onto the cinder track surrounding the pitch. Indeed, Joe Bolton came into a left flank that at Sunderland had something of a tradition of being populated by tough nuts. Ahead of McNab for most of the 1960s was winger George Mulhall, no shrinking violet, while preceding the swinging sixties trio of Mulhall,

Joe poses for a portrait.

McNab and Ashurst had been Billy Elliott, who during the 1950s had at one time or another occupied all of those left-flank berths, earning himself a reputation as being among the hardest players ever to play the game.

> *I always smile wryly when nostalgic football discussions hark back to the stereotypical hard-men footballers of the 1970s. The usual suspects are trotted out, you know them, Ron 'Chopper' Harris, Norman 'Bites Yer Legs' Hunter, Tommy 'Anfield Iron' Smith, blah, blah, blah. Yet the real 'Daddy' of them all, Joe Bolton, rarely gets a mention. Maybe that's because Joe was a genuinely hard lad whose tough tackling came naturally to him, and he didn't actually have to try and decapitate forwards in order to get his message of 'thou shalt not pass me' across like the aforementioned grapplers. Joe hails from Birtley in County Durham and was already a well-known character in the local neighbourhood long before he made his debut for the Wearsiders in 1972 against Watford. Often seen out and about while a Sunderland player, Joe was regularly resplendent during the Skinhead era of the early '70s in his Prince of Wales checked suit and lofas, complete with Suedehead haircut. What should never be forgotten about Joe, however, is that he was an excellent left-back. Had he played for a successful club in the manner he played for Sunderland, he would have won England caps. He was that good at his peak.*
> Tom Lynn, Sunderland supporter, Sunderland.

Bolton came through the ranks at Roker while Elliott was on the coaching staff, and indeed as Joe joined the club from school in June 1970 Ashurst had just played his last match and would remain a senior figure at the club during most of Bolton's first year. Joe certainly carried on the tradition of right-wingers dreading a trip to Roker Park. The crowd at Sunderland loved to see 'tackles' that would make even brave men wince. When you were tackled by Joe Bolton you stayed tackled! Sometimes he would get the ball, but he would always get his target!

Joe chuckles with a mixture of menace and amusement at the memories of those days and says 'Two tackles stand out. One was when Ken Knighton was manager. We were playing Nottingham Forest and I went into a 50–50 with Viv Anderson. I went into him so hard that Ken Knighton said to me it was one of the best tackles he'd ever seen. There was another one on John Chiedozie. He was fast, very fast. If he knocked the ball past you that was it – there'd be no catching him. He knocked it past me once, but fortunately as he was running past to get it he ran into my elbow.'

Bolton makes a crunching sound and laughs at the memory, almost like Muttley from *Wacky Races*. 'I didn't see any more of him after that,' he continues, 'like a lot of wingers he tried to swap over onto the other wing.' Of course, while opponents dreaded a Bolton bonecruncher, the fans lapped it up.

> *I remember a game at Nottingham Forest in the 70s when a young Viv Anderson came in for some rough treatment from Joe, and I recall Forest fans' shouting 'Viv, look out for their number three.' Joe loved the physical side of the game and never shirked a tackle.*
> Wayne Talbot, West Sussex based Sunderland season ticket holder.

Joe was one of those players who viewed a 50–50 as his ball without question. When crowds demand that players play for the shirt and get stuck in, inevitably players with the heart and commitment of Joe Bolton are bound to become favourites.

Speaking of his education, Joe explains: 'When I first started, a teammate in the youth team called Ian Harrison told me to let a winger know what he was in for. I learned that with the first tackle you let the winger know he was in a game, with the second the referee would come over and tell you to calm yourself down, and for the third one you'd get booked, but nowadays they get booked straight away for nothing. I've always admired players who could get hit, get hit again and come back for more.'

Joe's manual for getting his tackles in only extends to the third one and a booking, but by the time he left Sunderland no player in the club's history had been sent off more than the three times he had been dismissed. In today's climate where players seem to be cautioned for looking at someone the wrong way or taking their shirt off, Bolton and his fellow '70s hit men would not have lasted two minutes.

Joe's sending offs

Boxing Day 1977
Sunderland 2–1 Blackpool

'I was up against Alan Groves. He was a curly-haired lad. He'd jumped out of a tackle, and when I was on the deck he kicked me. I got up and he swung for me and missed. I swung for him and missed as well, but the referee only saw me throw a punch and I got sent off.'

9 September 1978
Burnley 1–2 Sunderland

'Mickey Henderson got sent off. He used to get so upset. Dave Merrington the assistant manager went into the dressing room to console Mickey, but about five minutes later I got sent off as well. I came in and Dave thought it must be half-time and the rest of the lads were behind me. He said "Alright Joe, what's the score?" and I said "We're getting beat one nowt, but we're still doing alright like." He said: "Champion," and I sat down and started taking my boots off. Merrington says, "Where's the rest of the lads?" so I told him "I've been sent off as well." And he just went "F***** hell!" and went off it.'

Known as 'The Battle of Turf Moor' this is a game fondly remembered by Sunderland fans who saw the nine lads that remained start the second half trailing to Burnley's 11 men and yet emerge as winners. Gary Rowell got both of Sunderland's goals that day and recalls: 'It was a massive game for our manager Jimmy Adamson and his assistant Dave Merrington as they were both back at their old club. At half-time Adamson was livid with us because we were getting beat and had had Mick and Joe sent off. He came into the dressing room, told us what he thought of us which wasn't much, and went out refusing to give us a team talk other than telling us how disgusted he was with us. We just sorted it out between ourselves and decided to have a go at them, reckoning Burnley would figure that we'd come out looking to sit back and go for damage limitation, so we caught them by surprise and managed to win the game.'

Joe watched the second half from the stand and met up again with Henderson a few years later when in the stands again, this time as a supporter: 'Mick's in the police now. He's a dog handler down at Sheffield. I was at a Sunderland versus Newcastle game with some of the lads and he spotted me and got hold of me from behind. I was shouting "I've done nowt!" when I turned around and saw it was him carrying on.'

7 February 1981
Middlesbrough 1–0 Sunderland

'I knocked a cross in and as I did so Terry Cochrane kicked me. I wasn't impressed so I butted him on the back of the head. The ref didn't see it but the linesman did. He spoke to the ref and the ref came over and said to me "You've just butted him." I denied it and he said: "Where's that blood come from then? Get off."'

Boro weren't bothered by Bolton's head-butt, they bought him five months later.

* Joe was later sent off for a fourth time in the red-and-white stripes of Sheffield United.

8 September 1984
Oldham Athletic 2–2 Sheffield United

'That was me and Glenn Cockerill who was with me at Sheffield. The referee was George Tyson from Sunderland. I'd seen him before the game and had a bit of a chat. It wasn't a good surface, it was slippery, and I went in, overstretched and took this lad out. Willie Donachie was playing right-back for Oldham, and he says "Send him off ref, the dirty b******." He got booked for swearing. I insisted that I'd just slipped, which I had, but then another time the winger came inside me across the front of me and Colin Morris tripped him up, but I got the blame for it and he sent me off.'

Joining Sunderland as a 15-year-old in the summer of 1970, Joe signed professional on his 17th birthday in February 1972 and made his first-team debut just two months later. It was not a bad start, Sunderland being 5–0 winners, but the so-called 'Sleeping Giant' of SAFC was comatose at the time, less than 9,000 watching this end-of-season walkover. 'It was Tuesday night versus Watford. Billy Elliott said to me: "You're playing tonight." I just thought it was reserves, but he said "No, it's first team." I was panicking. My dad was still working at Caterpillar, but he managed to get to the match thanks to a lift off one of his mates. The match was so nerve-racking. I was just hoping I could last the pace and that I'd get through the game.'

These days by the time youngsters begin to make a name for themselves they can have been at a club for years as Academies begin taking in players at Under-9 level, but in Joe's youth he had not been destined for Sunderland, despite being a local lad: 'There were one or two clubs that showed an interest, but I wasn't really a football fanatic. In fact I watched more games at Newcastle than I did Sunderland. I just went with my mates because you could jump straight on the bus from Birtley, whereas you had to get three buses to get to Sunderland. I wasn't that keen, but there were one or

Follow through.

two clubs interested. I went down to Coventry, I went to Leeds and I trained with Newcastle up at Hunters Moor on a Tuesday and Thursday night.

'Sunderland only came in quite late. Johnny Watters was the physio at Sunderland, and he used to go down to the dog track where he knew a friend that my dad worked with at Caterpillar. It was through him and a bookie called Tot McKinner that Johnny found out about me. Tot told Johnny that there was a young lad he knew who was a decent footballer. One of the scouts came and watched me, but they never approached me. Then Tot got a phone call from Johnny and said that [Sunderland manager] Alan Brown could come to my house on the Friday night straight after school.

'I'll always remember it. Our front door was on the side of the house, so we never used the front door. My dad was getting washed in the scullery in his vest and then there was a knock at the front door – it was Alan Brown and [chief scout] Charlie Ferguson was with him. My dad said "Ha'way come in this way," and I signed for Sunderland. I ended up leaving Lord Lawson School on the Friday and starting at Sunderland on the Monday. I never had my summer holidays!

'Ian Harrison was an apprentice at the time. His dad picked me up at the "Barley" and used to give me a lift. Going to Sunderland was nerve-racking. Luckily, I knew a lot of the lads I was an apprentice with. I'd played against a lot of them at schoolboy level against Sunderland boys, Chester boys, Jarrow, Hebburn and Felling. Some of us had played for the county together. There was Graeme Southwick, Robert Mitchell and Chris Kent. Graeme was so laid back, I think we started the same day. I settled in alright, it wasn't as though I was going anywhere strange. Robert Mitchell looked like he was going to be really good, but he got to one level and never got any better. We all caught up to him, but he was going to be a world-beater, Robert. He had a hellish left foot on him.

'There were enough there to field two youth teams and some smashing players. When you played, you got a game every other week because there were that many of us. There was Don Rankin, Maurice Hepworth, and you had Micky Horswill, John Lathan, Fred McIver and loads more. They were all eligible for the youth team as they were all under 19.

'Ray Yeoman and Billy Elliott were the coaches. Later Martin Harvey was coach as well and brought Kevin Arnott through. Ray came from Darlo, and he was a tough character as well when he played. I think I've only seen him once since he left.'

Sunderland indeed had a tremendous youth policy, of which Joe was one of its finest products. Astonishingly of the 24 players to represent Sunderland in Bolton's debut season of 1971–72, 19 were home grown. Furthermore, Sunderland had reached three of the previous six FA Youth Cup Finals, winning the trophy twice.

Some footballers insist they never read the papers, but Bolton instantly recalls the local scribe's summary of his debut, getting on for four decades since the line was penned: "A workmanlike performance" Argus wrote in the *Echo*, so I suppose I did alright. I didn't get dropped anyway,' Joe explains. In fact Joe kept his place for the last three games of the season and began the following legendary 1972–73 campaign in the side for the opening couple of matches.

'I played a few games and then Keith Coleman played,' Bolton recalls, but in typically modest fashion he attributes his progress to good fortune: 'I was lucky. I wouldn't have got in the team except through Bobby Park. He was a smashing player, but he broke his leg two or three times and he had to retire, so I was lucky to get in.' Park had broken his leg on the opening day of the 1971–72 season in a match played in torrential rain. That had been eight months before Joe's debut but Park, a midfield player, had tried and failed to come back. Given the huge number of youth players progressing through the ranks, as they always had under Alan Brown, it seems impossible to think that Joe would not have progressed but for Bobby Park's misfortune. Joe is correct in that Bobby Park was a talented player whose career was cruelly ended when still a teenager, having already played over 70 times, but there is no doubt that Joe's time would have come, regardless of Bobby Park's injury.

In one respect Joe Bolton's misfortune was that Bob Stokoe replaced Alan Brown. 'It's always the same in football, if you're playing you like the manager, if you're not playing you don't get on with the manager,' reasons Bolton. 'Alan Brown was strict, especially with punctuality. If you didn't get in the team the manager was crap. He gave me my debut, though, and I'll always owe him that. I remember one time we had a youth-team tournament at Washington, and we had to lay the slabs for the spectators all around the pitch. After training there was a big pitch roller, and he used to pull that himself – he was man-mountain. If he said "sh*t" you jumped on the shovel. A lot of people got on with him and a lot didn't.'

Stokoe, of course, transformed the club, and one of the ways in which he succeeded in doing this was by giving the team an injection of experience. One of the best products of Sunderland's youth policy of the Brown era was Colin Todd, who went on to gain 27 full England caps. 'Toddo' had been Sunderland's record sale when he left for Brian Clough's Derby in 1971, but he explains how Brown often used to bed in young players: 'Brownie would usually put you in for a few games and then take you out for a bit of a breather before putting you back in for another taste.' In Bolton's case as a 17-year-old he'd had a run of six games either side of the close season, and in those days of just a single substitute he was out of the picture watching fellow youth-team product Keith Coleman, four years his senior, hold down the left-back berth when Brown was sacked in November 1972.

Coleman would be the first player to be gotten rid of by Stokoe, who quickly gave Joe an opportunity when, as well as helping keep a clean sheet, he scored his first goal in a 4–0 win over Brighton in the first game of '73. 'Dennis Tueart pulled it back to me and I just hit it. Hit and hope, that's all it was, and fortunately it flew into the top corner. I felt embarrassed because I didn't know what to do,' Joe recalls.

That performance helped him keep his place in the opening couple of games of Sunderland's sensational run to become FA Cup winners, a third-round tie and replay with Notts County: 'I remember the Notts County game. I got a whack in the head. I didn't get stitched, but I was bleeding at the back. I can remember just after the game Stokoe said we were going to have a game of golf on the Monday. I didn't think he was including me. I turned to Vic Halom and asked, "Does he mean me as well?" Vic says, "Oh yeah, because you played." I'd never done that before with Alan Brown. I thought, "Oh well, he's changing things and including the young lads, and he's making it enjoyable for them as well."'

Having drawn 1–1 at Meadow Lane, where Jimmy Montgomery made a late save from Les Bradd as important as the one he later became famous for at Wembley, Sunderland duly disposed of the 'other' Magpies 2–0 in a replay where a first gate of 30,000 since the previous year's Cup campaign provided a glimpse of the Cup fever about to grip Wearside.

At this point Bolton had been on the losing side just twice in his nine first-team appearances, but four days after playing his part in the Cup replay over Notts County Joe was left out as Stokoe introduced his recent signing from Newcastle who would hold down the number-three shirt for the remainder of the Cup run, Ron Guthrie.

'I'd played a few games under Bob Stokoe including the games against Notts County, but in the meantime he'd bought Ron to add a bit of experience – that's what he said to me like. I didn't realise what would happen. I was in and out of the team, but I got on with Bob Stokoe alright. I was just the young lad, so I was the "gopher" really. I got into the team and I found him alright. With me being a young lad he kind of looked after me and so did all the lads as well. As I say I was the "gopher", but we used to have some right laughs.'

'Bob bought a lot of experienced lads from Newcastle, even later on with Bob Moncur a few years later. When he brought in Ron Guthrie I just thought my chance would come eventually, and it did. It was just a new face, it's happened at many a club, when a new manager comes in he brings people in, it just seems to lift the place. I hadn't really been into Alan Brown either. I was just a young lad at the time, I didn't know the things that were going on at the club.

'Arthur Cox did most of the training. I remember one time when we played Man City in the Cup. Bob Stokoe used to get so wound up at games. Some lads with greyhounds used to stand beside the players' entrance at Roker Park. Anyway, before the game Johnny Watters [the physio], who always wore a white coat, walked in with his white coat on and this greyhound with him with a little red-and-white scarf round its neck, and Bob just shook his head and looked at him and eventually smiled.'

As the Cup run gathered pace Joe appeared in seven of the final 15 games as Stokoe did what he could to ease the pressure on the Cup team. Having played in the first two of the nine games it took Sunderland to win the FA Cup, Bolton watched the 1973 Final on the bench, but only as a squad member with David Young the only substitute: 'If they'd had the number of subs they do now I'd have probably got a medal' says Joe, who did actually get a medal that week, but it was won at Roker Park rather than Wembley.

Having had three replays en route to Wembley and a number of winter weather postponements, Sunderland had been dealing with fixture congestion and had League commitments on the Monday before and after the Final. Forty-eight hours after Wembley, Joe played at Cardiff in a game which secured Cardiff's Second Division status, while at the beginning of Cup Final week he had been named as substitute for another game in London: 'The Monday before the Cup Final we played Orient. Trevor Swinburne was in goal as Monty was rested, and a few other lads like Brian Chambers, John Tones and Mick McGiven played.

'Some of us travelled back on the Tuesday with one of the directors, Mr Stewart. What a smashing bloke he was, he was a life-long supporter. In fact when I was there, the directors always came in, whether you won or lost, and said "Unlucky lads", or "Well done". There was Mr Collings, Ted Evans, Mr Ditchburn and Mr Thompson. We travelled back because on the Wednesday we played against Middlesbrough in the Northern Intermediate League Cup Final at Roker Park. It was a night when Tony McAndrew ruptured Maurice Hepworth's spleen.'

Young defender Hepworth's situation became critical. Indeed, having been with the Cup team in London at the beginning of the week and travelling home to play in his own Final, Hepworth did not even see the FA Cup Final on television as he was literally fighting for his life in hospital. Thankfully he got to hold the Cup, though, when the team turned up with it at his bedside on the night they brought it back to Wearside.

Joe did at least make it to Wembley and can be seen on DVDs sat on the bench wearing a dark overcoat, Dick Malone's as it happened: 'I'd travelled back down to London with the players' wives on the Friday and I had a few jobs to do at the match. I was still the "gopher". Before the game Stokoe says: "There's four tickets, get rid of them for me." I got outside and this lad shouts, "Joe, you got any tickets for me?" I said, "Aye." I gave him them, but when I was walking back in someone shouted, "Joe, they're Leeds supporters!" but I hadn't known that, so by accident I'd given them to four Leeds supporters instead of ours.

'I can remember I had Dick Malone's crombie on, and I had Billy Hughes' teeth in one pocket and Bobby Kerr's in the other. I thought, "Will I give them the wrong ones?" I thought they might

Joe Bolton in action.

go up to get the Cup with the wrong teeth in, and I was worried in case I gave them the wrong ones by accident. I'd already mucked up the tickets.

'We were walking to the tunnel long before the game, and Ron Guthrie says "You stick with me lad." We were as close as you are to me now, and I couldn't hear him. The atmosphere was amazing – the hairs were standing on the back of my neck. The noise was just so loud I couldn't hear anything.'

The atmosphere of course got even better. Porterfield got the all-important goal, Monty the all-important save and the Cup had red-and-white ribbons. Of course it was the greatest day in Sunderland's post-war history, but while Joe had played his part he did not even get to accompany the team on the lap of honour, in fact he did not even get to see it! 'After the game I ran over to Horswill because we used to be room partners. I saw Billy Hughes and asked: "Billy, can I run around the pitch with you?" He said "No, get the tea poured," so I had to go in and pour the tea.

'I was in the dressing room. When you get 12 sweaty blokes with kit all over it's chaotic. All the reporters and directors were in there, so I thought "I'm going in the bath me, I'm at Wembley and I've not even seen the lap of honour so I'm gonna get in the bath at least," so I jumped in. There's a picture somewhere of me, Vic Halom and Dave Young sat in the bath.

'Me and Sue were courting. She came down for the weekend, and after the game we were stopping at Park Lane in the Dorchester where the reception was on the night time. Suzie Quattro was on, with Sweet, and Emperor Rosko was the DJ. It was great. But I didn't drink because Stokoe was watching!'

Billy Hughes swapped his Cup Final strip for a gold record by Sweet, whose lead singer was fellow Scotsman Brian Connolly. Sweet's finest was not Hughesie's only Scottish musical pal, 'He was mates with Rod Stewart as well,' remembers Joe. 'I was either injured or I'd been coming back through injury and had played for the reserves. I was off the next day, and the first team were in training. Rod Stewart had been in training and I missed him, which was typical for me. That was at the gym at Washington. He was a funny lad, Billy.'

Knocking about with pop singers comes easily to Cup-winning footballers, but there were still two League games to play and Joe got a game in the first of them on the Monday, with the team delaying their homecoming until the Tuesday, and wrapping up the season by entertaining already promoted QPR another 24 hours later.

Perhaps the greatest cult hero of them all was Cup Final centre-forward Vic Halom who, like Bolton, was the essence of a cult hero and yet very different in character. Vic is outgoing and can be the life and soul of the party, whereas Joe likes to keep himself to himself, certainly not out of unfriendliness but of genuine modesty, even shyness. However, Joe has no bigger fan than Vic.

> *Halom, one of the hardest men to ever be seen in a red-and-white shirt, says: 'Joe Bolton was tremendous. Joe was fabulous. One of the hardest lads I've ever seen. I'm so pleased he was on our bloody side. He had a couple of games before Ron came in. He came with us and was part of it – in fact he remains part of it. I sometimes phone him up – he was a hell of a character. Last time I phoned him I left a couple of messages, but he didn't get back to me, which doesn't surprise me' says Vic with his usual knowing smile. 'Joe used to look after Hughesy and myself. When I got banned to the bedroom and had to be locked in – Joe used to go to the Chinese takeaway, and feed me through the window. That happened from time to time. I remember once we were playing Stoke in the Cup in 1976. We were staying in Buxton, but Bob [Stokoe] wouldn't let me out of the hotel room because I didn't have the "right" attitude! That was one of the times I had to rely on Joe.'*
> Vic Halom.

Having only turned 18 after playing in the third round and third-round replay, Bolton's career was still ahead of him at this point, but it was a fabulous start to a career that would see him give such great service to Sunderland and earn his own place in the hearts of Sunderland supporters: 'I'll never forget that Cup run because I was involved in every game,' he says.

Coming on as sub on the first day of Sunderland's season as Cup holders, Joe kept pushing harder and harder for a regular place in the starting line up. The breakthrough came at Fulham in October, where after coming off the bench he did well enough to begin to establish himself in the team, missing only three games until the final couple of weeks of the season.

He got into the side just in time to taste European Football. That may have been a sophisticated new experience for Sunderland, but Joe found he had more to concern himself with during the game than just the opposition: 'I didn't play the first games against Vasas Budapest, but I played against Sporting Lisbon home and away. The atmosphere was unbelievable. Although I was playing, I still had to carry the skips in and put the kit away. A mate of mine had travelled to Lisbon for the second leg, so I asked Bob Stokoe if my mate could help me carry the stuff in. He said, "Go on then." We took the kit in, and I had to set it out in the dressing room. Anyway, my mate disappeared, but later on during the game there was some commotion in the crowd, and when I looked it was my mate in the middle of the Sporting Lisbon fans with his Sunderland flag. I thought, "If Stokoe sees that and he knows that it's my mate causing bother, that'll be it."'

It was 'it' in effect as Sunderland lost out to Lisbon 3–2 on aggregate. Playing top European teams was one thing, but back in the day-to-day grind of Second Division football things went anything but smoothly. Having won the Cup the previous year, every team wanted to raise their game against the Cup holders, so it became a difficult time for Sunderland who finished sixth after spending much of the season becalmed in mid-table. In those pre-Play-off days sixth was of no use, although the fact the lads were only two points behind the third promotion place filled by Carlisle offered hope that the next year would see top flight status regained.

The 1974–75 season proved to be very different to the previous campaign, although it ended with the same result, Sunderland missing promotion by a couple of points. In contrast to 1973–74 though, where the Wearsiders had risen with a late surge, this time round they dropped out of the promotion places on the final day having been second or third for almost the entire season. Defeat at promoted Aston Villa marked the end of an era. Three of the Cup team had already left the club, and two more bowed out at Villa Park, including left-back Ron Guthrie who had been blocking Bolton's progress in his favoured position, many of his 20-odd appearances having been made in midfield from where he had managed to score in a couple of comfortable home wins.

'I played midfield when Ian Porterfield had his accident. I played at Blackpool.' National viewers remember Sunderland's seaside visit for Mickey Walsh's *BBC TV Goal of the Season,* but Sunderland supporters are more likely to recall Billy Hughes missing from the spot after the antics of a peanut seller behind the goal. Joe certainly has not forgotten, 'When we played I remember that bloke standing behind the goal in the white coat. They made a thing of it on *Match of the Day* – I was brought down for the penalty, and Tony Towers came over and told me, "Don't laugh, mind when you get up in case the ref sees you." He said I went down like a bag of sh*te! Ron was playing left-back and I was playing midfield. The lad who scored for them, Walsh, hit a hell of a goal.'

Home wins proved to be the order of the day in 1975–76, 19 of them accompanying two draws and no League defeats as Bob Stokoe won his second trophy at Sunderland, the Second Division Championship, with Joe the regular left-back. 'I was out of the team when we won promotion in 1980, but I was in the team when we won the Second Division in 1976.'

Promotion was clinched on Easter Monday before the last ever 50,000-plus crowd to squeeze into Roker Park, 'The stadium now is a beautiful place, but the atmosphere isn't the same as at Roker, that was some atmosphere' remembers Joe of a 2–1 win over a Bolton Wanderers side that included a young Peter Reid. The title was clinched the following Saturday, Joe keeping his only goal of the season for the occasion.

Joe had always been popular with the crowd as well as his teammates, and it was during the club's first-ever Second Division Championship-winning season that he first started to notice the crowd singing his name, although in typically shy fashion he was not about to milk it: 'The first time it happened I'd gone onto the pitch with Mel Holden, and the crowd chanted his name and he waved. Then they chanted mine, and I just put my head down and disappeared back down the tunnel, and they must have all thought "What's up with him?" but I just didn't know what to do with myself,' Joe admits.

Bolton never was one for the spotlight. In today's media-saturated game he would have rivalled Paul Scholes as a reluctant interviewee, like Scholes believing that the only worthwhile talking is done on the pitch and like Scholes never accepting that just because he was a footballer he was anything out of the ordinary.

'I went to a do recently,' he explains. 'My niece is going out with Paul Collingwood's brother Peter, and the do was at Shotley Bridge cricket club where there was a barbecue on. I agreed to go – but made it clear I wasn't getting up onto any stage to make a speech nor anything like that. It was a great atmosphere, and nobody ran across or anything to make a fuss. It was great because I was just there as part of the crowd, which is how I like it. I could just mix in with people and not be treated any differently to anybody else. I signed a couple of autographs and had a couple of photos taken, but I wasn't having to do this and that all night, it was very relaxed.

'I know a lad called Wayne Talbot who ran the Prudhoe branch of the Sunderland Supporters' Association. He asked me to come and talk to the branch, but I said "Wayne, I'm not into talking into microphones or anything like that." Some people can just do it, but I can't. I suppose if I'd had a few pints I'd talk all night about football and Sunderland, but that's talking to one or two people not a whole load at a time. I said to him, "I'll tell you what, I'll come and sit among 'yous' and just talk to people so then everybody isn't looking at me, because I'd get embarrassed talking to a group of people."'

Like a singer who is great belting out their hits but nervous on the chat show circuit, Bolton was best at the day job. No one who ever watched him slam into some poor unsuspecting winger ever noticed anything shy about him! The chant the fans came up with of, 'Joe, Joe, Joe Bolton!' seemed to sum him up. Away from the joyous lilt of 'Ole, ole, ole, ole, Marco, Marco' or 'Super, Super Kev' for great goalscorers in years to come, Bolton's ditty contained the same sense of brutality that 'Ooh Bally, Bally' did in providing the soundtrack to the sort of physical challenges with which Messrs Bolton and Ball would welcome opponents to Wearside.

'I just got stuck in', reasons Joe when asked why he thinks the crowd took to him as they did. 'I'll admit I wasn't the most skilful player out there, but I always gave 100 per cent. The crowd are not

Joe in action.

In the gym.

daft. They know when someone's pulling the wool over their eyes. That's what the crowd want – 11 100 per centers instead of 11 posers like some do now. Some players now are pinching a living. I think that's what it is. Being a local lad helped as well. I went through a bad spell like every player does, but because I gave 100 per cent and I wasn't afraid to get stuck in they always liked me.'

Having taken three years to get the club promoted after winning the FA Cup, the joy of promotion in 1976 soon turned sour for Bob Stokoe after a disastrous start to life in the top tier. It proved to be a season of trials, tribulations and transformation, with Bolton the only constant as the solitary ever present in a season that saw not only Bob Stokoe leave, but also Cup-winners Jimmy Montgomery, Dick Malone and Billy Hughes three of the 11 players to bow out. Beginning with three draws was not a terrible way to acclimatise after promotion, but with no wins in nine Stokoe felt he had taken the club as far as he could and resigned, Monty having played his final match in the previous game.

It was an unhappy time, and Joe reflects on the Stokoe era with his trademark honesty, 'You hear players say, "He was a queer bloke Stokoe," but because I didn't work with him every day in his early days at the club I didn't really know. Obviously I knew he came from Newcastle and had played for them for a long time, but I didn't realise he was so black and white through and through. I know in training he used to wind people up. I only ever saw "Pop" Robson get really mad once. We were in the gym playing five-a-side, and Bob kicked "Pop" from behind and 'Pop' turned on him, which wasn't like him. It was all a bit handbags. Bob used to wind people up like that. But he did what he had to do, and we won the Cup which was fantastic.

'He loved his golf, and we always took the golf clubs – ever since Stokoe came. He used to take us all over as part of training, just to change the atmosphere. The atmosphere was different with him. With the older players, he showed them more respect. I remember when I used to go away with them as a young lad I'd order a steak and chips and he'd be looking at me and saying "Are you sure you want to be eating that? It's not very good for you." If I'd had a pint of orange and lemonade he'd be like, "Watch what you're drinking, that's too gassy." I think it was just to get me in the right frame of mind and bring me on the right way. Even at the club parties, me and Graham Southwick were dying to have half a lager, and whenever he went out of the room we'd have a quick half. He'd come in walking by and ask, "What you had to drink lads?" He didn't rule the kids with an iron fist, but the kids were more wary than the first team. When it was the right time to relax it was alright. There's a time and a place for everything.'

Ian McFarlane took over as caretaker manager for seven games, picking up a couple of wins and a creditable draw at Manchester United, but still leaving the Lads one off the bottom when he was replaced. 'He was called "The Big Man"' recalls Joe, 'Smashing bloke mind. Bob had fetched Ian in. It was quite surprising because Arthur [Cox] was more or less getting the elbow. A lot of people felt sorry for him. Ian had been there before, he was there with Alan Brown. We'd been to Sweden on pre-season with Ian, he liked his golf as well. He was always wearing these brightly coloured checked shirts. He had massive feet – we were sitting in a café once, and his feet came round the corner before his body. He was wearing these red-and-white clogs, and they were gigantic!'

McFarlane tried to hold things together until a full-time replacement was lined up. That proved to be Ashington-born former Footballer of the Year Jimmy Adamson. 'When Jimmy Adamson came, the training changed. Everything we'd done – even pre-season – was different. Everything was so different, and so enjoyable. Dave Merrington was assistant manager. He's from Barley Mow – my dad used to cut his hair. My dad's more famous for cutting hair than I was for playing football. He was renowned in this area for cutting people's hair – only had one style. He had a "cree" in the back garden, and he used to cut all the lads' hair out there. I enjoyed playing under Jimmy. He very rarely lost his temper. It was Dave who lost it – he had a ginger cast and he was typically fiery.

'We played at Boro in the League Cup. Dave came into the dressing room at half-time, and he laid into the back four. Colin Waldron said, "Bollocks." Dave said "I beg your pardon?" and Colin went across and said, "Bollocks. Go on, hit me then." So Dave smacked him straight in the jaw. Dave used to just blow his top every now and again. He fetched in all the lads from Burnley. There was me, Jackie Ashurst and Bobby Kerr. It was all change because they brought in lads from Burnley. I must have been one of the last ones to move on from the team we had before they came in.'

That episode at Boro's old Ayresome Park ground came in Adamson and Merrington's second season. Sunderland had gone down the year before, having endured a record run of 10 games without even a goal to cheer before scoring a deluge of goals in a glorious but ultimately doomed battle to stave off relegation, only two defeats in 18 games preceding a final-day defeat at Everton.

That doomed 1976–77 season proved to be Sunderland's solitary year in the top flight during the 1970s and, as the club had found to their cost before, winning instant promotion was beyond them. Bolton remained a steady fixture in the side during a season of transition when Adamson's side failed to trouble the front runners. One of the few highlights of the season arrived on the final day when Joe came within one kick of becoming the first-ever Sunderland defender to score a hat-trick. He'd already leathered home two cracking shots in a pretty meaningless end-of-season game with Charlton when Sunderland were awarded a penalty. 'The first goal was one of those that you just hit and you catch it right, and it flew in. For the second one, Bobby [Kerr] ran in behind the full-back and pushed me in, and I scored. At half-time, Jimmy Adamson said, "If there's a penalty, let Joe take it." We got the penalty, and nine times out of 10 I'd have buried it, but I skied it. I sent the 'keeper the wrong way, but people keep saying even now "you hit me on the head with that ball when you took that penalty.'"

> *There is something indefinably exciting about tough-tackling left-footers. Birtley's original bulldozer combined a great physical presence with a tank-like momentum going forward. Joe's no-nonsense tackling was a feature of his play, but fans loved the unflustered way he went about his game. His consistently solid performances and thuddering challenges were his trademarks but will also be remembered for missing a penalty which would have sealed an amazing hat-trick.*
> Mike Love, SENSSA.

The person who would normally have taken that penalty was Gary Rowell. Joe was in the side with Rowell the following season when Gary included a penalty in his legendary hat-trick as Sunderland triumphed 4–1 at Newcastle. Being from Birtley, Bolton had plenty of mates on both sides of the North East divide. 'In my day, it was half and half. Sue and my dad were at the match. We stopped at the fish shop in Barley Mow on the way home. One of my mates is black and white daft, and I saw him and shouted "Come on the Reds" at him. He came and chased me until he realised it was me!'

A year and a half after skying his 'hat-trick penalty' Joe was almost put on the spot at Newcastle: 'We played Newcastle in the League Cup and we won on penalties. I was next in line to take one, and I was very relieved Barry Siddall saved their last one,' he reveals.

By the time of the 4–1 derby win (let alone the League Cup penalty drama, by which time Ken Knighton was manager) Adamson and Merrington had departed for Leeds, leaving Billy Elliott as caretaker manager for the second half of a season that came within a point of promotion and just two behind champions Crystal Palace. 'I knew Billy from the youth team and got on well with him. He was a smashing bloke. He was a hell of a player and could be fiery as well, he once had a go at Stokoe in the tunnel. People thought when Stokoe came Billy would be on his bike, but he was there long after Bob had gone.'

Elliott, though, was passed over for the manager's job in the close season, with Bolton less than impressed with his replacement, who was already coaching at the club, Ken Knighton.

'I used to have a mate called Joe who used to re-upholster chairs and things in working-men's clubs. I went around with him. We were in the players' lounge one day because he was going to refurbish the carpets and stuff, and I was helping him out. We just sat there having a glass of coke and Ken Knighton walked in and said something. I said, "Aye okay Ken", and he said, "It's boss now." He was a right champagne Charlie.'

'At the start of that season he made me captain, but later on he bought Joe Hinnigan. He said to me "I haven't bought Joe to replace you," but then he came up to me and said he'd leave me out because I was having a bad time, which was fair enough.'

Having skippered the side and been the last remaining player at the club to have played a part in the 1973 FA Cup win, Joe was jettisoned when Hinnigan debuted in Joe's number-three shirt in February. Hinnigan kept the shirt for the final 14 unbeaten games of the season as Knighton's men secured promotion with Bolton failing to even make the bench despite injuries: 'Joe Hinnigan could play centre-half as well and when Jeff Clarke got injured I thought he might move him to centre-half and bring me back in at left-back, but he put Gordon Chisholm in before me and left Joe Hinnigan at left-back.'

It was the second time Joe had won promotion at Sunderland. In 1976 as champions he had received a medal of course, but medals were also issued by the club for the promotion as runners-up in 1980, but Joe has since given that away. 'I've still got the medal from 1976. At the top it's got "Division Two Champions." The other one I gave to my mate John because his son's disabled. The one I gave away says, "Promoted to Division One."' In this day and age, when so many former sportsmen cash in on their glory days by auctioning their medals, it is typical of Joe Bolton that he thought of someone else in giving away that promotion souvenir, but perhaps given the way he went from hero to zero that season the medal did not hold the sort of memories it should have.

Back in the top flight, Bolton came to the fore once again, only ever present Stan Cummins surpassing his 39 League appearances: 'The season afterwards Joe got injured at the start and I hardly missed a game.' Nonetheless, he continued to feel his days were numbered under Knighton's regime: 'We went to Norway for pre-season. There was [assistant manager] Frank Clark who I got on with great, Ken Knighton and Peter Eustace who was his coach. John Cooke and Rob Vincent who were young pros coming through were there. We got to the airport, and there Ken Knighton stood. He said, "Come on Joe and get these bags." I thought "He wants to make me look small, they want me to leave," but it just made me think "I'll show them," and after getting back into the team for the first game the only games I missed were when I was suspended after getting sent off at Middlesbrough.'

In fact Bolton stayed longer than Knighton, who left in April. 'I heard on the wireless he'd got sacked and Mick Docherty took over.' Docherty had four games to prevent Sunderland slipping straight back down in the first year after promotion as they had done in 1977 and as they would do too many times in the future. Knighton's big signing Tom Ritchie famously hit a hat-trick in the first game after the manager's sacking, having failed to score for the man who had bought him, but desperate defeats at West Brom and at home to relegation rivals Brighton left Sunderland needing to win their final game to be sure of staying up. The problem was it was against Liverpool at Anfield, but win they did.

The Wearsiders were helped by two key factors: Liverpool had a European Cup Final coming up later that month, and with nothing at stake for them in the League it was perhaps timely that in Bob Paisley they had a manager who had grown up as a Sunderland supporter in Hetton-le-Hole. 'Mick Docherty went to hand the team sheet in and came back having seen Bob Paisley,' recalls Joe. 'Docherty said, "We'll be alright just watch the tackles." They had a European Final to play.'

Things were going swimmingly for both sides, Sunderland were heading towards a positive result and Messrs Hansen, Souness, Rush & co. were not likely to need a shower after the game when Joe in his inimitable fashion almost altered proceedings, 'There was one there to be won and I went for it, but I just had to calm down and not make any more like that,' he admits, adding 'Mind, the goal Stan Cummins scored that day was right in the corner. There's no way their 'keeper would have stopped that, no 'keeper would – not even Monty would have stopped it.' Sure enough Cummins's goal sent home a happy red-and-white army that gave Anfield a gate 9,000 higher than Liverpool's previous home gate against Manchester United. Sunderland did their bit to help Paisley's men win

Playing for Sunderland at Middlesbrough who he would join in 1981.

the European Cup three weeks later. Joe had restricted himself to just a solitary 'tackle'…and Sunderland born Alan Kennedy duly scored the winner in the European Cup Final against Real Madrid.

Sadly that win at Anfield proved to be Joe Bolton's 325th and final game for Sunderland. A couple of generations earlier another Sunderland hero Len Shackleton infamously entitled a chapter in his autobiography: 'The average director's knowledge of football' and left the page blank. Joe evidently thought along similar lines when he went to Sunderland chairman Tom Cowie and one of his directors about a new contract: 'I went in, and Tom Cowie was in charge of the contracts and had Peter Fraser with him. Peter had a farm in Scotland, so he liked his shooting. Mr Cowie offered me a contract, and I said I wasn't happy. I thought I'd merited more money and that was the only time I'd ever argued over a contract. I'd always just signed. Other lads had gone in and said, "I want this and that" and they'd hang on and get it. Cowie asked me "How can you merit more money?" I told him, "I've just played every game of the season bar three I missed through suspension." He said, "but you seem to have lost interest. You never win the Man of The Match award in the papers." I said, "Well, if that's how you judge players you can forget it, I'm off."'

> *Joe was similar to Vic Halom, a hard man, but he was a straight, honest bloke. Not devious or anything. As chairman you occasionally meet a player who's a bit devious, but not Joe. He was straight on...but he frightened a few wingers!*
> Keith Collings, Sunderland chairman 1971–80.

These were the days before agents, and for all the horror stories surrounding them in the modern game perhaps that was an occasion where an agent might have smoothed the path towards agreement, but the summer appointment of new boss Alan Durban failed to keep the ever popular and loyal Bolton at the club.

'When Alan Durban came Arthur Cox wanted me to go to Newcastle. I'd had talks with Boro, and the only reason I went to Boro is because they were in the First Division. If Newcastle had been in the First Division I'd have gone there.

'I went to see Bobby Murdoch at Boro, and I came back and had to have a meeting with Alan Durban. Durban said he wanted me have a trial for 12 games before he offered me a contract. I said "You're joking. I've played against your team in the past, surely you know all about me. What happens at the end, if you don't want me other teams will be fixed up," so I told him to forget it and went to Boro.'

Bolton's Boro debut came in an opening-day defeat at home to Spurs, and things did not get much better as the Teessiders ended up bottom of the table with Sunderland once again just escaping the drop. Nonetheless, Joe found much to enjoy at Ayresome Park and played twice against his old team, a goalless draw at Boro and winning 2–0 on Wearside. 'It was a new challenge. It was just the way I was treated, which was much better. I hadn't got over Durban wanting to put me on trial after the number of games I'd been at the club and the fact he'd already seen me play. When I came back to Sunderland to play for Boro I didn't want to prove anything to the crowd, just to the board of directors because I would have ended my career at Sunderland if it wasn't for them, but that's life.'

Joe had cost Boro a reported £200,000, a sizeable fee at the time for a defender, but after a second season during which he played regularly as Boro struggled in the lower reaches of Division Two he was released on a free transfer.

'I went to Sheffield United with Ian Porterfield.' It was a good move. Porterfield also had Joe's old Roker teammates Kevin Arnott and Mickey Henderson in his line up, as well as former Sunderland youth-team goalkeeper Keith Waugh. Joe arrived in time for the second game and from there played in every game as promotion was won from the Third Division by the tightest of margins, only goals scored lifting them above Hull.

Bolton stayed with the Blades for another two seasons, playing over 100 times for them including a 1–0 home win over Sunderland in March 1986. Just over a month later a tame 1–1 draw with nothing at stake between Crystal Palace and Sheffield United marked the 441st and final League appearance of Joe's career.

One of the hardest men in the game gave him a chance to continue, 'Norman Hunter was manager of Rotherham. I went there from Sheffield United, but I'd hurt my knee and finished when I was 31' says Joe, who did not seek an immediate return to the North East after hanging up his boots.

'I lived in Baslow after I finished playing football. The money wasn't great and we moved to Chesterfield. I had a spell playing for Matlock Town. I had about four games as caretaker manager and I enjoyed that, but I didn't put in for it. I just thought that naturally they knew I was interested as I was doing it as caretaker, but in fact Dave Pugh got the job. He'd been at Rotherham and Doncaster, but I did enjoy being manager.

'I was on the dole at the time, but some of the lads were coming up from places like Caernarvon. They were getting back at three in the morning and then getting up for work so they could play non-League. They weren't getting much money, in fact it probably hardly covered their expenses.'

It was not just management that Joe tried his hand at, he had a go at a sport some might think him well suited for, 'My son played rugby at Chesterfield. I encouraged him but I wasn't going to force him, I wouldn't want to force him to do anything. They had some dads v lads games. I played about four games at Chesterfield and scored a couple of tries. My son played a few games but then packed it in. He's 22 [in 2008] and he's into his dogs like me. He's called Joe, I'm Joseph and my dad was Joseph as well.'

Having made a career of steaming into wingers with the elegance of a juggernaut, Bolton tried long-distance lorry driving as a new career before coming home. 'I had my own wagon for a while, but that went pear shaped. The main reason I came back was because I never had any money when I finished playing. I was never any good with money – I was never into gambling or anything like that. I just could never look after my money. I've been with Sue since I was 16 years old, I went in one night from work, sat down with Sue and said, "You alright?" She told me, "We're behind on the mortgage." I said "Is that all you're worried about? Right, we'll sell the house and go back home." So that's what we did. I wouldn't care, I've got programmes. I used to get a programme from every game I played in. I kept them, and when we moved back from Chesterfield I've put them down and can't find them.

'Football passes me by these days. I like to see Sunderland doing well, but to me it was just a job. I was lucky to be in the position to do it, and to be honest I don't think I realised how lucky I was. I wish I could meet Roy Keane, I'm not just saying it because he's our manager, but I've always said that there's only one player at Manchester United who was on what he was worth, and that was Roy Keane. He was up and down. He was the only one who merited £100k. Some players now walk around like they're God's gift. I would put them all on the same basic wage and put them on appearance money. I remember when Sunderland staff were made redundant a few years ago and Michael Gray had just bought a new Ferrari. I know a bloke at Sunderland who has been there since before I played and he's still there. He knows the players, and when I last saw him he said some of them will pass you by and not even say hello. He said when Arca was there he always spoke, he's supposed to be a canny lad.'

To some extent, of course, every generation of footballers looks at the current crop of players in comparison with their own era and sees massive differences, but in Joe Bolton's case even when he was playing all he wanted to do was to be accepted as like any of his mates. Asked if he realises how much of a hero he is to Sunderland supporters, Bolton does his best to shrug off such an accolade: 'People keep on saying things like that, and I say "nah, I'm just one of the lads." I get embarrassed

Joe Bolton in 2007 in his native Birtley.

though. To me it was just a job, I didn't want to be any different to anyone else. When I was out with Sue, we just wanted to keep ourselves to ourselves, and people would say, "Ah, he's a footballer so he thinks he's better than us, he won't talk to anyone." If I was out with the lads, and we were having a laugh and that with people, everyone would say, "Look at him, showing off because he's a footballer." You couldn't win, but I just wanted to be like anyone else.'

As far as Joe was concerned he just went to work at a football club just as any of his pals might have gone to work at the pit or the local factory. Being a hero never entered his mind, yet ironically it was this very down to earth nature, combined with the fact that when he wore the red-and-white shirt he dished out the sort of treatment to opponents that his mates would have loved to, that made Joe the cult hero he undoubtedly was, and equally still is to the generation of supporters for whom the cry, 'Joe, Joe, Joe Bolton!' still brings a shiver and a look to see if a stretcher's on the way.

SEEDAAALLL

BARRY SIDDALL

Goalkeeper
1980 promotion winner with Sunderland.

Born: 12 September 1954, Ellesmere Port.
Signed for Sunderland: 29 September 1976
Transferred: 22 August 1982 to Port Vale, free

Bolton Wanderers:	January 1972, 137 League appearances
Sunderland:	29 September 1976, 167 League appearances
	192 total appearances
Darlington:	(Loan) 2 October 1980, 8 League appearances
Vancouver Whitecaps:	(Loan) June-August 1981
Port Vale:	August 1982, 81 League appearances
Blackpool:	(Loan) October 1983, 7 League appearances
Stoke City:	January 1985, 20 League appearances
Tranmere Rovers:	(Loan) October 1985, 12 League appearances
Manchester City:	(Loan) March 1986, 6 League appearances
Blackpool:	August 1986, 110 League appearances
Stockport County:	June 1989, 21 League appearances
Hartlepool United:	March 1990, 0 appearances
Mossley	
Carlisle United:	November 1990, 24 League appearances
Chester City:	July 1991, 9 League appearance
Northwich Victoria	
Preston North End:	November 1992, 1 League appearance.

'I could see the likeness when they called me Basil. It was the 'tache. On one occasion I was playing for Port Vale at Southend, and the Southend fans spent all afternoon shouting "Basil" at me. In the end when the ball was at the other end I did the funny walk for them, and they killed themselves laughing. I got a letter a few days later signed by four Southend fans saying they'd spent years being depressed by watching Southend and I'd made their day and given them the biggest laugh they'd ever had at the match.'

Barry Siddall was never short of a laugh. He was a good goalkeeper and had to be as the man signed to replace the one and only Jimmy Montgomery. The fact that from the day Siddall took over

'Basil' portrait from a football sticker.

from Monty in 1976 the club's all-time record appearance maker never managed to add a single further appearance to the 627 he had made prior to Barry's arrival is testament to the quality Siddall brought to the side.

Like a lot of other players, Barry came to the club at a difficult time. Sunderland were struggling soon after finally winning promotion three years after the sensational Cup win of the early 1970s, but Siddall was an instant hit with the supporters despite the less than flattering nicknames they came up with for the former Bolton 'keeper. In addition to being 'christened' Basil after John Cleese's Basil Fawlty, Siddall soon had other monikers, 'I know the Sunderland fans used to call me the "Flying Pig" but I didn't think I was fat! It was all a good laugh, though, and they all used to shout "Seedaaall" when I took a cross or made a good save.'

Barry was not fat. In his first season at Sunderland he was recorded as 13st 2lb, but compared to Monty's lithe 11st 9lb Siddall was not slim either and when he launched himself to take a cross the nickname did not take the fans long. It is said that if a goalkeeper leaves his line he should clear everything in his path and make sure he takes the cross; the way Barry battered all and sundry out of his way was certainly sufficient to make mincemeat out of most forwards.

'The crowd took to me straight away and vice versa' confirms Barry, 'I always got a big buzz out of playing at Roker Park, especially in front of big crowds. I had a great rapport with the fans, and having taken over from Jim Montgomery I was delighted to have them on my side. I was young and a cocky bugger and lapped it up. I've seen Jim when I've been a guest on his table at matches at the Stadium of Light in recent years, and he's a decent fellow. At the time he'd have been sad that his time was over after being a hero for so many years, but time moves on for everyone.'

Infamously dubbed the 'Flying Pig' because of his rather square-looking and unflattering physique, Barry Alfred Siddall [couldn't get a more English name, could you?] was in fact a pretty capable custodian who has gone down into Wearside folklore because of the brilliant relationship he developed with the Roker regulars. He had a tough act to contend with, following Monty and competing with Chris Turner, who was kept out of the team for long spells by Siddall but who still was good enough to be later signed by Man United. Siddall was a real character who always had a laugh with the fans during warm-ups and used to enjoy a few beers in The Saltgrass, mixing with mates and fans in a friendly, outgoing manner. Barry Siddall was just your regular bloke who happened to be good enough to play professional football…and very well too.

Tom Lynn, Sunderland supporter, Sunderland.

Siddall had six years at Sunderland before his time was up. For the first three years of that spell he was the undisputed number one before facing a challenge from the excellent Chris Turner. In a career spanning two decades, over 600 League games and 13 different League clubs, Barry played more games for Sunderland than any other club and created a lasting impression on Wearside. 'Years later I did the half-time draw on a day when Sunderland stuffed Oxford 7–0 at the Stadium of

Light. I got a fantastic reception then and to get that so many years after I'd finished playing for the club was unbelievable.' That occasion was 16 years after Siddall left Sunderland, but it was not the first time the fans had shown their appreciation.

'When I was with Blackpool we played Sunderland at home, and I got a fantastic reception from the Sunderland fans. There was a huge contingent of them behind the goal, and when you get a reception like that from fans of a former club it's something you remember the most. Sunderland won 2–0 that day, I can remember John MacPhail scored both of the goals, one of them with a penalty. I got a terrific reception when I came back to Roker Park with Blackpool, as well as I had when I'd been back before for a game I remember Sunderland won 1–0, with a goal from David Hodgson.' That occasion, in fact, was Siddall's Stoke debut on a day when his defence included a young Steve Bould, later to endear himself to Sunderland fans himself at the other end of his career.

Sunderland's supporters had left a telling impression on the young Siddall in Barry's time at his first club Bolton. He first played against the Lads in what was just the Wearsiders' eighth home League game after winning the Cup in 1973. He had debuted for Bolton in October 1972, a month after his 18th birthday, and in the autumn of 1973 played twice against Sunderland in the space of three weeks. It was in Sunderland's promotion season of 1975–76, though, when he really saw what his future club was capable of. Phenomenal travelling support contributed to Bolton's home gate, with Sunderland being 18,000 higher than their second-highest crowd of the season, while on Easter Monday over 51,000 squeezed into Roker Park for a game that sealed promotion for Sunderland against a Bolton side that, as well as Siddall, included a young Peter Reid: 'Playing at Roker Park in front of the huge Roker End and with the chanting from the Fulwell End sticks in your mind, especially as a young player' recalls Barry, 'Peter was a couple of years younger than me and was an apprentice when I was a young pro. He was very dedicated to the game and did the simple things well. You always knew what you'd get from Peter once he had the shirt on. If he'd had more pace he'd have probably won more England caps.'

At this point Barry had not missed a game for Bolton since before his first appearance against Sunderland two and a half years earlier. Indeed, he was ever present for the Trotters for three successive seasons, but after being among the leaders all year he saw Bolton miss out after witnessing Wearside's promotion party. Little was Barry to know that before long he would be a Sunderland player himself, although the unexpected sighting of a former Sunderland player, George Mulhall, by now assistant manager at Bolton, panicked him at first.

'Sunderland came in for me in the September. The thing was, at Bolton we weren't supposed to play golf from a Thursday onwards, but I was playing at Dunscar on a Thursday, and I saw George Mulhall's car approaching so I hid. The following day I got called into the manager Ian Greaves's office, and thought I was in for a bollocking, but he said "Don't worry, we know you were playing golf, but Sunderland have come in with an offer for you." He already had my boots in his office and he'd lined up Jim McDonagh as my replacement so he just gave me my boots and said "Get up to Sunderland and sign for them." Sunderland almost tripled my wage from £70 a week to £190, and the bonus list was a lot better as well so I couldn't say no. I knew Sunderland were a big club. It was only three years since they'd won the Cup, they'd just won the Second Division and they got big crowds. For me the biggest thing about a club's support is its travelling supporters, and Sunderland travel in massive numbers. I'd seen huge numbers when they'd come to Bolton, and that stood out for me.'

Mention of Siddall's replacement at Bolton, Jim 'Seamus' McDonagh, will send shivers down the spines of Sunderland supporters who recall his later spell at Roker with horror, although in fairness to McDonagh he had a good career and was well thought of at many clubs. It simply did not happen for him at Sunderland and, had it not been for Siddall's strength of character, 'Basil' could easily have become 'Fawlty' at Sunderland.

Into October without a win, manager Bob Stokoe resigned following a home defeat on Siddall's debut. With long-serving Montgomery, Dick Malone and Billy Hughes three of 10 players making final appearances around the time Siddall arrived and three managerial changes during the season, a 10-game run without so much as a goal scored and eventual relegation, the situation could have made lesser characters wonder what they'd done in moving to Sunderland, but Barry remained undaunted: 'If I'd been older I'd probably have thought "What have I done coming here?" but I was young, and I just got on with things. When you're young you don't let things like that bother you. I was a cocky lad, and to me it was all just a big new adventure.'

Caretaker manager Ian McFarlane was in charge when Barry was beaten twice without reply at QPR on his away debut. Not every player's cup of tea, McFarlane soon moved on, and by the time of new boss Jimmy Adamson's first match Siddall had played for three managers in his first nine games. 'It was hard to judge Ian McFarlane. He was an honest sort of fellow and a decent coach, but I don't think he was management material. When Jimmy Adamson was appointed he came on the field to warm me up in his first game. As he was doing so he said: "Do you realise you're being warmed up by a Footballer of the Year?" and I thought he was a bit cocky, but I got on well with him. I thought Adamson was a shrewd bloke. He let his assistant Dave Merrington do all the volatile stuff. I'm an Evertonian, and Jimmy Adamson reminded me of Harry Catterick [Everton's Championship-winning manager of 1970] in that he had an overview of everything and surrounded himself with good coaches.'

Look at Sunderland's fixture list for Siddall's first season at the club. At first glance, anyone of a

red-and-white persuasion might hope it is a misprint. In the middle of the season where the scorers should be is just a vast empty space. After Billy Hughes tucked away a penalty in a defeat at Ipswich in November two games before Adamson arrived, Sunderland went 10 long games without finding the back of the net. Going into a Friday night home match with Bristol City three days before Valentine's Day, they were six points from safety when it was still two points for a win and had played two games more than the side just above the drop zone. After that night, eventual champions Liverpool took 22 points, and Sunderland matched them, but such Championship form over 17 games

Running out of the Roker Park tunnel behind Jeff Clarke.

proved to be not quite enough, with what would have been the greatest escape since Steve McQueen, Dickie Attenborough and co-enacted the great World War Two tale, falling agonisingly short in circumstances so controversial that even now only Newcastle and Leeds cause more antipathy among most Sunderland supporters than the name Coventry City.

A cold February evening had seen Mel Holden end Sunderland's goal drought against Bristol City who would feature again in the tale at the end of the season. Having remembered what that net hanging from the opposition's goal was for, Sunderland began to make up for lost time, so much so that they ended the season having scored six goals more than 12th-placed Middlesbrough. Sixteen goals in three games began with four put past the Teessiders as confidence flooded through a side given an injection of youth.

Going into the final game of the season on a Thursday night at Everton's Goodison Park unbeaten in nine, Sunderland knew a point would keep them up but even a defeat would not be disastrous unless Coventry City and Bristol City drew with each other at Coventry's Highfield Road. In that tale of two cities neither could rest easy. A win for either would keep them up and condemn the other, with a draw keeping Bristol up at Coventry's expense if Sunderland avoided defeat.

The games were meant to kick-off at the same time, but Coventry delayed due to crowd congestion, with Sunderland's starting on schedule even though both matches attracted gates of 36,000. It was a match too far for Siddall's Sunderland who lost 2–0, but there was still hope as long as the Coventry – Bristol City game was not drawn. Had the games ran parallel to each other, Coventry would have had to go for the win, but when Coventry City put Sunderland's result on their scoreboard for all to see the last 15 minutes or so became an exercise in simply avoiding defeat and condemning Sunderland. The Bristol team contained Norman Hunter, while Coventry included Terry Yorath. Both had played for Leeds against Sunderland in the Cup Final four years earlier, and they must have had a good night, but for Barry Siddall and Sunderland it was back to the Second Division they thought they had left behind.

'There was a bit of skulduggery at Coventry. Their kick-off was delayed by 15 minutes, which left them knowing all they needed was a draw after they got our result. There weren't many shots after that news came through! It left a bad taste in the mouth as that sort of thing really shouldn't happen. We were never in the game at Everton and came off hoping the result had been what we wanted at Coventry, only to learn that they were still playing and could see out the game knowing what they had to do.'

In the next two seasons Barry missed just one game, racking up a tremendous total of 103 consecutive League appearances stemming from his debut before he was ruled out of a March 1979 trip to Millwall. In the first season after relegation a poor start meant Sunderland never threatened the front runners, indeed the sixth place they reached with two wins in the last week of the season was the highest they had been. A year later, from the end of November onwards, Sunderland were never out of the top six, only to eventually miss out in typical Sunderland fashion by an agonising wait on the final day.

Two games stood out that year. In the first Barry had to be at his best as he could not expect much cover, as Sunderland were reduced to nine men having had both full-backs sent off in the first half at Burnley. Astonishingly, the nine men scored twice to win the game, which Siddall says typifies their spirit: 'We basically had a young side which had no fear. There are one of two ways young sides go, they either fold or they roll their sleeves up. We had people like Shaun Elliott, Gary Rowell, Kevin Arnott, Barry Venison and Bob Lee, so we were a decent side, and we had some lads with real character. Jimmy Adamson let us play, and certainly if that Burnley game had been on TV it would have been great to watch.'

Within a month of 'The Battle of Turf Moor' Adamson had jumped ship to Leeds, followed shortly afterwards by Dave Merrington leaving club stalwart Billy Elliott as caretaker manager from before Christmas until the end of the season. Losing 2–0 at home to Cambridge United was not a great start for Elliott, but the team gradually got into its stride, a Gary Rowell hat-trick in a 4–1 win at Newcastle kick starting a run of seven wins in eight games that propelled the side right into the thick of the promotion race. Having turned the tables on Cambridge by beating them 2–0 on their own patch, Sunderland had the chance to go top of the League with two games to play.

To do this, Sheffield United needed to be beaten by a four goal margin. Local lad Wilf Rostron took the headlines with a hat-trick that featured two penalties and two goals in the last three minutes to have the crowd in raptures as the four-goal margin needed was reached with a minute to spare. There was still time, though, for referee Mr Richardson to give the Blades an injury-time penalty. The points were safe, but that four-goal margin and psychological lift of topping the table for the first time since relegation two years earlier was at stake when Gary Hamson stepped up to try and deny Sunderland top spot. 'Seedaaalll', though, became the hero with a full-length save backed up by bravely smothering the rebound. Barry had made two terrific saves earlier in the game and the dramatic penalty save was one of his finest moments.

Three days later, mid-table Cardiff came to Roker and undid all Sunderland's good work by inflicting a home defeat. It left Sunderland facing a final-day trip to Wales, where the red-and-white army decamped en masse six years to the day after the 1973 FA Cup Final. Wrexham's Racecourse Ground was splitting at the seams as 19,133 squeezed in, Sunderland's travelling support far exceeding the 7,113 that saw Wrexham in League action the same week…at St James' Park, home of Newcastle United. Sunderland duly defeated Wrexham but needed Notts County to take a point at home to Stoke. Without the shenanigans of scoreboard announcements Sunderland faced the same sort of wait they had endured at Goodison Park two years earlier, but when the news filtered through Stoke had won 1–0.

Mathematically, a glimmer of hope still existed in that Sunderland were still in a promotion position, but they had completed their fixtures, while Crystal Palace had one game left and if they won that would be that, and Sunderland would miss out as they had so many times before. It was no surprise at all when, six days later, future Sunderland striker Dave Swindlehurst was on the score sheet as Palace eased past Burnley and into the top flight, leaving Sunderland to try again. 'They were frustrating times,' remembers Barry, 'because in 1978–79 we'd done well all season but just missed out. Dave Merrington was another of those fellows who are better coaches than managers. When Billy Elliott took over he was OK, but he leant on Ken Knighton quite a bit and Ken did a lot of the coaching.'

One place behind Sunderland in the table that year were West Ham United, who were FA Cup-winners a year later and looking for a new goalkeeper as Barry explains: 'During that spell West Ham came in and bid £190,000 for me before they eventually signed Phil Parkes from QPR. I didn't know about that until much later on. Billy had asked Ken about it and Ken had said: "Don't let him go." I'm not saying I would have gone to West Ham, but I didn't get the chance to even think about

Barry Siddall in his Sunderland days.

it, and £190,000 was a big fee.' As it happened Parkes was brought in for his Hammers debut a week after Sunderland had played at Upton Park, but come the end of the season it was all change at Sunderland too, and despite being rated by new Sunderland manager Ken Knighton at the time of West Ham's interest the two were not to get on once Knighton became the gaffer.

111

Barry began what would be the promotion season of 1979–80 in the side but was under pressure from new signing Chris Turner, and it did not take long for the new boy to take over. 'Right from my debut from Bolton I'd never missed a game if I was fit, and it had been the same since I'd been at Sunderland, so being out of the side was something I definitely wasn't used to until Ken Knighton signed Chris Turner. He'd been with Chris at Sheffield Wednesday, and Ken and I didn't see eye to eye. He'd sent me home once from a pre-season tour, so after that I knew that any mistake I made I'd be out, so I felt under a bit of pressure when Chris came in, especially as I knew they'd been together at Hillsborough. Chris was a very different 'keeper to me, very agile and quick and different in stature. He was a good 'keeper.'

Losing his place after a 2–1 League Cup defeat at West Ham at the beginning of November, Barry was to be restricted to just five of the remaining 29 League and Cup games, not featuring at all in the final four months of the season as promotion was won. In fact Sunderland supporters went for just over a calendar year without seeing 'The Flying Pig' in action as Turner cemented his place as Knighton's number one.

Having been passed over for the Sunderland manager's job, Billy Elliott resurfaced as boss of Darlington and was only too pleased to take Barry on loan. 'I went on loan to Darlington to play football. Throughout my career if I've been out of the side I've given it a couple of months and then gone to see the manager. It's not a case of chucking my dummy out, I just wanted to play. When I played it wasn't as if you even had a sub 'keeper on the bench. These days you see 'keepers in the Premier League who might be on something like 16 grand a year – a week I mean – and they might play 40 games in eight or nine years. I'd sooner play at a lower grade than be second choice.'

The slip of the tongue regarding amounts of money some people do not earn in a year being made weekly by reserve-team footballers is understandable. No doubt there'd have been some people at Darlo delighted to be on £16k a year when Siddall joined them on loan in the old Fourth Division. Barry began and ended with clean sheets in narrow away wins among his eight games for the Quakers.

Returning to Roker Park to wait for his chance to play top-level football again, Siddall finally got the opportunity at Southampton at the end of January. Once in he stayed in, playing the final 15 fixtures. While he'd missed out on the excitement of promotion he was to experience another red-and-white relegation battle. Defeat at Stoke cost Knighton his job with four games to play and Sunderland hovering perilously on the cusp of the drop zone.

With Mick Docherty as caretaker manager the Lads went into the final home game with relegation rivals Brighton knowing a point would just about keep them up. The silence could be cut with a knife when Gary Williams volleyed a winner for the Seagulls at the Fulwell End with seconds to go. It was a disaster, and if the Sunderland crowd have ever been so suddenly and eerily stunned into silence it was when that goal went in. As the crowd trudged out of Roker Park they faced the prospect of a second successive first-season relegation following hard-won promotion. There was still a chance of redemption, though – all Sunderland had to do to be safe was win their final game…away to Liverpool.

Reigning champions Liverpool had already locked the League Cup in the Anfield trophy room and, having disposed of Bayern Munich in the semi-final, were looking forward to a European Cup Final in Paris against Real Madrid.

'What a place it was to have to go for the last game of the season needing a result' says Barry. As related in Joe Bolton's chapter, Liverpool's Hetton-born manager Bob Paisley would not be losing any sleep if Sunderland managed to remain on Liverpool's fixture list for the following season, and famously Sunderland managed to come away with a victory thanks to a cracking goal from Stan Cummins combined with a clean sheet from Siddall, who remembers one unexpected danger, 'Liverpool weren't at their best and had their Final in mind. The only real danger was late on when they brought on a young lad up front who was playing for his future. He buzzed about a bit, but we kept a clean sheet which was the main thing, and Stan scored the goal we wanted.'

Colin Russell was the young forward trying to make a name for himself that afternoon. It proved to be his first and last appearance for his home-town team. He went on to play over 200 League games but, thankfully, for Sunderland he remains a tiny footnote in top-flight history rather than someone like Tommy Harmer, Tony Cascarino, Jason Euell or Clive Mendonca: names that loom in the nightmares of Sunderland supporters.

The goalkeeper beaten by Stan Cummins at Anfield was Ray Clemence. He had spent that season playing alternate England games with Peter Shilton. Now at Sunderland, with Knighton gone and caretaker Docherty having followed, the appointment of Alan Durban as manager in the summer of 1981 gave Barry cause for optimism about his future, even after missing the start of the season due to the commitments of a summer spell playing across the Atlantic for Vancouver Whitecaps. 'I respected Alan Durban. I'd seen him a lot when he played for Derby County. He was a very good coach and a decent manager. He was always fair with me and Chris Turner. The situation was that the goalkeeper in form kept his place, and that was fair enough. Chris and I were closely matched I think. When Chris Turner came some fans wanted him to play and some wanted me to play. We'd both get shouts of "Put Turner in!" or "Put Siddall in!"'

Turner played the opening three games under Durban, conceding six goals. Make no mistake about it, Chris Turner was an excellent goalkeeper and a terrific servant to SAFC. When he eventually left it was to Manchester United for a record fee, so he was no mug, but as Barry says there was little to choose between the two of them, and he got his chance to show what he could do at home to Wolves, where a clean sheet set him off on a run of 29 consecutive League and Cup appearances. The last of those at Notts County in a 1–1 draw at the end of February 1982 was to be Barry's last for the club. Sunderland were in dire trouble at the bottom of the League, but despite being part of a struggling side Siddall had not been beaten more than twice in any of his last 10 League games when he was discarded, so did it feel harsh to be left out? 'Yes, although I was coming to the point where Alan Durban had it in his mind that he was going to give me a free transfer. I understood that and there was no animosity. I've seen him since when I was coaching at Lincoln, and there's no bad feeling at all.'

Having signed for Newcastle's 1960s centre-half John McGrath at Port Vale, Barry added another promotion to his CV in his first season when he played regularly, other than for a mid-season spell when a young Neville Southall came on loan from Everton. Southall became renowned as being a goalkeeper in the Barry Siddall mould, so although he never turned out for the team he supports perhaps Barry played his own role in Everton's mid-80s success, when his old Bolton teammate Peter Reid was the fulcrum of their glory years. For Barry Vale Park was a far cry from Roker Park, however, not just in terms of the level of football but in terms of his rapport with the fans, 'I never took to the fans in the Potteries. We had a good side under John McGrath and went up but the following year we were second bottom and all that was forgotten. They weren't nice fans to play for.'

During his second season at Port Vale Barry went out on loan to Blackpool, although for the rest of the season, other than his trip to the seaside, he remained first choice for Vale. There is no love lost between Port Vale and local rivals Stoke City, but mid-way through the following campaign Barry moved between the two, jumping from the Fourth Division to the First in the process.

Football being football, Barry's return to the big League saw him debut for Stoke at Roker Park, where a David Hodgson goal gave Sunderland the points, but ultimately Sunderland and Stoke would be relegated that year. Stoke were in desperate trouble – it was the year they set a record low points tally of 17, which they were happy for Sunderland to take off them in 2006. Having watched Sunderland fail to score in a run of 10 top-flight games in 1976–77, Siddall was involved in damage limitation as Stoke struggle to score, finding the net in only four of his 15 appearances for them that season.

Increasingly, Siddall was becoming a soccer nomad, always on the move looking for a game. Early the following season he was out on loan again, this time turning out for former Bolton teammate Frank Worthington at Tranmere and in March came a final opportunity to play top-flight football with half a dozen end-of-season games on loan to Manchester City, where the centre-half in front of him was future Sunderland manager Mick McCarthy.

Come the end of the season Siddall joined one of his former loan clubs, Blackpool. Of the 13 League clubs he represented they were the only one after his first two of Bolton and Sunderland that he would appear 100 times for. 'Blackpool fans were good to me. I initially went there on loan from Port Vale, and I enjoyed it there.'

Stockport County, Hartlepool, West Brom, Mossley, Carlisle, Chester, Northwich Victoria and finally Preston North End all took Siddall on at some point: 'It wasn't easy. I based myself in the Blackpool area and travelled to wherever I was playing. When I played for Chester we trained at Nantwich and played our home games at Macclesfield.

'I went to Hartlepool to help Cyril Knowles out. I liked Hartlepool's fans. I did a bit of coaching for them but didn't really train there. I used to train with Blackpool and then just travel to join up with Hartlepool for games usually. "Pop" Robson was coaching there at the time, and I was just helping out.'

Siddall's 609th and final Football League appearance came on 12 December 1992. It was his first and last game for Preston North End, a 5–2 home defeat by one of his old clubs Port Vale being an inappropriate end to a career that had seen him give great service to the game, exhibit a love of simply playing – hence all the loan moves – and always give good value for money. First and foremost Barry Siddall was a very good goalkeeper, but whether doing the 'Silly walk' for the 'Basil' baiters at Southend, or convincing Sunderland supporters that pigs really can fly, he was never less than one of the game's most colourful characters.

'I probably could have played on for another year, but in the end packed it in because I'd travelled enough. I did a bit of coaching for a while as a freelance, but the thing is there's no work when the pitches are frozen and there's no work in the summer. I last coached at Blackpool and was still doing a bit until Steve McMahon left. I'm a typical old player really in that I only go back to football when I'm invited. I go to Bolton a couple of times a season, and I've been up to Sunderland and enjoyed it, but I don't even watch much on the TV. I like to watch the World Cup and Euro Finals, but I don't bother with the group games. I've had my time and enjoyed it.'

In the modern game, with reserve goalkeepers capable of earning £16,000 a week, when players call it a day earning a living often is not a necessity. However, if an exiled Sunderland supporter in the right bit of Lancashire has ordered this book they might find it is delivered to them by a flying pig doing a silly walk – or at least a former goalkeeper now delivering the post. 'I've been a postman since June 1995,' says Barry. 'It was in a small village called Freckleton, and a couple of lads I knew were already postmen. They told me a job was going, so I went in to see about it. They asked me to start the following day, and I've been there ever since. There are a few people who I deliver to who know I used to be a goalkeeper. Once on Radio Five they were asking people to ring in if they knew anyone famous, and someone phoned in to say "Barry Siddall's my postman." I didn't half get the mickey taken at work.'

No Sunderland supporters would ever take the mickey out of Barry. He was and remains a highly respected goalkeeper, and should there be a Sunderland supporter on his round he would know because as he opened the letter box he would be certain to hear them yelling 'Seedaaall!'

SUPERDICK

DICK MALONE

Right-back
1973 FA Cup winner with Sunderland.
1976 Second Division Championship winner with Sunderland.

Born:	22 August 1947, Carfin, Lanarkshire.
Signed for Sunderland:	13 October 1970, from Ayr United, £30,000
Transferred:	6 June 1977 to Hartlepool United, free

Ayr United	July 1964, 173 League appearances, 19 goals
Sunderland:	13 October 1970, 235+1 League apps, 2 goals
	281+1 total apps, 2 goals
Hartlepool United:	6 June 1977, 36 League apps, 1 goal
Blackpool:	November 1978, 48 League apps, 1 goal
Queen of the South:	1980, 42+1 League apps, 2 goals

'If you've got the Cup Final on DVD watch it, and just before Jimmy's save you'll see me stumble. You watch why I'm stumbling – Allan Clarke had actually tripped me because when the ball was coming across to Trevor Cherry. I could have headed it clear, but he tripped me, otherwise I'd have cleared it, but Trevor Cherry headed it goalwards and Peter Lorimer had a dig. I felt if that had gone in I would have chinned the referee. I would have stuck a right hook on the referee because he cheated us, because he must have seen that, he must have seen it. You watch it, Clarke tripped me. Steve Kindon is the only player who has ever mentioned it to me. He spotted it.'

Most of the other players featured in *Sunderland Cult Heroes* were hard, tough players – especially the full-backs – but this is Dick Malone speaking, Sunderland's cultured right-back from the 1973 FA Cup Final explaining his view of Jim Montgomery's legendary double save that ranks as the best ever seen at Wembley. It was Malone who cleared the ball when Monty's wonder save from Lorimer's close-range shot rebounded from the bar, but as you can see he does not believe Monty should have needed to make the saves. Thirty-five years on from the free-kick he did not get, Malone remains livid about it. Never a hothead, nor a dirty player, Dick Malone had a style all of his own and a usually calm but not weak personality. It turns out, though, that referee Ken Burns' decision to not give a free-kick is not the only thing that annoys him.

One of four Scots in Sunderland's 1973 FA Cup-winning team, Richard Philip Malone was born on 22 August 1947 in Carfin, Lanarkshire. He is and always has been a man of integrity

Left to right: Dave Watson, Dick Malone, Jimmy Montgomery and Ron Guthrie. Only Ritchie Pitt is missing from this 2003 picture of the 1973 FA Cup-winning defence.

and principle, qualities built into him through an upbringing short on money but big on learning how to be independent, and to do things the right way.

'My father had died three months before I was born, and it was tough. My mother brought me and my brother up. We had virtually nothing at all. That would fit the criteria for a lot of people, but we had nothing and we struggled to have food on the table. We were always guaranteed bread and tea every day, so we had that. My mother used to go out to work doing some physical, manual work for some pennies, not enough to give us the sort of food that we eat on the table now, but it was enough to give us at least bread every day. We had no extra money for toys or sports equipment, bikes etc. so really all I could do was play football, that was my pastime – playing football.

'I used to go out for walks a lot because I didn't have money to do anything else, so I walked a lot and played football every night after school. I'd come back out at five o'clock and play till about 11 at night in the summer. In the winter we would play in the street with a little ball, which developed techniques and skills that I was able to put to good use in later years. That was the sort of upbringing I had. We had no decent clothes, going to school every day in baseball boots with holes in the soles, and the socks I was wearing for school were football socks. They had hoops in those days, so it didn't look the sweetest thing.

'I had a bit of an introvert personality at that time, so whenever anyone or any clubs were showing interest in me, not quite at the professional age but junior football teams or whatever, I felt a bit overawed by going to these people, but as it happened I was very intelligent as a kid.

'I went to play for a junior football team. I played for various amateur teams, good amateur teams. There were a lot of professional footballers came out of those teams and I ended up at a junior team called Shotts Bon Accord, which was the equivalent of non-League football down in England.

Shotts is where Bill Nicholson was born. The club's claim to fame was that they had the biggest playing surface in British football, and it was quite amusing because in the first half of every game at Shotts other teams looked dead sharp against us, but in the second half they couldn't raise a gallop, and we just used to slog them so we always trounced them.

'I sometimes played right-back but mainly centre-half for Shotts. They always did well in the junior Leagues and the junior ranks, and they attracted some decent professional players. I was a kid of just turned 15 playing with these guys, so I was still a bit reserved about myself. As it happened we won the West of Scotland Junior Cup, after which there were various offers from professional clubs at the time wanting me to sign – but I wasn't interested.

'I had started work as an apprentice electrical engineer, and I didn't really want to be a professional footballer, believe it or not. The outcome of that was I nearly got killed in my job. I was very close to being killed and that stopped me in my tracks. I didn't want to do the job any more, so I packed in. I was about an eighth of an inch away from coming down off a crane on to live cables for the crane which were 660 volts. There was no safety guard on it, and I don't know what made me look down, but I looked down and just saved myself. I was 15–16ish then. At the time my mother married again. My brother Frank played professional football for Kilmarnock. There were clubs coming in for me but I didn't want to play professional football.

'Ayr Utd came in. Bobby Flavell was the manager then. He was the first British player to sign for a South American club – Bogota. He thought I was the bees knees and he said "Ok, look. You don't want full-time football, why don't you try part-time with us?" My stepfather and my brother said "Well, you are playing part-time football now, you're training twice a week in junior football and playing on a Saturday, you will be playing at a better standard and getting more money for it." So that was what I tried, initially playing at centre-half, and obviously it worked out well for me.'

Making his debut in a Scottish League Cup tie at Morton on 26 August 1964, by the end of January he had become a regular in the Ayr side that finished one off the bottom of Scotland's Division B as it was then, and Dick was to enjoy some tremendous times with the team known as 'The Honest Men'. He was still in his teens when Ayr won the B Division in 1966, with Malone an ever present in the side. The top flight proved too much for them, Ayr finishing bottom with Dick still a regular. He then played in a second promotion-winning team in 1969, enjoying his football under the man who later would manage Scotland in the 1978 World Cup Finals, Ally MacLeod.

'I had a fair bit of skill on the deck with the ball, and Ally obviously homed in on that and said I was an accurate striker of the ball. I was a very, very accurate striker of the ball. Ally had been a left-winger, having played in the Blackburn Rovers days with Bryan Douglas and Derek Dougan.' MacLeod had played in the FA Cup Final of 1960 – the one where Wigan chairman Dave Whelan broke his leg – and had scored against Sunderland during the Cup run.

'He decided to play me at right-back and told me the one thing wingers hate is chasing back, "They hate it with a vengeance" he said, "so all I want you to do when you get the ball is just go past all these wingers so they will disappear." I did that, and that is exactly what used to happen. That is how it worked out really, he was a very clever manager, absolutely brilliant in fact, probably one of the best managers I have ever known for tactics and motivation. We played total football, we played in triangles all the time, and we had a very, very good team to the extent that we beat clubs like Rangers.

'For a provincial club like Ayr Utd to hammer them, and we hammered them to the extent that the Rangers fans were throwing their scarves onto the Somerset Park pitch, was great. We played very well even though John Greig, Willie Johnston and Willie Henderson and all these guys were playing. We trounced them, we played some lovely football. It was a treat to play, great.

'I was still naïve, but I was beginning to get more self-confidence because I was playing well, hitting all the headlines, and there were a lot of clubs chasing me according to the press. I had no reason to disbelieve them, so I became more self-assured on the park but I was still naïve.

'Obviously every club has a price of a player and, although they didn't want me to go, Ayr were prepared to sell me at that time. I went down to London to Fulham. who were keen on signing me. They were a bit of a glamour club at the time, Johnny Haynes [who had captained England] was still playing, Allan Clarke [who would play for Leeds in the 1973 FA Cup Final] was a centre-forward and George Cohen was right-back, so I'd need to dislodge the man who had won the World Cup with England the year before.

'Ally told me he knew the manager, Vic Buckingham, and he even explained to me what he'd be wearing, a jacket with leather patches. When I got there it was the same jacket! We had a brief chat about what we would do, and this guy took me out into the middle of the park. I've told you my upbringing, so I'm standing there and he booms,

"THIS COULD BE ALL YOURS!"

"God this guy's a nutter" I thought.

"YOU WILL BE THE KING OF CRAVEN COTTAGE!"

I thought, "I don't know what to say to this guy." I really didn't know how to answer that.

'So he ranted on like that for about 10 minutes before we went up to his office. "Right, what I want is for you to play an attacking sweeper's role" he said when we got there. I thought this guy is definitely an idiot because I've never heard of an attacking sweeper, so I hummed and ha'd for a little bit, and he could tell by my hesitancy that it didn't spark a light with me at all.

'He said to me "You just don't want to sign for me because you don't like me." I just didn't know how to handle that, I really didn't know what to say, so I fumbled about for something to say and eventually said "Mr Buckingham, I think sweeper and attack are opposites, it's a contradiction and I cannot get my head round it."

"You leave that to me. I will play you. In fact you will play for Ayr on a Saturday, and I will fly you down on a Sunday, you can train with the lads and play in the reserves on a Tuesday in that position. I'll fly you back up to Ayr to play with Ayr on a Saturday, and we'll do that for a month. If you're comfortable with that, and I have no doubt that you will want to play that position, then we'll complete the transfer."

'I just wanted away. He said "Let's go and do some training," so I went and trained. This was a Monday and they were playing on a Tuesday in a Cup game against Man City, and I trained with Johnny Haynes. I can tell you I've done some stiff training in my life, really hard training, and this training on the day before a game was the hardest I've ever done in my life, it just kept going on and on, running and running. Afterwards we went back, and he wanted to talk. He asked, "Now can we talk turkey?"

"Well I don't think Mr MacLeod will go along with that"

"Well let's phone Ally," so he phoned Ally, and Ally said,

"Put Dick on the phone,"

Ally said to me, "I know you cannot talk, but if you mean yes say no, and if you mean no say yes. Do you want to sign for Fulham?"

Ayr United v Celtic line ups.

Bottom: Ayr United v Celtic, Scottish League Cup semi-final programme, 1969.

I said, "Well yes, yes, it's great, it's really great, I'm enjoying it, it's really great."

Ally said, "Right, OK. I'll talk on a few more minutes and then you can put him back on."

Ally just told him that he wasn't prepared to risk injury, so it got knocked on the head then. As it happened, George Cohen got an injury after that, about a week after, and it finished his career, so I probably would have ended up playing right-back!'

Vic Buckingham was a previous manager of Ajax and a future coach of Barcelona, winning the League in Holland and the Cup in Spain. He'd won the FA Cup as manager of West Brom in 1954. Prior to becoming manager of Fulham, he had preceded Alan Brown as manager of Sheffield Wednesday, leaving them after the scandal of some of his players taking bribes. Dick trained with Buckingham's Fulham ahead of their League Cup tie with Manchester City on 1 November 1967. Fulham won the match 3–2 against a City side that would win the League that season. Fulham, on the other hand, would finish bottom of the

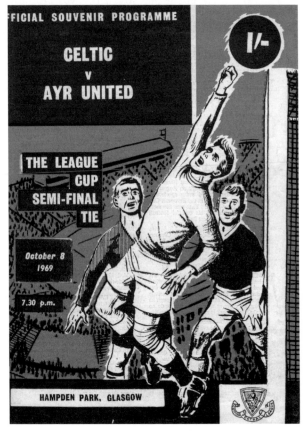

pile, Buckingham being sacked and replaced by Bobby Robson two months after trying to lure Malone to London.

Happy to return to Ayr, Dick continued to enjoy his football as MacLeod's side continued to punch above their weight. In October 1969 they met Celtic at Hampden in the semi-final of the Scottish League Cup.

Cup success was waiting for Malone at Wembley, but Dick has a lingering belief that he should have had the opportunity of a Scottish as well as an English Cup medal to his name, 'We hammered them, we should have won. Bertie Auld came on with 10 minutes to go and hit a hopeful shot from about 25 yards – it went in the net. Everyone raved about the game, we played brilliant football, I can't stress that enough, played absolutely brilliant football. At that time at Ayr you couldn't wait, you dreamt about going out to play the next game because the football was so sweet. Everyone who came and watched us, the write-ups they gave, the quality of the football we played was unbelievable.'

Capped by Scotland at Under-23 level against France in 1969, Malone was hot property and now 23 rather than the naïve teenager he had been when turning down the chance to go to Fulham. There was no shortage of interest in him from south of the border, and Dick was made directly aware of it, 'There was a club came on and tapped me up. I was panicking in case the manager found out about it. It was a First Division club, a big one, so I told the manager. I said "Look, I've been tapped up and I'm just telling you in case you hear anything, but I want you to know I didn't start anything, they phoned me."

'Anyway, we played Airdrie on the Saturday and they beat us 4–2, but I had a good game, I know I had a good game. I made both our goals, but he more or less accused me of not trying. He only said that because I had told him I'd been tapped up, because no one needs to tell you when you've had a good game, and no one needs to tell you when you've had a bad game – you know. So I told him that was the last time he was going to say that to me. To be honest, I was financially set for life at Ayr United because they had worked out a business plan for me that was going to see me right. I put my letter of transfer in on the Monday, and I was transferred on the Tuesday. I made an agreement with myself that if I liked the manager that comes in I'd sign, because I didn't want to get into a situation where I'd have to choose should I sign for this manager, or should I sign for that manager?

'The first manager who came in was Alan Brown on the Tuesday and I liked him. I liked the way he spoke, he spoke about the same way of playing as Ally Macleod, even though I must say he didn't quite play like that when I actually got to Sunderland, and I felt a bit like a fish out of water.

'The people were brilliant at Sunderland, very friendly. I got on great with the players, but it wasn't quite in the triangle football I had been used to. Whenever I got the ball in the early games it was difficult. The first time I got the ball on my debut I was waiting for two players to come to me, but all they did was run away, and I thought – God, what is going on? That happened every time I got the ball, I was looking to pass it, but the crowd were shouting, "Get the ball up the park!" I thought, "God what's going on here?" and I held on thinking someone would give me the option of a short pass, but they never did, so I just ran into brick walls.'

To make matters worse, Malone was injured on his first Sunderland appearance. 'I got a real clout on the bone in my hip, God it was painful, it was really painful, which isn't a good start. It's the last thing you want because it's hard enough trying to settle and you just get in the team, and then you're out and you're trying to get back in again. It puts a bit of pressure on you.'

Sunderland at least recorded a 1–0 home win over Bristol City in October 1970 on Malone's debut when he played alongside Jimmy Montgomery, Bobby Kerr,

Dick Malone.

Malone in action.

Ian Porterfield, Billy Hughes and Ritchie Pitt, all of whom would join him in climbing the steps at Wembley two and a half years later. Dennis Tueart missed Dick's debut but was also already in the side and Dave Watson arrived two months later.

No one knew that these players would become living legends in 1973. In Malone's early days times were fraught at Sunderland. The club had just suffered its second-ever relegation. The first in 1958 had robbed Sunderland of its proud boast of being the only club never to have played League football outside the top flight. It had taken six years and several near misses to get back. Wild celebrations had greeted promotion in 1964, but it hadn't been built on, the team had fallen apart with a change of manager, a change of attitude and a drinking culture taking hold of the club before the return of Alan Brown, the promotion-winning manager who had left after falling out with the directors.

Brown remains much admired by his players and is attributed with being the main managerial influence on Brian Clough and, in turn, Roy Keane among many others, but to the supporters he was an aloof figure responsible for the only two relegations in the club's 91 year history. Victory on Malone's first appearance lifted the side from 12th to 9th, but in those pre-Play-off days when only the top two went up immediate promotion was already looking a forlorn hope. Hope, in fact, was disappearing as quickly as the crowd, the average gate of 15,780 being over 6,000 less than the previous post-war record low.

'The fans were unhappy, they were going to listen to or believe anything that they read or heard. They were unhappy with the club. The press didn't help; they didn't like the manager, they wanted him out, and they proceeded to continue giving him bad press until he left. Alan Brown probably wasn't the most tactful with them, but he was a players' manager, and he didn't like the press unfairly criticising players when it wasn't true. He would always take them to task on it, and they resented that. You've got to use the press, you cannot like everything that they say, but you've got to accept that they are there to sell papers and if that means crucifying certain players at certain times, well, that's what they will do.'

Dick replaced long-serving Cecil Irwin, a loyal one-club servant who had debuted as a 16-year-old in 1958 and been a stalwart of the side throughout the 1960s. Irwin switched onto the left flank following Malone's acquisition, but his first-team career was to have less than a year to run.

Once Dick returned to fitness Sunderland remained frighteningly inconsistent, and for a club who have made a tradition of being involved in last day of the season 'nailbiters' they remained locked in mid-table, with the fans becoming even more dismayed with one of the two players they liked – Colin Todd – being sold ('keeper Montgomery was the other).

Prior to Dick's purchase the Sunderland crowd had a chant that went: 'In Dublin's fair city, where the girls are so pretty, I first set my eyes on sweet Molly Malone, and she wheels her wheelbarrow, through the streets broad and narrow, crying…Sun'land!' The new right-back from Ayr United was therefore destined to be dubbed 'Molly' and in his early days was anything but a cult hero before the fans took to him when they recognised that in fact he was a decent player trying his heart out to play good football and taking responsibility to want the ball and try to use it purposefully.

'I stuttered my way through those games in the first few months because I wasn't very confident' remembers Dick. 'At the time I can remember Ritchie [Pitt] was playing centre-half, and Ritchie was struggling to cover his partner in defence as well and so it was exposing us a little bit, so I would come off my man and think I'll cover Ritchie. This was after Colin Todd went, and I was leaving my man, and it made me hesitant. I can understand when you don't have confidence in the way the team is playing. When Craig Gordon first came he was uncertain about certain things and he took a pounding. When you're not confident about what's going to happen you tend to be hesitant, and that's what happened to me initially, but as the players began to play more and more together we began to improve.

'After about three months Bobby Kerr and I started to play as a unit, and we formed a great partnership. We worked hard at that, and in the end Bobby and I didn't need to look up, if I had my back to the wing and I received the ball I knew where he would be. I knew that he would either be square with me to receive it or making a beeline to make a run down the wing, and equally when Bobby was in possession he knew I'd be there backing him up and making a run for him.'

February and March saw a run of one goal in eight games, but things improved with a 5–2 thrashing of Swindon followed up by a 1–0 home win over Orient, a game which saw Dick score the first of his two goals for the Lads, and it was a beauty, a shot from at least 30 yards screaming into the Roker End goal. 'When I was at Ayr Ally McLeod always used to have us practising shooting. He always professed that everyone at some time during the game will have an opportunity to have a shot at goal, and he always had us practising shooting. We had a goal with two boards with gaps on the right and left hand side and we had to get the ball in that space. I became very accurate and that was one of the reasons, because we were always practising. I was a regular scorer up at Ayr [In 1968 – 69 Dick scored 13 goals in 46 League and Cup games] but when I came down here and was having a shot from maybe 35 yards I was told not to do that but to play someone in. When you stop doing things you get out of the habit, but I would have normally had a dig from 40 yards at

Dick in action for Sunderland in his early days at the club in 1970.

times if the opportunity was there to do so, because even if you don't score they can take deflections and a lot of goals are flukes because anything can happen.'

Neither of Malone's goals for Sunderland were flukes. They were both great but very different goals and both scored at the Roker End. They were separated by three and a half years, the second coming at the end of a typically storming run from the back by the 6ft 1in right-back. That goal was almost a carbon copy of a memorable goal he had scored for Ayr at Alloa in 1967 during the period when he found the back of the net on a regular basis. Indeed, in October 1968 he became the only full-back in Ayr's history to score a hat-trick, Stenhousemuir being on the receiving end. Dick's second and last for Sunderland was part of a 4–1 thumping of Portsmouth on a day when Sunderland played magnificently. Orchestrating that performance was Ian Porterfield in sublime form. Sadly that weekend Porterfield would be terribly injured in an horrific car crash.

> *Six-foot full-backs are a rare phenomenon, and successful ones ever rarer, however his place in Sunderland folklore was as much to do with his attacking forays as his defensive stability. His upright almost statuesque stance proved a deceptive weapon as he jinked his way down the line in an almost mesmeric fashion. Expectation filled the air each time 'Super Dick' touched the ball as no one was quite sure what would happen next (possibly even himself). The crowning glory came at Wembley, but most fans will remember the solo goal against Pompey, which was long awaited and produced scenes of wild celebration.*
> Mike Love, SENSSA.

At the point of Malone's previous goal, however, Ian Porterfield's world renown as the scorer of the most romantic goal in Cup history was far away. Indeed, Dick still had one more game to play at Ayr's Somerset Park. In arranging Malone's transfer Sunderland had agreed to visit the Scottish club for a pre-season friendly the following summer.

Dick had given great service to Ayr United. He had been one of their best players in the best spell in their history. He had turned down the opportunity to leave them for top-flight English football in London in 1967 and given them three years further service before commanding a £30,000 fee for a club which he had cost nothing, yet his welcome home was not even lukewarm with the reason remaining a mystery: 'Every time I got the ball they tried to kick me off the park' says Dick of what became a bad-tempered friendly. Ayr's programme for the match was a

SOMERSET NEWS 5p

71 - 72

AYR UNITED

Pre Season
Friendly

SUNDERLAND

Wednesday
4th August
Kick-off 1930 hrs

Ayr United v Sunderland programme.

neat 24-page issue affording ample opportunity to welcome back their former player. However, there was not a single mention of Malone in either manager MacLeod's notes or the 'News and Views' welcome to the game. A bog-standard paragraph-long pen pic of Dick among the visitors' pen pics read, 'Joined Sunderland last year for a reported £40,000 figure after 7 years at Somerset Park and representing Scotland at Under-23 level. Dick has made a big impression on Wearside with some powerful displays in a No. 2 shirt. He was unlucky to be injured in his first match with his new club but has now settled down to become a firm favourite with the Sunderland supporters.' Nothing wrong with that (except the exaggerated reported transfer fee) but hardly a warm welcome 'home', and neither was Malone among the six Sunderland players pictured.

Declining to handle the programme, Dick says 'It surprised me. To be honest I don't know why, it is bad writing anyway. It [a welcome to a returning player] should have been done, whether they were sincere about it or not is academic. It should have been in, but it didn't happen.'

The match finished 1–1, with Malone booked and Sunderland's ex-England international Gordon Harris being sent off after missing a penalty. The scoreline would be repeated in Sunderland's first two League games of Dick's first full season, in fact five of the first dozen games were 1–1, but a transitional period continued with four players making their final appearances in the opening seven games. Progress was being made, however, and from Christmas to the end of the season Sunderland hovered between third and sixth place. Only the top two went up, though, and Sunderland were three wins behind runners-up Birmingham in the final analysis.

Missing just a single game all season, Malone had cemented his place and was given a glimpse of the glory days ahead when Cardiff City visited Wearside for a fourth-round FA Cup replay. The match was played on a Monday afternoon due to a floodlight ban in operation because of energy restrictions caused by a miners' strike.

Forty-eight hours earlier, just over 15,000 had seen a routine Second Division win at home over Oxford, but despite the problems of the fixture being on a Monday afternoon over 39,000 turned out, illustrating that while the weekly gates had dropped there was still a huge number of people ready to come back as soon as there was a flicker of a revival. 'I don't remember much about the game at all, but it did give me an insight into what the club was capable of achieving by way of crowds etc. The fans were always very, very emotive and passionate about it and vociferous. They would always voice their opinion, and even if they hated you they would still be there the next week.

'Everyone asks me when you're playing in these games do you try any harder, and it's hard to put it into words because you don't try any harder but you know what it means to the crowd, for bragging rights alone. Whether you're playing a derby match or a big Cup game, you know that you need to perform. So you are keyed up and you're on your toes, you are thinking, and when you get into the dressing room all you want to do is get out on the park and get the first touch because you know the first touch is important. If it hits you and goes out of play your favourite six supporters are going to be there shouting, "Get off that pitch Malone!" Then you think if the second ball does the same "I'm a goner." It's funny, because everyone said the crowd was shouting, but once the game was underway I realised I couldn't hear the crowd, I wasn't good enough to listen to the crowd, I just got on with the game.'

That Cardiff replay proved to be yet another 1–1 scoreline, Sunderland losing the second replay at Manchester City two days later. Had they progressed to the fifth round, Sunderland would have entertained Leeds United who went on to lift the trophy. That showdown between old foes would

Dick was always an accurate striker of the ball.

have to wait. Nonetheless, without ever being especially good Sunderland had improved compared to the football they were playing when Dick signed.

'It still wasn't the same football that Ayr played. We'd played English teams in pre-season friendlies when I was with Ayr, and it was so sweet. Some of the press cuttings we got I've kept because some of the comments are unbelievable. However, I found that once I had built up a relationship with Bobby [Kerr] on the park it was a lot better. Most of the play used to start with Monty, who would feign to play the ball to the left but throw it to me on the right, then it would be Bobby and me, and that's how the play would normally start. We worked on that in practice. I always looked for the ball, I always wanted the ball. Even if I was having a nightmare, I wanted the ball again to try and show people that my touch was okay, even if it was bouncing off me, because you go through games and it's very difficult to maintain a high standard in every game. I think that's what supporters appreciate, the fact that you don't hide, that you keep going even when you are having a nightmare. I think that when people talk about the cult heroes that is the main contributory factor to the support of that player.'

Dick's analysis is as accurate as his shooting had been at Ayr. Supporters do like seeing someone who comes back for more time after time, like a boxer who will not go down but keeps looking for that one punch with which they can redeem what has gone before.

Everybody knows that it was Jim Montgomery that made the save in '73, but less may remember that it was Dick Malone that mopped up. That his clearance was scuffed is no surprise, unorthodox is a word that was often used in reference to Malone's style, and yet he always seemed to get the job done. Sunderland supporters have a history of taking full-backs to their hearts, instigated no doubt by the sight of Malone's forays up the wing. There was something good about the way he looked in thin vertical stripes too.
Andrew Smithson, Sunderland supporter, Sunderland.

The 1971–72 season ended with Sunderland taking part in the Anglo-Italian Cup, playing a couple of games in Italy and hosting return games with those sides in early June. British referees officiated at the games in Italy, with Italian refs taking the games in England. Sunderland had participated in the inaugural tournament in 1970, while the defending champions from the 1971 competition were Blackpool…managed by Bob Stokoe, who had led the Tangerines to victory in Bologna. Of course Stokoe's next silverware would be with Sunderland, but the Wearsiders' efforts in the Anglo-Italian tournament came to nothing other than providing Dick Malone with a taste of European experience and a bad taste of refereeing in the opening game away to Atalanta in Bergamo, where a 2–0 half-time lead was turned into a 3–2 defeat: 'We played really well and the referee, Clive Thomas, I felt cheated us; I think he booked me. I didn't rate him at all. He was such an arrogant little sod. The referee was ridiculous, he was the difference between us winning and losing.

'Our second game took us to Sardinia to face Cagliari. At that time Luigi Riva was the centre-forward for them, although he wasn't playing in the team that night, but he was the Italian cult hero. To put you in the picture of what they thought of him they put the taxes up in Sardinia to pay for his increase in wages. That's how much they felt for him. I think we murdered them, we beat them 3–1. They didn't like it, and a big fight started on the park, it was hilarious. After the game their players were taking their boots off and throwing them at us, and the crowd were throwing cushions and seats over the barriers.

'It took us an hour and a half to get away from the ground. It was a nice quiet end-of-season game! We found it quite hilarious actually. After the game the "Bomber" [manager Alan Brown] said, "No we don't want any" when they offered drinks. Our tongues were swollen because it was very warm and we were choking for a drink, but he insisted, "No we don't want a drink." He thought the drinks might have been tampered with. We had to wait not only for an hour and a half to get away, but then the trip to the hotel, which was the Forte Club on Sardinia, which wasn't the cheapest. It's still going now, it is a beautiful place, but that night was hilarious, real good fun.'

Fun was something in short supply under Alan Brown. A third season out of the top flight really had to bring a promotion campaign, Sunderland was still a club shocked at being out of the top flight. Although an opening day defeat at Middlesbrough was the last until the ninth game of the season, that second defeat left Sunderland in 10th place, languishing a long way off the pace-setters. A run of three defeats followed by a goalless home draw had Sunderland 14th when the axe fell on Brown at the start of November.

'It was getting to the stage where we were expecting something to happen, and anything that Alan Brown said the press crucified at any opportunity. Dave [Watson] was useless, I was useless. They would pick up on anything and blow it out of all proportion; he can't do that, he can't do this, and Dave was a centre-half playing centre-forward to help

Header.

the team, but they did him for it. In the end I just stopped reading any newspapers; I didn't read any reports on football whatsoever because it was all bullsh*t they were coming out with. It was getting so that every game you weren't getting the right result you were expecting the worst, and eventually it happened, they got rid of him and they brought Bob Stokoe in.

'I don't know why they picked Bob Stokoe, I honestly don't know that at all because it wasn't as if he was a famous First Division manager and, not only that, he'd played for the black and whites – so why they picked Bob Stokoe, I don't know. Maybe it was because he'd had relative success with low-budget teams, he could make something out of not a lot.'

Stokoe shook the sleeping giant of Sunderland awake. A winless month under caretaker Billy Elliott meant that Sunderland had not won in nine and were fourth bottom when he took over. Five months later they were Cup-winners, having outplayed three of the country's most powerful teams. Does Dick accept the common belief that the main thing Stokoe did was to take the 'shackles' off the team, allowing them a drink and to express themselves after the tight disciplinarian regime of the 'Bomber'?

'It's fairly accurate,' agrees Dick before outlining the context, 'You have to understand that when Alan Brown was brought back Sunderland were in a terrible mess with a drink problem. I think that was one of the reasons they brought him back – to bring a bit of discipline back to the club. There had been a disastrous tour in Canada and America in '67 and they were still paying for it years after. The drinking culture had taken a grip at Sunderland, and it needed to be put back into perspective again. Alan Brown was obviously a hard man, but he was a generous manager, a big man, and he had scruples and principles about everything. If he agreed something with you, for instance if he promised you'll get £70 a week, you wouldn't need to have anything filled in, he would get you to sign a blank contract and everything you agreed would be fulfilled. That was the way it was. He was an honourable man, but he just fell foul of the press.

'Maybe he took his discipline to an extreme level where he stifled a few of the players and after all not everyone has got the same mentality. When you are dealing with a lot of people, if you tell them, "No drink when you are representing the club" – and that's what he did say, he knew some would have one or two. As soon as you say they can have one or two, they would have five or six which leads to nine or 10, and I think that's what he was afraid of because the club had just come from that.

'That was the background when Bob came. He realised what the players had had before and said – and meant – have a couple. Bob wasn't a drinker himself, but he respected grown men to have the ability to say, "I've had enough thank you." Managers are not daft, they know what happens, so I would say that it's accurate that that was the reason, and by lifting the complete alcohol ban it made the atmosphere in the club more enjoyable. When the "Bomber" was there you felt a bit reserved. That was his role, it had to be, he was brought in for that and Bob came and made it a bit looser. You could have a bit of a laugh, could take the mickey out of him, although we used to take the mickey out of the "Bomber" on the field as well.'

Stokoe enjoyed some massive strokes of good fortune when he arrived. His first game was a home defeat to Burnley, but as he had only just arrived and Burnley were en route to winning the League no blame was attached to him. Moreover, he had pulled off a masterstroke with the supporters by immediately re-introducing the club's traditional black shorts instead of the white ones worn in recent seasons. His second game away to Portsmouth resulted in goals in the last three minutes,

Dick (second from right) at the unveiling of the Stokoe statue with, from left to right: Ritchie Pitt, Bobby Kerr, Bob Stokoe's daughter Karen and Jim Montgomery.

turning a 2–1 defeat into a first win in 11 games, followed by a goalless home draw – and then came his biggest piece of good fortune.

'We got the flu, and there was a break which gave us the chance all to unwind, relax, not play ,and that took the pressure off the team and the new manager.' From the Portsmouth game nine days before Christmas, Sunderland did not play again until 6 January when the fixture that presented itself was a home game with Brighton who would end the season bottom of the table. It was the first game of 1973, Sunderland romped home 4–0, their biggest win of the season setting the side up nicely for the next game at Notts County, the start of the Cup run.

Bob Stokoe was such a resounding success at Sunderland that he became known as 'The Messiah', and a statue of him now stands outside Sunderland's Stadium of Light home.

Stokoe added little in the way of personnel to the team he inherited, but he gave them responsibility and belief and was blessed with a few important things going his way. Reflecting on the qualities a successful football manager needs, Dick – who later turned down the chance to join this precarious profession – observes, 'In defence of the Board of Directors it's very difficult for directors to know what to do because what makes a good manager? I get asked that all the time, "Is he going to be a good manager?" The answer is that you don't know. I've known managers do everything right and get the wrong results, and I've known managers who do everything wrong, everything a manager shouldn't do, drinking and whatever, and get the right results. But who is a good manager? It's a difficult question, and the answer is, "Don't know, all you need is some luck" – if you haven't got the luck you can close the door.

'Sunderland were unlucky in their first season in the Premier League under Roy Keane because they got robbed with referees. In another season they might be very lucky and get another 12 points on top of the 12 that we should have had in 2007–08 and finish sixth top, you don't know, so what plays a big part in any manager's success is the rub of the green.'

Replays were required to progress past Notts County and Charlie Hurley's Reading in 1973 before the fifth round paired Sunderland with Manchester City. City had disposed of Liverpool, who would win the title that year, in the previous round and they had home advantage…sort of. Massive Sunderland support was present at Maine Road, and that support came home with a massive dose of Cup fever after the best Sunderland performance in years earned a replay which would be voted the greatest game ever played at Roker Park when the ground closed almost a quarter of a century later.

Dick recalls the occasion, 'In the first game we never once thought we were going to get beaten. I can honestly say that. There were over 50,000 squeezed into Roker Park for the replay. We started well, and after about 10 minutes I remember thinking, "God we are going to thrash these, we are moving sweetly tonight, we are on fire." We were playing that well, the players certainly always felt we were going to win, and that is my main memory.'

Sunderland demolished City 3–1, 10 days after the 11 who beat City and would win the Cup had played together for the first time, slamming Middlesbrough 4–0. The Boro match had been Vic Halom's home debut. Vic was the final piece in a jigsaw that had had eight of the 11 pieces since a couple of months after Malone's arrival over two years earlier. From the games with City 'Stokoe's Stars' were unstoppable: 'I always felt we were capable of beating anyone,' Dick agrees, 'We had such a good team. That was born out of playing together a lot, we knew each other's play, we were confident with each other and we were totally honest with each other. If I hit a bad pass, someone would run and try to make it into a good pass. Everyone gave 100 per cent for everyone else, the camaraderie was there.'

Fellow Second Division outfit Luton were seen off in the quarter-finals with the semi-final pairing giving Sunderland the task of preventing Arsenal reaching a third successive Final. 'During the game we didn't feel we were going to thrash them as we had Manchester City, but we never thought we were going to get beat. You begin to wonder sometimes, we had played well but you are going to have a bad game sometime, and that was always at the back of my mind. With the history Arsenal had and the players that they had, we knew we needed to be on our toes and make sure that the game went our way. We were moving the ball about sweetly, it was a dream to be at the club at the time, and to qualify for the Final was exactly that.'

That famous Final could have seen Malone playing against Sunderland rather than for them. 'Three months after I had signed for Sunderland I went into a toilet at a night club. I never drank when I played, but I was at the night club to watch a friend of mine who was one of the acts. In the toilet this guy said to me,

"You're Dick Malone, aren't you?"

I said, "Yeh yeh."

"Well you are a 'bleeping' idiot"

"Well obviously you've seen me play then" I replied.

"No, I'm a scout for Leeds, and we chased you for two years. You were top of Don Revie's shopping list and you go and sign for this shower here."

'I knew there had been several clubs after me when I left Ayr, but it wasn't until this conversation I knew about Leeds, so it was quite ironic that it was Leeds I'd play against at Wembley.'

Malone was at the centre of the pre-match hype, pundits predicting that Leeds would target him by feeding left-winger Eddie Gray, who they felt would get the better of the full-back, but Dick was completely unperturbed by such speculation and when supposed match-winner Gray was substituted (in the days of just one replacement) the fact that Malone had seen him off only added to his reputation.

'Bobby [Kerr] and I always worked as a unit. Bob [Stokoe] didn't need to say anything to us about specifically dealing with Eddie Gray. I never felt anything about it at all. Apparently the pundits felt because of the marauding runs I was known for Leeds would be able to get Gray in behind me and that he'd expose me, which was fair comment. What they failed to understand is I knew that's what they thought, so I wouldn't do the marauding runs up the park and give them the space to do that.

Striking the ball at 'Boro.

'Having said that, there are two things about that game: Eddie Gray had spent a long time off – he may have been running fit, but he certainly wasn't mentally fit for the game in my opinion. I thought Eddie Gray was Leeds United. He won most of the games for Leeds, he was so clever on the ball. I must admit it did worry me that it was raining heavily and the pitch was very slippery, because when you are up against a player like Eddie Gray who can turn on a sixpence, he can put you on your backside very easily. That really did bother me at times. If you look at the Cup Final again you'll see Dennis [Tueart] on his backside a lot, that's how slippery it was, but it didn't pan out that way. Gray didn't get the space, and he gradually moved further and further back. In fact, he ended up moving back where Bobby was, and in the end I didn't even need to mark him, to the extent I didn't know when they took him off because I wasn't really marking him. He didn't come up as far as me; he didn't have the space.'

> 'Super Dick, Super Dick' chanted an ecstatic Fulwell End as a 40-yard rocket shot crashed into the back of the Roker End net against Orient, if my memory serves me rightly, in the '70s courtesy of Richard Philip Malone, the Scottish right-back signed by controversial Sunderland boss Alan Brown in October 1970. Malone was as honest as they come, a marauding defender who often bore all the trademarks of a frustrated right-winger, such was his desire to get forward. The most famous Malone story in my mind was the one about the ITV football panel on The Friday Night Programme on 4 May 1973 which previewed the next day's massive Sunderland-Leeds FA Cup Final. Including the likes of Derek Dougan and Paddy Crerrand, they were particularly scathing of Dick's ability to cope with Leeds left-sided flanker Eddie Gray, then one of the best players in the world in that position. As history proves, however, Dick had his most effective game ever in a red-and-white shirt, and Gray was subbed.
> 'Nuff said.
> Tom Lynn, Sunderland supporter, Sunderland.

Sunderland, then, had sussed out how to handle Leeds, but despite Sunderland's elimination of Manchester City and Arsenal Dick feels they still caught Leeds by surprise: 'What they failed to understand is that we were playing in the Second Division at the time, and when you play in the Second Division you've got to play a similar type of football to the division you're in, maybe a little bit different if you are a better team. More times than not it's less skilful and you've got to outshine the opposition as far as effort and desire is concerned before in the end class will tell. You stutter and stammer in lots of games because you are trying to match all this effort, and huffing and puffing. When you get into the First Division, which is now the Premier League, you get more space, and they would never have really seen us in that territory before so they wouldn't know what we were capable of or what they were going to get from us, but we knew what we were going to get from them. It was very easy for us to do the damage to them, but it wasn't quite as easy for them to do the damage to us.'

The win shocked the rest of the country, but it didn't shock Sunderland. The players had been utterly convinced they would win, and the Cup fever that had gripped Wearside meant that the fans were actually expecting to win, many pointing out that the only time the Lads had won the Cup before, the numbers 73 had been reversed.

Unfinished League business in Cardiff delayed the homecoming until the Tuesday after the Final. 'I remember how dangerous it was with the crowds hanging from buildings in the town. I kept thinking people are going to fall. They were hanging out of windows and off roofs. I'm sure some of them must have had a few drinks, and I was worried someone was going to get badly hurt. The size of the crowds I couldn't believe, and that was from Carrville all the way to Sunderland. The enormity of the crowds was unbelievable. If I'd been told there'll be massive crowds I could have believed it would be the case in the town centre and at Roker Park, but it was unbelievable all the way from Carrville, and that is what stuck in my mind.'

Winning the FA Cup brought entry to Europe in the old European Cup-Winners' Cup, Dick creating Sunderland's first-ever goal in a major European competition when his free-kick was headed home by Billy Hughes. 'We murdered Vasas in Hungary. We were a great team then,' Dick sighs before lamenting, 'I honestly think the club then let the fans down by letting that team break up. I know that Dennis and Dave felt they probably needed to move on to further their England careers or whatever, but I can tell you that if the club had made an effort financially for all the players – and we deserved it, really – then I don't think the team would have broken up.

'They undervalued the Cup team greatly. In retrospect, maybe if I was in that position I might have done the same, but we brought in a lot of revenue to the club and we didn't really get a lot of reward from it. In those days footballers weren't negotiating deals as they do now with agents. In my situation, and I dare say 80 or 90 per cent of the players would be the same, they came from tough backgrounds and had nothing, so anything better than nothing was acceptable. You didn't really know what you could and couldn't ask for. You would go and ask for a tenner rise, and if you came out with a fiver you'd do handstands. The clubs abused that a little bit, I don't know where the money went, but I believe that mentality left the door open for agents to get a foothold in, and now it's gone to a ridiculous level where they are strangling clubs. I would shoot the lot of them personally – why anyone should be getting the sort of money they are throwing about, it's ridiculous!

'In '73 we agreed £1,000 each, Leeds were promised £10,000. We never thought we would get to the Final when the bonuses were drawn up, and the club could very easily have done something about that, I can tell you that, they could have very easily done something for us, but they didn't.'

How much further success the Cup team might have had if the side had been kept together and the squad added to will have to remain a matter for conjecture. Perhaps if they had there would have been more European football to enjoy in addition to that ECWC involvement, 'We played really well against Vasas. We also played really well against Sporting Lisbon, and they were lucky! We should have beaten them, and they were the favourites for the competition. We missed a few chances and one of the goals in Lisbon was hilarious. My recollection of it is that when Jimmy had the ball he always used to look to the left and throw it out to me on the right, well he did that, saw the winger was coming towards me and tried to pull it back but only managed to direct the ball to the winger. I've never seen the goals again on TV so I don't know how accurate my memory is, but that's what I can remember.'

Rather like Glasgow Rangers whose success was curtailed due to a fixture pile up in 2008, Sunderland's European campaign suffered in 1973–74. Ten games were played in 28 days during October, with four fixtures squeezed into the fortnight between the two-leg clash with the Portuguese.

Two of those games were pulsating League Cup ties against an excellent Derby County midway through a spell of two Championships in four years. 'We'd drawn two each down there when we had John Lathan up front. The amount of people who have said to me that the replay was the best game they had seen for years and years is amazing. People had come down from Scotland to see me and told me it was the best game they had ever seen. We tossed up for the second replay, and we won the toss, played them again at Roker Park a couple of days later and beat them in another fantastic game of football.'

To progress Sunderland needed to return to the top flight, but there were three long years to wait between Wembley and promotion. When elevation to the top flight finally arrived in 1976 it was done on the back of an unbeaten home record, where only two teams took home as much as a point. Sunderland's first-ever Second Division winners were delivering only the club's second trophy in 39 years, but unlike the promotion team of '64 or the Cup-winners of '73 they had a very different make up, completely lacking the bond that has been maintained for a lifetime by the men of '64 and '73.

Dick scores brilliantly against Portsmouth in December 1974.

'It didn't have the same camaraderie,' says Dick 'I couldn't tell you the line up.' Whereas most Sunderland supporters of a certain age can trot off the regular '64 team and the '73 Cup team as easily as their address and date of birth, it is a rare fan who can do better than name the odd individual from the Second Division champions of 1976. Six of the Wembley heroes were still around to pick up a second medal: Malone, Montgomery, Kerr, Halom, Porterfield and Hughes, the latter two playing half a season each, although in Halom's case the final game of the season was his last in red and white.

The rest of the regular line up was completed by Joe Bolton, Tony Towers, Bobby Moncur, Mel Holden, Bryan 'Pop' Robson and in the latter half of the season Roy Greenwood, but there was a vital ingredient missing from the mix: 'Arthur Cox was part of the set up, and after he'd been sacked he was missed. Since Arthur had been at the club he was the main coach. Billy Elliott more or less took a back seat, having contributed a lot to the club over the years, and obviously he passed on a lot of his experience to some of the younger lads who would come through when he was coaching reserves and so on. Arthur was more key to it and was part of the team. Even in industry or sales it's always about a team effort, I'm only as good as the guys I've got working for me and vice-versa. Arthur was at the forefront of it because he was coaching the first team and the players got on very well with him. I could only speak very, very highly of Arthur.'

For a while it looked as if Sunderland might achieve a promotion and Cup double in 1976. Oldham and Hull had been routinely disposed of at home before a thrilling fifth-round tie with top-flight Stoke. A goalless draw in the Potteries brought them back for a fifth-round replay under the lights that rekindled memories of the Man City game at the same stage just three years earlier. Sunderland edged a thrilling game in extra-time, and when the quarter-final draw presented the Lads with a home tie against Third Division Crystal Palace the path down Wembley Way looked to be opening up. 'I thought we were doing it again. I really did, especially with our home record,' remembers Dick, but the infamous north-east wind blew those hopes away.

Malcolm Allison had reason to recall Sunderland's Cup pedigree, having coached Man City in '73, but as the fedora waving Palace manager he soaked up the stick he got when winding the crowd up before the game as well as his side (captained by future Sunderland assistant manager Ian 'Taff' Evans) soaked up pressure throughout the game with Palace sneaking victory: 'There was a breakaway, and Alan Whittle got the only goal of the game for them. We just couldn't buy a goal that day, we did everything but score. We would have won it that year as well. I was sure of that.'

A repeat of FA Cup glory was not to be, but the wait for top-flight football was over and Sunderland started brightly enough, holding their own in three successive draws. In the side for those games, Dick was missing for the following match when the wheels came off in a 4–1 hammering at fellow promotion-winners Bristol City that signalled the start of six defeats and a draw that left Sunderland adrift at the bottom of the table, and, even worse, without a manager after the resignation of Bob Stokoe.

It was a time of major upheaval, Dick was in and out of the side, record appearance maker Jimmy Montgomery played what proved to be his final match in Stokoe's penultimate game, 'The Messiah' resigning following a dismal 1–0 home defeat to Aston Villa on the day he gave a debut to new 'keeper Barry Siddall and a second appearance to his £200,000 club record signing, striker Bob Lee. New coach Ian McFarlane was unpopular with several of the players and during six weeks as caretaker manager sold 'Pop' Robson and Bobby Moncur.

After the long fight to get a team who had thrilled the world in winning the FA Cup into the top flight, Sunderland's undoing was largely down to showing that team to the world according to Malone: 'The directors, in their infinite wisdom, had taken us on a month long 10-match tour at the end of the previous season. We went all the way round Australia, New Zealand, Singapore and

Malone in action against Oldham at Roker Park.

Tahiti. It was a really, really tiring tour. I can remember coming back after playing in every game. Some players had relaxed a bit, but I'd trained hard and when I got home I sat upright in a chair and never moved. I didn't even flicker for five and a half hours I was that tired.

'We'd kept crossing the international date-line. In the first 10 days of the tour I'd only managed 18 hours sleep. I couldn't relax, couldn't unwind. I'm sure that tour contributed to us struggling. I felt jaded. I didn't want the season to start, and that wasn't me, I just wasn't ready for it to start. I was flat and had no sharpness at all.

'I was very friendly with Bob Stokoe, I liked him a lot. I argued with him all the time, and the lads will tell you that the team talks were often aimed at me because Bob was a defender, an old-fashioned defender and that's the way he thought the defence should be, but I didn't want to play like that so him and I would be arguing, and if the lads wanted a break, if they were tired on a Monday, they would just say, "Dick you start it" and so I would. It wouldn't go any further than me and him and that was it, but we argued all the time. I respected him a lot and he respected me, and the fact is he played me even though we disagreed a lot. When Bob resigned it cost him money, and he regretted that.

'Jimmy Adamson replaced Bob a few weeks later. He was a clown, a bad man manager, terrible. He wanted rid of all the guys who'd been there and I understand that. All he needed to do was to say "Look, the team hasn't been doing so well, I'm going to change a few things to bring a fresh breeze through the club or whatever. I might have to play you although you won't be my first choice, but I'll help you get away and make some money." What he did though was not even tell me if any team came in for me. I had 10 teams phone me up, which was illegal of course, but when I asked him, "Has anyone been in for me boss?" he'd snap "No", and I had to sit and take that – and people wonder how agents ended up taking a strangle hold on clubs. I ended up having to go to devious means to get a free transfer. In Jimmy Adamson's defence I must say he was a brilliant coach, but as for man management, well he wasn't a manager. He would have been great as an assistant who could have coached the players.'

Youth-team product Jackie Ashurst was gradually pushing harder and harder for a regular place. Indeed, Adamson only played Malone in his second and third games leaving him out after a 2–0 derby defeat at Newcastle two days after Christmas. He never picked him again, soon bringing in Mick Docherty at right-back.

Fit and available for selection, Malone spent the last six months of his seven years at Sunderland languishing in the reserves. 'I was disenchanted with football and I was going to pack in, really, I wasn't going to play again. I forced Jimmy Adamson to get me a free transfer because they weren't going to. He told me: "There's no one been in for you, but I'll make you available for a nominal fee so you can make a few bob, because you've been a great servant to the club." He said it with a stupid smile on his face. I could've put his teeth down his throat. I wish I had. I said "If I've been such a great servant then free me," to which he replied: "No f***** chance," but in the end I eventually did leave on a free.'

Having had respect for Ally MacLeod, Alan Brown and Bob Stokoe, Dick found the Adamson regime at Sunderland intolerable. Having failed to score a solitary goal in any of Adamson's first nine games in charge, even a superb second half of the season inspired by the young triumvirate of Gary Rowell, Kevin Arnott and Shaun Elliott could not prevent relegation, and as Sunderland sunk to Division Two Dick was going even further, joining Hartlepool United who had once again finished in the bottom four of the Fourth Division.

An accomplished and well-respected professional, Malone had plenty of options from higher-placed clubs and was only 30, but he followed the well-trodden path from Sunderland to Hartlepool, something Brian Clough and Len Ashurst had done in recent years in commencing their managerial careers – although that prospect did not appeal to Dick. 'I'd had other offers, but I went to Hartlepool for geographical reasons. I'd been going to pack in altogether, but the Hartlepool chairman, a guy called Vince Barker, came to see me. He wanted me to be player-manager, and I thought "God, that's the last thing I want" and I told him "But you've got a manager Mr Barker." He said: "Ah, Billy [Horner] won't mind, but why don't you come and play, and then when you want to hang up your boots you can manage the club?" I told him I'd think about it, so I went and joined them. I played, and I was happy tinkering along. Billy was a nice guy, he wasn't a manager either. He was a good coach, but he lacked discipline. There needs to be an aloofness between a manager and player so there's a respect there, and Billy was too much of an "Aye alright?" kind of personality and was too easy on certain players that needed controlling. He didn't do that, but we had a good team. There was Eric McMordie, Derek Downing, Tommy Gibb and Alan Foggon, all of whom had played at a high level.'

Clearly Hartlepool had enough to turn it on from time to time. Although they again finished in the bottom four and had to seek re-election under the old system of assessing Football League status, they had a decent Cup run, defeating Tranmere, non-League Runcorn and Second Division Palace before going out to eventual winners Ipswich Town. Dick's second season at Hartlepool was short-lived: 'It ended up backfiring a bit. Billy wanted to go for man-for-man marking, well I think if you do that you've run out of ideas. I disagreed with that and said I was going to leave. I got left out and Bob [Stokoe, now managing Third Division Blackpool] came in for me. He'd been after me anyhow, and I just agreed to sign for him, although that's not strictly true because in fact I never signed a contract for Blackpool, I just played for them.

'It was brilliant at Blackpool and they treated me like a king. The chairman was forever chasing me to sign a contract, but I always said "I'm happy the way it is. This way if I want to stop playing I can do." But I was playing absolutely brilliant. I was playing better than ever, I was fit and oh God I really enjoyed my time there. Bobby Kerr joined us so that was great, the fans were great, I played great and played in different positions. I had a few games in centre-midfield and played as a centre-half or sweeper.

'I can remember the first time Bob asked me to sweep up at centre-half. I had the flu really bad and a bad chest infection. The doctor said to me "Because of your bad chest infection I'm going to give you some anti-biotics, but they're double strength. They'll shift it, but they'll give you diarrhoea as well." So I had the flu and diarrhoea and a cough when I went in. Bob wore his heart on his sleeve. You always knew if he was on a downer by the expression on his face. When I saw him I knew what he was going to say to me.

He asked, "How are you son?"

I told him, "I was okay until I realised you were going to ask me to play tomorrow."

He said, "Oh God, is it that obvious?"

"Where do you want me to play?"

"Where do you want to play? I've got eight injuries so I'm going to mix and match. I'll either play you centre-midfield or centre-half."

'When I went there it was centre-half, sweeper. Over the years when I was playing, even at

Sunderland, during the games I was up and down the park all the time and I'd often tell Ritchie [Pitt] or Dave Watson I was knackered at half-time and they'd say they were alright, so I used to think I wasn't fit. I'd tell Arthur Cox I was going to come in every afternoon for the following week because I didn't think I was fit enough and he used to insist, "You're one of the fittest guys around, that's rubbish," but I'd still go in.

'I played in this game with flu and diarrhoea and it was muddy and energy sapping, but the game started and I was playing well and the crowd were applauding every time I got the ball. I found I had so much time and then it started to dawn on me…centre-halves don't really run! I thought no wonder Ritchie and Dave were never knackered, I thought "God, they don't run, centre-halves don't really run." Arthur Cox had always fancied me to play sweeper. It's all grafting on the flanks. You bomb forward to support your winger and as soon the move breaks down you've got people shouting at you, "Hey Malone, you're out of position, you've left your man" and you're thinking I'm doing my best to be in two places at once. Honestly, at centre-half I strolled the games. I was Man of the Match in that first game despite feeling ill, but I absolutely strolled through it.'

A mid-table finish was not enough for Blackpool, who sacked Stokoe in the summer of '79, replacing him with coach Stan Ternent who had been at Sunderland during the Stokoe era, but Ternent's tenure was to be brief. 'Stan was the coach to Bob and took over when Bob left. It didn't pan out, and I would say that Stan was unlucky, because he knows what he's talking about and as I've mentioned before some managers do everything right and get the wrong results, and I've known managers do everything wrong and get the right results. Stan did everything right, but unfortunately things didn't go his way due to certain circumstances, but you could say that about a lot of managers.'

Ternent was replaced by former Blackpool player and England World Cup winner Alan Ball, an opponent of Malone in the 1973 FA Cup semi-final: 'Alan Ball was great with me, but he wanted to play a certain style of football that didn't suit me. He wasn't the greatest man manager, but he was great with me. I'm not being derogatory about him, but he's another guy who would have been a great guy to have as an assistant.'

Griffin Park, Brentford, was the venue when Dick Malone kicked a football in anger for the final time in English League football. It was 23 February 1980, and like a coal mine that closes before the seam has been exhausted Malone retired when there was plenty of football left in him; he was only 33. 'I could have stayed at Blackpool, but I'd had enough so I packed in, walked out and signed on the dole. I'd had enough.'

A bit like a smoker who gives up and later has to have one more cigarette, there are several players featured in this book who, like Frank Sinatra, have later come back for one more encore. Dick was one of these players, albeit a reluctant one. Nonetheless in September 1980 he was tempted back into action with Queen of the South in the south west of Scotland, playing a total of 43 times for them, 30 in his first season as promotion was won as runners-up in the Second Division, and 13 more in 1981–82 in what was the middle tier of Scottish football, some 18 years on from his debut up the west coast at Ayr.

'I had a gap after finishing with Blackpool and didn't intend playing again. Out of the blue I got a phone call from George Herd.' Herd was a former Scottish international who had played over 300 games for Sunderland during the 1960s and coached at the club. 'George was managing Queen of the South and when he rang me up his words to me were: "Dick, I need you to help me. I've got a

Dick, second from left in the front row, at an October 2007 reunion of players to celebrate the 50th anniversary of Player of the Century Charlie Hurley signing for Sunderland. Back row, left to right: Dean Whitehead, Cec Irwin, Martin Harvey, Ian Rodden, Septimus Taylor, Ritchie Pitt, Charlie Hurley, Ambrose Fogarty, Bobby Park, Len Ashurst, George Mulhall, Johnny Crossan and Brian Usher. Front row, left to right: George Herd, Dick Malone, Paul McShane, Bobby Kerr, Jimmy Shoulder, Winston Young, Jimmy Montgomery, Nicky Sharkey and Gary Bennett.

right shower here and I need you to come and play." I told him I wasn't fit, but he persuaded me, telling me that even if I wasn't fit I was going to be more use than the players he had so I went up. I only travelled to games on matchdays, even though that meant some very long trips for away games.'

Dick also turned out for North Shields, but that was only for a game or two: 'That was just the odd fleeting game as they were struggling and I was helping a friend out,' confirms Dick, but by 1982 the curtain had come down on his final encore as a footballer.

'My next stop was working in the haulage trade for TNT, who I worked for for 17 years. I then set up on my own, but that backfired because without mentioning personalities I got shafted. It cost me a lot of money, but I moved on and I'm still in transport. I work for Crawford transport in Washington, and I'm working part-time with an ex-director of TNT at setting up a dedicated Irish service from the North East.'

Having become vice-chairman of the Sunderland Former Players' Association, Dick remains a hugely popular and respected figure at SAFC more than a third of a century after helping bring the Cup to the club. 'The Former Players' Association is thriving' he says, 'With Niall Quinn as chairman of the club the Cup team feel welcome in and around the ground. Niall's opened the warmth out, and it shows from the top all the way down.'

Under Quinn's leadership Sunderland are searching for success, and there is optimism that the modern-day Sunderland will remind the country that Sunderland never were 'giant killers', they were and are giants of the game. Dick Malone became a cult hero of Sunderland fans. They took to their hearts a player who at first looked ungainly and awkward, a full-back who gave the term 'mazy dribble' added depth. What the fans liked in Malone was that he was a trier, he was not going to be put off his stride no matter what, he may well have been unorthodox, but he was a vital part of a great team, and a player supporters could identify with. He was never flash but modest and unassuming, a player the crowd grew to love, 'My relationship with the crowd was brilliant. I always got applauded, even when I tripped up! I always gave some sort of entertainment during the game I gather. I guess that was why the crowd liked me. And I tried, I kept trying and I wasn't such a bad player. I know that because there were a lot of teams after me. That's how I know that, not because I thought I was a good player.'

All cult heroes have a chant. Up the road at Newcastle at the time their hero was called 'Supermac' – a player Sunderland fans said was the answer to the quiz question, 'What's taken to the Cup Final and never used?' – at Roker Park the fans had one man in mind as a retort to Tyneside about the relative qualities that distinquish 'Canny Owld Sun'land' from the airs and graces of the self-appointed 'regional capital', so Malone, the marauding, mazy dibbling right-back was christened 'Superdick'. The chant repeated over and over would resonate whenever Malone had dribbled 'broad and narrow.'

Dick laughs at the memory, 'It was great to have a chant it was an endearing term and I felt proud that the supporters took the time and effort to shout my name. I just hope they didn't think it was literally true! I wasn't in those rotten films I've heard about.'

HE SAYS NO, NO, NO!

NYRON NOSWORTHY

Defender

Born: 11 October 1980, Brixton.
Signed for Sunderland: 10 June 2005 from Gillingham, free transfer

Gillingham: 1997, 151+23 League apps, 5 goals
Sunderland: 10 June 2005, 80+8 League apps, 0 goals
                          84+8 total apps, 0 total goals

Sunderland statistics up to start of 2008–09 season.

Nyron Nosworthy has the credentials necessary to be classified as a cult hero. For a start, from the moment he arrived supporters could be pretty certain that if they chanted: 'There's only one Nyron Nosworthy' they would be factually correct, although that chant was not needed as Nyron's own inimitable style soon led to the creation of other songs in his honour.

Signed in 2005 on a free from a team relegated from the division Sunderland had just won, the acquisition of Londoner Nyron failed to impress fans who were looking for Sunderland to add quality to a promoted side in preparation for the Premier League. Nosworthy had been signed as cover for right-back Stephen Wright, but injury to Wright early in the opening game of the season propelled him from the bench and into the limelight. He had a less than auspicious start, letting a simple pass roll under his foot and out for a throw-in the first time the ball came to him. The side proceeded to break Sunderland's own unwanted record for the fewest Premiership points, and when the first win of the season eventually arrived at near neighbours Middlesbrough Nosworthy succeeded in causing flutters of panic with a horribly miscued back pass from the halfway line that conceded a bizarre and unnecessary corner.

And yet somehow Nyron quickly became a cult hero. True, many in the crowd initially thought him useless, and perhaps those who took to him did so to begin with because they thought he needed all the help he could get, having left a much smaller and only previous club in Gillingham to come and perform in the demanding atmosphere of a struggling Sunderland team in the top flight. What the fans saw that they liked was a lad giving his all. A player who may well not be the most talented footballer in the country but one who was evidently playing with his heart and soul and fighting for the badge on the shirt without patronising the fans by kissing it.

What is more, people began to realise that Nyron had some great attributes such as speed, strength and athleticism to go with his commitment. Nonetheless, as one seasoned observer put it:

In action, 2006.

'The ball is not his friend.' At times Nosworthy would combine the most basic mistakes with moments of sublime skill, so much so that fans would struggle to fathom how a man who could beat an opponent by delicately flicking the ball over his head before deftly cushioning it and laying it off would at other times struggle to trap a simple pass.

Nyron's penchant for combining the brilliant and the ridiculous had already earned him cult hero status among those who adored him before his transformation from raw right-back to colossal centre-back midway through the Championship-winning season of 2006–07, a hiatus that led to him claiming the Player of the Year award despite making only a smattering of appearances by the campaign's halfway point.

Nyron himself has long been aware of his one time tendency to undo all his good work through the odd aberration: 'One of the things that the youth-team coaching staff at Gillingham all said was that I have all the attributes to be a top-class player, but the things I had to work on were my distribution and concentration level. That let me down sometimes at Gillingham, and it is something I work on all the time, but these things happen. It seemed to happen to me quite regularly. On my Sunderland debut the ball went under my foot, and things like that stick in your mind even if you do something well afterwards.

'I try not to think about things like that, though, because I know I need to go on and perform again. That's the most important thing – performing in the next game. You're the only one who can change it. I've made mistakes over time, but the main thing is to redeem them and do the correct thing. If you keep that attitude, things will come good for you.'

Football fans respect pride and commitment and at Sunderland, rather than castigating Nyron's errors, the fans got right behind him from the start and showed their appreciation of the fact that any occasional errors were not down to lackadaisical commitment. This was illustrated by the first of the chants created in Nyron's honour, a simple 'Come on Nyron' repeated over and over again to the tune of the old Gary Glitter *Do You Wanna Be In My Gang?* hit.

Certainly the chant helped Nyron to feel part of the gang and accepted at the Stadium of Light. 'Gillingham fans hadn't really had a chant for me, and when I heard the fans at Sunderland chanting my name for the first time it felt brilliant, although I tried not to think about it too much and just tried to concentrate on the football.

'When my family come up they always talk about the supporters. They love the fact that the fans are really passionate. I would like to sit there and listen to what they're saying – you can hear them roar. That makes you want to play better. If we lose the ball I want to chase the opposition down and win it back. The fans like to see you working for the team, and they like to see entertaining football. I'm an entertainer as well as a professional sportsman, and I try to give the supporters what they want.'

Nyron's infamous back pass at Middlesbrough only served to add to his reputation. In similar fashion to how Kevin Ball is able to laugh about hitting his own crossbar from 40 yards in the 2–1 win at Newcastle in 1999, and how Niall Quinn escaped punishment courtesy of Tommy Sorensen at the same venue a year later after conceding a late penalty, nothing ill came of Nosworthy's calamity. 'I was thinking, today I've been consistent in my passing, just taking it easy and doing the right things. I had the chance to chip it up, but was closed down quickly so I thought "a good solid back pass to Kelvin in goal," but I'd taken my eye off the ball, and I just seemed to hit it so hard. I thought "That's typical, that is." Just when everything was going my way, I was playing well, and then I go and do something stupid. I laughed about it. The gaffer [Mick McCarthy] let it rip, but I've got broad shoulders, I just took it on the chest. If they'd scored I think that would have done me more harm.'

As it was, Sunderland won that match 2–0 at Middlesbrough, but what is often forgotten is that the nearest Boro came to scoring that day came at a crucial stage of the match when they broke from a Sunderland corner to bring a terrific save out of Kelvin Davis who did well to parry the ball, but had it not been for Nyron having raced back at Olympic sprint pace to rescue the situation there would have been an easy tap-in for the onrushing home forwards.

> *Defies the maxim that defenders cannot be entertaining and effective. A superb athlete who combines pace and strength with a Caribbean swagger. His flamboyance verges on the suicidal at times, but it is this maverick trait that has fans expecting the unexpected. His excesses are more than compensated by a fierce competitive spirit and defensive solidity.* Mike Love SENSSA.

Nosworthy was having to learn quickly having been thrown in at the deep end. With Sunderland releasing previous reserve right-back Mark Lynch during the close season, Nyron had been signed to put pressure on first choice and former Liverpool player Stephen Wright, but when Wright limped out of the opening game of the season suddenly Nosworthy found himself required as a regular in the side. Indeed, in that first season on Wearside only three players appeared more times than the former Gill.

'It worked out for me pretty well. On the first day of the season I was watching from the bench and thinking: "Oh that's a good player" and so on but then I was suddenly on the pitch. Afterwards I found out Wrighty's injury was serious and the next game is at Liverpool – you're playing and that's it. You have to prove your worth. I think that helped me a great deal. We struggled to get results, but on a personal level I was playing and I knew I was doing my best.'

'Nugsy' – the nickname is a childhood one 'Given to me by my dad because he reckoned my head

was shaped like a nugget', and used by Nyron as a personalised number plate – had been in the situation before, albeit at a lower level, but just as nerve wracking as his Sunderland debut was, so was his League debut with Gillingham. That came in November 1998 when a last-minute goal from Robert Taylor gave Gillingham victory over Kevin Keegan's Fulham, who were en route to promotion with over 100 points: 'I actually remember being told I was going to be on the bench, and I was thinking "I'm going to be sitting on the bench watching this game". But after 10-15 mins our left-back got injured, and the original right-back Mark Patteron moved over to the left and I got on and played on the right. I came off for the last 10-15 minutes, so I wasn't on the pitch when we scored, but it was a great win.'

Nosworthy's debut came just as he had turned 18, and the teenager added a couple of further substitute appearances that season as Gillingham reached the Play-offs, but at that stage he was not sure that football would prove to be his career path: 'I signed as a YTS when I was 18. Before that

I was playing, but I wasn't signed on the scheme. I was playing part-time and wasn't sure if I really wanted to do the YTS and waste my time as I didn't know if I was going to take it seriously. Eventually I was training hard enough so the youth-team manager really liked me, and I spoke to him about getting me signed up, and he sorted it all out for me. I wasn't too sure what else I'd do if I didn't become a footballer. I did Leisure and Tourism – most people do that after school, but I didn't know which avenue I was going to go into.

'I had no trials. There was interest from word of mouth – it was between Gillingham and Charlton. Gillingham got back to my coach for my Sunday team. There were eight or nine of us, practically the whole squad of us played against Charlton for our first game, and we did pretty well, although none of the other lads made it as footballers, even though there was a lot of talent there to be honest. I wasn't a defender then, I was a dynamite midfielder, a midfielder in a holding role, but I did score quite a few goals.'

Gillingham were being managed by Tony Pulis, who created a disciplined and well-organised side that reached Wembley in the Play-off Final for promotion to what is now The Championship at the end of Nyron's debut season.

This was the season after Sunderland's Play-off Final with Charlton that saw the Lads lose on penalties after sharing eight goals, and Gillingham's match was to prove equally heartbreaking. Nyron watched from the bench as the Gills led Manchester City 2–0 with just two minutes to play, only for late late goals from Kevin Horlock and Paul Dickov to force extra-time and subsequently spot-kicks, which Gillingham lost 3–1: 'I was on the edge all game, taking it all in because I hadn't been to Wembley for anything. I just remember taking in the atmosphere, and watching individuals, watching their reactions. Everyone was on their toes, and when we went one up with less than 10 minutes to go it was like "this is it" and then we scored again, and I thought "this is unbelievable." Then there was a crazy two minutes, and in a moment it was all gone. It was a great experience, though, I really enjoyed it apart from the disappointment of the result."

Someone else who was disappointed was Pulis, who was sacked by Gillingham, who brought in Peter Taylor for another crack at promotion, which was achieved via the Play-off route again. Sunderland fans think they have seen a transformation in Nosworthy from a right-back to a centre-back, but Peter Taylor had other ideas for Nyron: 'That whole season he saw me as a striker, so he'd have me coming off the bench and causing havoc. Peter Taylor was brilliant. He was very different and I wasn't at all surprised to see him do well as part of the England set-up with the Under-21s, but even back then he was really keen on developing the youth. I played a lot of positions. I came on against Oldham in midfield, played at right-back. In fact I played anywhere I could get a game basically.'

Gradually establishing himself in the side, Nyron played in two thirds of the Gills' League fixtures, starting as many times as he was used as a sub. His physical presence when used up front was a valuable asset, and he grabbed his first goal on the anniversary of his senior debut. It came in a big away win at Scunthorpe, and from Nugsy's own description it sounds like he was living up to his own billing as an entertainer: 'I remember that game because the floodlights were out for about 15 minutes. I was just warming up, messing around – everyone was getting impatient. When my goal came both centre-halves collided, and I thought I'd keep it low and it went through the 'keeper's legs. It looks great on video tape, although the celebration was quite erratic. I was just jumping for joy. I didn't have anything mapped out, I just stopped and was like "I scored!" There was a little bit of relief.'

As Sunderland had done, Gillingham came back strongly from Play-off penalty defeat: 'It was hard, because Gillingham is seen as a very small club and we were always punching above our weight, but when I was there there were a lot of older players that I really looked up to, and if I could say one thing it would be that they were really good to the younger lads and really looked after us.'

It was largely those experienced players that Taylor turned to for the pressure cooker of the Play-offs, Nosworthy appearing as a sub in the second leg of the semi-final, won in extra-time against Graham Kavanagh's Stoke, but when Wigan were beaten at Wembley in another extra-time victory Nyron remained unused. However, he had gained a taste of big-game experience when playing at Stamford Bridge against Chelsea in an FA Cup quarter-final: 'I remember thinking "This would be a good game to go out and express yourself." We had nothing to lose. I came on in the second half and was doing all sorts of tricks. I don't know what came over me. I came on up front, so I thought I had to elaborate on things a little bit and was running around everywhere. I was just this crazy young boy trying to impress, and I really enjoyed it, but it was one of those games where Chelsea were in second gear. We enjoyed it anyway and gave it our all, but they won it comfortably.'

Promotion and a Cup run earned Peter Taylor a move to take over at Leicester City, but his departure was a backward step for Nyron who saw teaelpermmate Andy Hessenthaler take over as player-manager and restrict him to a mere couple of substitute appearances until March: 'Part of it was a new manager. Andy brought in a lot of players, and favoured others, so I couldn't get on. It was a disappointing season for me really, because until then I'd been featuring quite a lot, so to be out of it was really hard. I just got on with it.' Persistence paid off as Nyron finished the season with a run in the side. He had to be patient the following season too, but once given an opportunity two months in he remained a regular in the side at right-back as a creditable mid-table Championship finish was achieved.

However, unlike at Sunderland, Nyron was not the darling of a section of the fans, and at times they gave their youth-team product a hard time: 'I wouldn't say that I was a cult hero at Gillingham, but in general I was popular, and the crowd used to give me a bit of encouragement when I was playing up front. I did get a little bit of a hard time sometimes, but it was minor. I enjoyed the fans there.'

Brixton born, Nyron grew up as a dedicated Arsenal fan. In years to come at Sunderland when Gunners' full-back Justin Hoyte was taken on loan, he and Nosworthy became almost joined at the hip. Since Hoyte's return to Arsenal Nyron has been delighted to see him progress: 'I'm happy for him. Coming up to Sunderland was good for him. He might not have warmed to it at first because it was a long way away from home for a young boy, but he came up to the North East and took it in his stride. He's laid back like me. I think that's why we got on so well, he was like a little brother. Justin is a really nice person who I was happy to see get his chance and play well for Arsenal, even in the Champions League which was good for his portfolio.' Indeed, when Arsenal reached the Champions League Final at the end of Hoyte's season at Sunderland, Nyron made sure he pulled in a favour by ensuring that Justin got him a ticket for the match, and the pair travelled together to Paris for the showpiece: 'It was unbelievable. The whole build-up, it being the real crème de la crème of football was awesome. We were really well looked after. We had a nice meal on a boat and spent the day together. I'd bought a video camera for the game. Little did I know I'd bought a camera without a video tape. I was really fed up about it and had to get most of it on my phone. Just to see Ronaldinho warming up was brilliant.'

For such a dedicated Gooner, being left out of a Gillingham side that drew Arsenal in the fifth round of the FA Cup in 2002 was devastating. Although he was playing regularly when they met at Highbury, criticism from the Priestfield Stadium regulars contributed to his omission. 'That one hurt me' Nyron admits, 'At the time we'd played a home game about two or three weeks before and the crowd were getting on my back, but I wasn't bothered by it because you have days like that. The manager seemed to think at that time that he didn't want to play me anymore, he wanted to leave me out of the side, which had me raging. I just had to keep all the frustration inside and basically take it on the chin and get on with it. I knew hopefully I'd play again, if not at Gillingham then somewhere else.'

Nugsy came back strongly, though, started the following season (2002–03) in the side and rarely missed a match. Mainly he operated at right-back, but he finished the campaign with a flourish as a striker: 'What happened that season was that we were struggling. We didn't have any strikers and everyone knew that I'd done the job up front before. The manager came in and everyone was smiling. He pulled me in and said "We're going to put you up front." I played four or five games up front and all the boys were putting money on me to score goals – I got some good odds! We played Coventry away, and I came really close, but one of their lads wiped me out and I basically missed an open goal. That was the closest I came. I thought I wasn't gonna score. It came to the last game of the season away to Crystal Palace and some of the family said they were coming. I was really trying to think like a striker, like a poacher – like David Connolly. I was just floating around and anticipating things. The ball came to me in the first couple of minutes and I got the better of the defender, so I just hit it low with my left foot and it went in. I was just buzzing after that. The adrenalin was really good, and I scored again almost straight away. The second one was a really good strike into the top corner. It was just my day really – everything was coming my way. I had another chance, which would have given me a hat-trick, but we won 2–1 and I was buzzing because of my performance. As a striker I was over the moon with that performance – everything was working.'

Boosted by his two goal salvo, most of Nyron's early-season games the following season were up front where he added to his goal haul with a late League Cup winner at Cambridge: 'That goal sticks in my mind 'cause that was a cracker by any standard. I don't care what anyone says. My best friend kept saying "I don't think you meant that." I said, "Look at my action, the way I am – I'm starting to score." That game we played against Cambridge, they were by far the better side. I played up front, and we just couldn't get going, but we found a bit of form in the second half. John Hills crossed the ball for me, just dinked one back, and it swung at an awkward angle, quite tight. I watched it come over, I was stretching. I jumped and volleyed it over the 'keeper's head. People were saying it was like Van Basten! I'd tried it since and haven't managed it again, but I've done it now so I'll leave it alone! I've got it on video – I've got all my goals on video. I just kept rewinding and rewinding that goal and thinking "I can't believe that I did that". It's nice to look back in your career on something you've done.'

Good as it was, that rocket marked the end of Nugsy's goalscoring for the Gills, and before long he was back in his more familiar role at right-back. The season proved a slog for the Kent side, who, after three mid-table placings following promotion, found themselves in a relegation scrap. Moreover, it was one they had to battle in without Nyron's help as a hamstring injury ruled him out of the last three and a half months of the season, which included Gillingham's first trip to the Stadium of Light, although he had played in a 3–1 home defeat by the Black Cats earlier in the season, his first connection with Sunderland.

In the end Gillingham stayed up on goal difference by a single goal. With the simple twists of fate that football has a talent for producing, Gillingham's final fixture saw them travel to Stoke, managed by Tony Pulis, the man they'd sacked after losing a Play-off Final on penalties. The Gills had leaked five goals at home to Coventry the previous weekend but battled for a crucial point in a goalless draw that sent Walsall down. 'I remember that game clearly because I travelled to Stoke even though I was injured. Tony Pulis was very professional. I think he'd fallen out with the Gillingham chairman towards the end. I was on the edge of my chair, thinking, "Please, please blow up". I couldn't wait for the final whistle, especially as they had a couple of late chances, but we just held on.'

Joy turned to despair 12 months later when, instead of surviving by a single goal, Gillingham were relegated by a single goal. Crewe Alexandra, who had not won for 20 games, managed to collect three points on the final day, leaving Nosworthy shell-shocked on his final appearance for the club, despite a draw at Nottingham Forest who were also relegated.

Nyron played 37 League games in his last season at Gillingham, but two of the nine he missed were against Sunderland and on one of those occasions he managed to miss the kick-off, even though he had to be at the game. 'I got there late when Sunderland came to Gillingham. I would have played but wasn't fit. I remember getting there, and it was pretty quiet, so I was thinking "Oh, it must be 0–0," but it was already 3–0 to Sunderland, and it ended up 4–0 with Marcus Stewart getting a hat-trick. I was good friends with Ian Cox, who is a centre-half, but he was playing right-back that day instead of me, and I remember people saying that he got tortured by George McCartney and Julio Arca who terrorised him. I didn't play in the return match either, although I

Celebrating with the fans at Luton in 2007.

Celebrating in the dressing room with Danny Simpson at Luton after sealing the Championship in 2007.

travelled. I was injured. I'd done my ankle and I had to have a scan. I remember thinking "I have to travel all the way to Sunderland to have a scan – that's a long way," but the club wanted me to get it done. I remember the boys played really well.'

Gillingham had brought in former Sunderland coach and reserve player Stan Ternent in an effort to stave off relegation. Always a colourful character, Ternent certainly left an impression on Nosworthy: 'He was mad. I've never come across anyone like him. I liked him. His methods were different. If we were playing a small side, he'd eff and blind and say "Just put it in the bloody corners". He made it very simple. His methods were different, but very good. If you weren't involved it probably would have been quite frustrating for you, but he had his methods which were working for us. He came at a time when things were really bad. We couldn't win. He came but didn't turn things around enough unfortunately, even though we only lost one of our last 12 games.

'Neale Cooper came in as manager, but I never played under him. I felt that it was time for me to move on. So it wasn't a case of not being offered anything by Gillingham. I wasn't sure what I wanted to do but I wanted something new and in a higher League than the level we'd been relegated to.

'There were a few clubs that came in for me, but I came up to Sunderland and obviously the facilities up here are amazing. West Ham were interested and I think there were a few other First Division sides as well. When I was at Gillingham people would ask me if I would go up north, and I always said "No way. I'm not leaving family and everything, it's too far." I thought about it – you have one life to live, and I thought it was the opportunity of a lifetime. I'm quite spontaneous as well, so I thought "Just do it". I wanted to prove it to myself that I could do it.

'My family like it, they love seeing where I live. I've got three sisters and three brothers, I'm in the middle. My older sister has a family of five who are my "crazy nieces". I love them to bits. My eldest brother works with kids as a mentor, and I have another brother who is more of a ladies man. He's a sweet boy who is into TV presenting on a music channel on Sky. His name is Dwayne Nosworthy. He seems to be doing alright for himself and is working hard, but it's a difficult industry.

'It's quite relaxing in the North East because in London it's all mayhem. If you're not loaded, you're constantly thinking about stuff you've got to pay for, but to come up here and just get away from it all, you can just really chill out. When they come up here they don't really want to go anywhere, they like to just put their feet up and chill out. I love living on the coast looking across the sea. I'm enjoying my time here.'

> *Nyron is the sort of person who I would describe as 'salt of the earth.' He always gives 110 per cent effort for the team and is an excellent role model for young players and young supporters alike.*
> Doris Turner, Sunderland supporter, Hetton-le-Hole.

Quick to respond to his new fans, Nyron threw himself wholeheartedly into the spirit of things when asked to make appearances at events on behalf of the club, and for causes such as 'Show Racism the Red Card.' 'I think it's very important. I play football, it's what I do. I'm easy going. Some people see you as something bigger and better, and it's nice. I never really had a sports person that I really wanted to see and meet and look up to as such. I just wasn't really bothered, but up here football is the main thing. You see kids up here with their parents well into it. It's a good feeling, especially when they're asking questions and you're giving them good information and knowledge. You hope it helps, if not all of them, then two or three of them.

'With racism a lot of violence used to happen. Some people are quite ignorant – they don't know any better. Especially if they're in a gang, and they just follow – some people are just lemons. They think it's much easier to follow than it is to be a leader themselves. That's the way it is. There's good and bad in everything, you can only do your bit to try to help. You've got young kids, and their parents might be telling them one thing, and they'll be going to school and possibly hearing something else. It's a multi-cultural society, and sometimes someone might say something hurtful, but if you can teach them that if they all get along then everything will be okay, then that is a positive thing to do. It's enjoyable and nice to see everyone getting along.

Cooking something up.   *King of the kitchen.*

'When I was with Gillingham Millwall were the main rivals. I remember getting more abuse than anything from the Millwall fans. That can affect a young lad, but I'm quite relaxed – I wouldn't let it bother me. You just get over it, show that you're a bigger person.'

Significantly, at the end of his first season at Sunderland, Nyron, along with his pal Justin Hoyte, were the last two players to leave the pitch after the final home game. A season that had taken the description 'dismal' to new depths had just had the curtain brought down on the home programme with the only home win of the season. Sunderland had fought hard enough, and to their credit they had never thrown the towel in, and no one had hammered them out of sight despite the undeniable fact that in terms of quality they were without doubt one of the poorest teams ever to play in the Premier League – their 15 points, a record low at the time, illustrates that. Nonetheless the crowd had never turned against them, recognising that whatever faults existed they had no quarrel with the attitude and commitment of players who as a team simply were not good enough. Those without the necessary heart were not being picked. The final home game took place on a Thursday evening that happened to coincide with local elections. Not for the first time the BNP had targeted Sunderland as a place where they might make inroads, and not for the first time the people of Sunderland had delivered them a monumental 'V sign' by not even electing a single one of their candidates. Nosworthy and Hoyte receiving such warm applause despite Sunderland's relegation was a poignant counter-balance to the attempts of those who looked to divide people.

Former Sunderland skipper Gary Bennett was a trailblazer for black footballers when he came to Sunderland in 1985. He was not the first black player to play for Sunderland, but he was the first good one, and the fans took to him. Bennett has maintained a lifetime's connection with Sunderland, done immense good work in combating racism and observes: 'I think in watching Nyron Nosworthy become a cult hero, sometimes I look back and think those were the sorts of

Training in Malahide, Republic of Ireland, 2007.

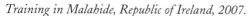

Entering the pitch against Reading in 2007, ahead of Nugsy is Dickson Etuhu while Paul McShane follows him.

things I was producing as well. Running out for Sunderland wearing red and white you've got to know what it means, not just for yourself, but to the supporters as well. I think if you give 100 per cent, even if you've not got the best ability, they can appreciate that and that's shown with Nyron. No disrespect to him, but he isn't blessed with the most ability, but what he does do is give 100 per cent, and as long as he gives 100 per cent, the Sunderland fans will appreciate that.'

A revolution took place at SAFC during the summer of 2006, with the Drumaville Consortium led by Niall Quinn taking over the club and installing Roy Keane as manager after a brief spell where chairman Quinn held the reins. For Nosworthy an injury picked up in the final pre-season friendly could hardly have come at a worse time as he tried to impress the new people running the club.

By the halfway point of the campaign he had featured only fleetingly, before one day Keane informed him he'd be playing centre-back: 'He didn't ask me to play centre-back, it was just a case of here's the team sheet, Nugsy's at centre-back and I had to get on with it.'

From that point until the end of the season Nyron started all 19 games, during which time Sunderland went from 10th place to top, lifted the Championship trophy and lost only once. It was no surprise when the club's Player of the Year award went to Nyron, whose performances at centre-back alongside youngster Jonny Evans were immense. Former manager Mick McCarthy, who signed Nugsy, had tried him at centre-back with disastrous consequences in a pre-season game at Vancouver shortly after his arrival, but Keane took Nosworthy's game onto another level. Those occasional errors Nyron had made at full-back where his concentration sometimes wandered became a thing of the past, as at centre-back he was more in the thick of the action.

Before long the fans had a second song in his honour, but in contrast to 'Come on Nyron' that recognised the need for improvement the new ditty, a version of the Amy Winehouse song *Rehab* simply extolled his ability: 'Try to take the ball off Nyron, but he says No, No, No.'

> *Never in all my years of watching professional football have I seen a transformation in a player like that of Nyron Nosworthy under the Keane regime. Signed by Mick McCarthy from Gillingham as a right full-back, Nyron just never displayed anything like consistent form, and with all due respect, he was awful at times. However, his strength of character shone through because he always gave 100 per cent and football fans always appreciate that basic, but much needed, attribute. When he was initially moved to centre-half many people thought: "What on earth is Keano doing?" But from his first match against Ipswich at the SoL in that position he has looked a natural centre-back. Indeed, he has impressed so much that Niall Quinn has hinted at an England call-up, which really would cement one of the greatest manager's transitions of all-time. Nos is a genuine, pleasant bloke who has a fantastic rapport with the fans. The photograph of him at Luton after the last match of the 2006–07 season is one of my all-time favourites, as he poses with fans with a pork-pie hat on. The crowd at that point were singing their adaptation of the Amy Winehouse classic 'Try to take the ball off Nyron but he says No, No, No'. Nugsy, I take my hat off to you, man. Your success as a respected Premier League performer has been achieved against all the odds and your cult status is well deserved.*
>
> Tom Lynn, Sunderland supporter, Sunderland.

Showing appreciation to the fans at the end of the 2007-08 campaign.

In action against Arsenal, May 2008.

Who else but Nugsy could sign on a free transfer, play in the worst season of the club's history and single handedly raise the blood pressure of Wearside every time he got the ball, yet still have a back catalogue of terrace chants that would put the Rolling Stones to shame?
Andrew Smithson, Sunderland supporter, Sunderland.

Recognised jointly with his captain Dean Whitehead as North East Player of the Year for 2007, Nosworthy's second attempt at the Premier League was a marked improvement on the first, as rather than breaking unwanted records for managing fewer points than any other team, Sunderland under Roy Keane shook off their reputation as the ultimate 'yo-yo' club and secured their place among the elite with two games to spare: 'It's very satisfying and rewarding' accepted Nyron, 'From a personal point of view as well as a team point of view I think it's a fantastic thing that we've achieved. Staying up in the first year after promotion is a great step in helping to establish Sunderland in the Premier League.'

A fixture in Sunderland's newly promoted side until November, his team badly missed Nosworthy after he limped out of a derby match with Newcastle, Sunderland shipping seven goals at Everton in his absence. As in the previous season Sunderland's upturn in fortunes coincided with Nyron being partnered with central-defensive partner Jonny Evans, who returned for a second spell on loan from Manchester United. Having kept a solitary clean sheet (at home to dead men Derby) since the opening day of the season, Sunderland registered three consecutive home shut-outs once the pair were re-united in central-defence, and in the next dozen games only twice did Sunderland concede more than a single goal.

Having been tarnished by being part of the '15-point team' along with the likes of Whitehead and Danny Collins, who survived the purge of players to help Sunderland climb back into the Premier League and stay there, Nyron took satisfaction from proving that he could cope in the top flight: 'The 15-point season was terrible for everybody. You reflect so much on what you could have done and how you could improve. Many games we were losing by one goal and sometimes you would question your ability and ask: "Are we doing the right things, and are we good enough?" Obviously we came straight back up from the Championship and held our own.'

Not only did Nugsy hold his own, but at one point he was shown to be the most effective defender in the Premier League by the Actim Index stats which base their findings on a detailed statistical analysis of every player's contribution in games. Like most footballers, Nosworthy does not get carried away by statistics, but nonetheless it did give the ex-Gillingham defender a boost to be rated higher even than England defenders John Terry and Rio Ferdinand: 'It was nice for me. I came here as a full-back and the best thing for me was moving to centre-half because it really pushed my career on. It's nice to have stats that show you are doing the right thing.'

Nyron's success in his second season, dealing with the best the world's toughest League had to offer, brought him into international contention with Jamaica calling him up, although due to a combination of injuries and fixtures being called off the season drew to a close with Nugsy still uncapped. Who knows, if he keeps saying 'No, no, no' when people try to take the ball off Nyron, and if he keeps popping up at the top of the Actim Index, the Brixton boy might just make it into one of Fabio Capello's England squads. Stranger things have happened, not least that a free-transfer man from Gillingham should be such a mix of magic and mayhem when he first came to the North East, and yet could become a star performer only after he'd already established himself as a cult hero of the red-and-white army.

SHOOT!

CHRIS MAKIN

Full-back
Championship winner with Sunderland 1999.

Born:	8 May 1973.
Signed for Sunderland:	5 August 1997 from Olympique Marseille, £500,000
Transferred:	7 March 2001 to Ipswich Town, £1.4 million

Oldham Athletic:	Associated schoolboy June 1987
	Professional September 1991, 93+1 League apps, 4 goals
Wigan Athletic:	(Loan) August 1992, 14+1 League apps, 2 goals
Preston North End:	(Loan) 0 apps
Olympique Marseille:	August 1996, 29 League apps, 0 goals
Sunderland:	5 August 1997, 115+5 League apps, 1 goal
	136+7 total appearances, 1 goal
Ipswich Town:	March 2001, 78 League apps, 0 goals
Leicester City:	August 2004, 21 League apps, 0 goals
Derby County:	(Loan) February 2005, 13 League apps, 0 goals
Reading	August: 2005, 11+1 League apps, 0 goals
Southampton:	August 2006, 24+3 League apps, 0 goals

'It grew into something. It really blossomed and I had a fantastic relationship with the Sunderland fans. It was the best relationship I ever had with a set of supporters. Every time I got the ball they'd all yell "Shoot!" at me. It got a bit embarrassing in the end because I'd get the ball in my own half and they'd still be shouting "Shoot!". There was one occasion I was coming out of a supermarket, and there was a band playing outside the front entrance

Chris Makin in 1997.

raising money for charity. They saw me, stopped playing and all got up and shouted "Shoot!". It was embarrassing, but it was a good laugh.'

The name 'Shoot!' came about because, like many a Sunderland right-back both before and after his era, Chris rarely looked like scoring. When he did find the back of the net it was a 'pearler', after which the fans gently teased him to try again virtually every time he got the ball!

There is something about full-backs that Sunderland fans take to. Dick Malone, Joe Bolton and John Kay are all featured in this collection of cult heroes, as is Nyron Nosworthy whose cult hero status was established before his transformation to centre-back from right-back. Others such as Richard Ord, who spent much of his Sunderland career at left-back, and Poland international right-back Dariusz Kubicki have also had their dedicated admirers among Sunderland's support. Chris Makin slots right into the cult heroes bracket because, when Sunderland were flying under Peter Reid with the front two of Niall Quinn and Kevin Phillips the most lethal goalscoring partnership in the land, right-back Makin still managed to be many supporters' favourite player, and that was some achievement.

> *When we were flying in the late '90s Kevin Phillips and Niall Quinn got all of the headlines and rightly so as goalscorers, but it's a team game and Chris Makin was a vital part of that team He was my favourite because he seemed to sum the team's attitude up. He wasn't going to let anybody get the better of him, and he always looked like he was enjoying playing for Sunderland. His partnership with Nicky Summerbee was fantastic, and the pair of them were perfect for each other.*
> Dave Smith, Sunderland supporter, Durham.

Once a player has that kind of affinity with Sunderland fans, he can count on it forever so long as he does not blot his copybook in their eyes, by for instance rejecting a potential return or wearing a dodgy T-shirt – not that Lee Clark, good player though he was, was ever a cult hero on Wearside. For Makin there are no such blemishes and in 20 years time if he wants to turn up and do the half-time draw he will still be guaranteed a great ovation, complete with the invitation to 'Shoot!'

'Every time I played against Sunderland I got a fantastic reception. The fans at Sunderland were unbelievable towards me. I came back with Ipswich for the first game of the season a few months after I'd left and got an exceptionally good welcome. That was great because it's always good to know you've been appreciated by supporters.' That kind of reception, whether turning out against Sunderland at home or away, was maintained right up until his final appearance at the Stadium of Light in Southampton colours in November 2006.

Chris played for 10 clubs in a career spanning 16 years and over 400 League appearances across England and France. Inevitably in such a career there were ups and downs, not only in terms of success on the pitch but with fans too: 'I got on well with the Marseille fans, they were good supporters. To start with I had a good relationship with Oldham fans, but it got a bit weird when they got onto me for being a big Man United fan. It soured things because I was taking a bit of stick for that, which was stupid because I'd been with Oldham since I was about 10 or 11.'

Having started training with Oldham at such a young age, Chris signed as an associated schoolboy with them in the summer of 1987 and had a glimpse into the future less than a year later when he sampled playing a home game at Sunderland. That was in an England shirt when he played at Roker Park against Brazil. 'We were just kids and we were very excited to be playing Brazil, but they were a poor side and we beat them twice, at Wembley and at Roker. It was a night game at Roker Park, and I got on for the last 15 or 20 minutes' remembers Chris, then representing Bury Schools FA as part of an England team that included two other schoolboys destined to become Sunderland players: Lee Clark and Marcus Stewart.

By the time Chris was wearing England white on Wearside he had been drafted into the national School of Excellence at Lilleshall, a hot house of schoolboy talent where he progressed, going on to sign as a professional for Oldham Athletic in September 1991.

Latterly the Latics have sunk to the lower divisions they've been traditionally known to populate, but when Chris signed pro they were sitting in the middle of the top flight having won the Second Division a year earlier, swapping places with Sunderland who were relegated. Indeed, Oldham were founder members of the FA Premier League when it began in 1992 as Oldham progressed under manager Joe Royle, who by that time had been in charge at Boundary Park for a decade and had succeeded in delivering top-flight football to the club for the first time since before the war.

Just as Oldham's stock has fallen since the start of Chris's career, Wigan Athletic's has risen massively. At the start of his first full season Chris joined them on loan in the Third Division at their modest Springfield Park home, Dave Whelan and his millions having not yet arrived to transform the club into one of football's nouveau riche. It was under the tutelage of his manager, former Northern Ireland international Bryan Hamilton, that Chris took his first steps in the League. Playing at left-back, Makin made his bow at Swansea, doing well enough to play 15 consecutive games in his three-month loan.

Astonishingly the man called 'Shoot!' at Sunderland took only four games to score! Netting in a 2–2 draw with Hartlepool he repeated the trick the following month with the winner against West Brom! On that occasion he did have more of an opportunity, operating in midfield as he had often done as a youngster.

While the Wigan loan spell was a great success, things could not have been much worse when Chris made a temporary move to Preston: 'I went there as a young lad and wished I hadn't. I didn't want to go but was persuaded to. John Beck was Preston's manager at the time, and it was all about long balls and long throw-ins. They had a plastic pitch that people wore tracksuit bottoms to play on. As it happened, after I joined them on loan I got shingles which was very painful, so I never played for them and went back to Oldham.'

Makin's big break came in October 1993 with his top-flight debut for Oldham at home to Arsenal. Joe Royle's men were struggling and had a problem at left-back, where Chris became the fourth man used in that position in the first dozen games. Up against the likes of Ian Wright, Alan Smith and Anders Limpar, the debutant had his work cut out, helping his side to keep a clean sheet against George Graham's Gunners, who were temporarily missing the 'one' bit from '1–0 to the Arsenal' as it was their third in a run of four successive goalless draws.

Chris kept his place playing his part in a 1–0 win away to Chelsea followed up with four further consecutive appearances, the 'goal machine' scoring the winner against Norwich on only his fifth start!

From Christmas onwards Makin did not miss a match as he established himself in the team. For a young lad making his way in the game, a first top-flight season becalmed in mid-table would still be an adventure, but there was never a dull moment for Chris as Oldham battled unsuccessfully against the drop while also going on a fabulous Cup run.

After conceding in a 2–1 third-round win over Derby, Oldham's defence remained unbreached in four games taking them to a Wembley semi-final against Manchester United, where they led through an extra-time goal from Neil Pointon. Just as it looked as if a fifth clean successive Cup clean sheet would be chalked up Mark Hughes broke Oldham hearts, with one of the best of all the spectacular goals he scored in a sparkling career, to earn United a replay, which they won convincingly at Manchester City's Maine Road.

Chris bounced back from the double disappointment of relegation and Cup heartache to end the season with a medal, being part of the England Under-21 team that won the Toulon tournament in France. Beginning with a substitute appearance against Russia, he played five times in nine days, starting the other four games including the Final which saw England beat Portugal. It was not the first Final Chris had represented his country in, having been part of the National School squad who lost 2–0 to Spain in an Italian tournament six years earlier.

Returning from France, Chris was to have two more seasons at Oldham before crossing over the Channel again, this time in search of club football. Season 1994–95 saw him play over half of Oldham's games, but he missed Latics' trip to Roker Park as he would also do in the following campaign. He did, though, come up against Sunderland for the first time in a goalless January 1995 home draw and again as Sunderland won 2–1 at Boundary Park midway through a run of nine successive wins en route to the 1996 Championship title.

As Sunderland prepared for a first-ever tilt at the Premiership, Makin was calling time on his first club and looking further afield, moving into French football.

'Marseille was fantastic' says Chris. 'At the time I was determined to go, and I was one of the first Bosman moves. Marseille is an unbelievable club and the fans are much more passionate than in the rest of French football.' It was their first year back in the top flight after they had been punished by relegation after the match-fixing scandals that led to the banning of their president Bernard Tapie.

Playing 29 times in a 38 game season as Marseille comfortably finished in mid-table to consolidate their place back in the French First Division, Chris was content to stay and look ahead to moving onwards and upwards as Marseille sought to re-establish themselves as France's leading side, but the best spell of his career was beckoning him on Wearside. Peter Reid had been interested in Makin when Chris was at Oldham, but with the player bound for France on a Bosman the Sunderland manager had to be patient in his search for the full-back.

'Reidy came in for me to try and bring me back to England, but I really didn't want to leave. Once Marseille knew they could get money for me, though, that was it. Then, as now, French football is always desperate for money, and I was threatened with all sorts if I didn't leave and let them take the fee. I was told I'd play in the reserves all year and wouldn't get a game.

'Obviously the pull of the North Sea meant I couldn't resist the possibility of leaving the South of France, so I came to Sunderland. I had talks at Roker Park, which was being demolished and I stayed in the Seaburn Hotel. I looked out of the window at the sea that was just so grey and thought, "What have I done coming here?" I went to the opening game at the Stadium of Light against Ajax, though and thought "I'll have a bit of this" because in the end, while living in the South of France, is like being on holiday all of the time, in the end your choices as a player are not about the lifestyle but about football, and there were good football reasons to come to Sunderland. I already knew Sunderland's reputation for their fans, and I could see that for myself at the Ajax match.'

Sunderland paid a reported £500,000 for the former Oldham full-back, and it quickly began to look like money well spent, as at 24 and coming into his best years Makin the Mackem was born. Making his home debut in the first-ever competitive game at the Stadium of Light meant he was in tandem with the club at the start of a new era, and for a Manchester-born lad the opposition of Manchester City were a team he could not wait to get stuck into.

'I've always been a big Man United supporter, but I'm from a family of City fans so to make my home debut for Sunderland against Man City was brilliant. It was a Friday night and the atmosphere was just superb. We beat City 3–1, and as we had the weekend off I had a few pints with my dad afterwards in the hotel, but the thing I remember most about the match was Sacko [assistant manager Bobby Saxton] going absolutely off it afterwards because we'd let them have too many chances and he wasn't at all happy.'

Playing every game until injury in mid-Autumn, Makin was an instant hit with the fans but, though he ended the season with just over 30 appearances, for much of the campaign he found himself on the bench: 'Darren Bullock had really done me in a game against Swindon. He should have been sent off but he got away with it even though he'd damaged my ankle ligaments. By the time I was fit again the team were on a massive run and Darren Holloway was doing really well, so I couldn't get back in. When I did play I managed to help make a few goals, and when we ended up in the Play-offs I just wanted to be as fit as possible so that if I got the chance to play I was going to be an asset.'

Used at left-back in the first of the Play-offs away to Sheffield United in place of Mickey Gray, Chris was not involved at all in the fabulous second leg against the Blades. Back then, only three subs were named, but Chris made the cut in the Final and was on the bench at Wembley for what proved to be an epic with Charlton: 'Clive Mendonca turned the lads inside out that day and Darren Holloway had a poor first half, which was unusual because he had been playing really well. I had a feeling I'd get put on, and when I did I was determined to enjoy it and was running around like a headless chicken.'

The match, of course, is remembered as a classic, with Sasa Ilic's penalty save from Michael Gray the moment emblazoned on the memory. Gray was Sunderland's left-back, a local lad who bounced back to show he was the best in the country when capped the following season. As is well documented, Chris Makin was not exactly renowned for his goalscoring prowess, but while Gray's failure is indelibly imprinted in supporters' minds it should be remembered that Makin was one of those mentally strong enough to step forward and put his neck on the line.

In such situations the walk for the taker from the halfway line to the penalty area looks dreadfully long from the stands. It must be a form of torture for players, especially on such a high-pressure occasion when the stakes are at their highest. Gray has to live with the memory of his miss, and for a heart-stopping moment Makin thought he would be the player with that weight to carry: 'I definitely thought he'd saved it. I knew which way I was going to put it but as I smacked it I saw he was going the right way and I thought "He's going to stop it". Then for a fraction of a second I thought it's going to hit the post. As it happened, the 'keeper got a hand to it, but the shot had enough power that he couldn't quite keep it out and it trickled in. The sheer relief at that moment was unbelievable.'

Football can be like a soap opera and nowhere more than at Sunderland. For too many seasons the goings on at SAFC could have been renamed 'Deadenders' or even 'Bore-a-nation Street.' Players become characters, some loved more than others, and in a penalty shoot-out the players know who is taking the spot-kicks but fans have to wait until each new penalty to see the next 'victim' of that manager's 'Russian Roulette', as the next penalty taker steps forward from the group and begins the long walk forward. When a favourite emerges there is no need for discussion. There is a collective inner feeling of 'Oh God, if someone's going to miss please don't let it be him.' That was certainly the feeling with Chris, who after all was anything but deadly in front of goal.

'The reason I volunteered to take one was that I'd had a disappointing end to the season. When the game went to penalties there weren't many volunteers stepping forward, so I decided to stand up for one rather than spend the rest of the summer wishing I had done,' says Chris, giving an insight into his mentality, indicating that wish to stand up and do his bit. In the circumstances it is a clear example of why the supporters took Makin to their hearts and why, it should be said, no one ever thought the worse of Micky Gray.

It was not the first time Makin had stepped forward in a penalty shoot-out. He had scored one for England as a 15-year-old in a 10–9 Nordic Cup victory over Denmark. The same tournament had seen 'Shoot!' Makin join Robbie Fowler, Trevor Sinclair and Garry Flitcroft on the score sheet in a 4–0 win over Finland.

Defeat was hard to take; although as in the Milk Cup Final of 13 years before – also dependent on a penalty miss – the red-and-white army took it on their chin, congratulated the victors and looked to the future. Having scored four goals and all of their first six penalties, surely only the soap opera that is Sunderland could score 10 times at Wembley and still lose.

It was a long, long journey home from the Play-off Final to the North East and an even longer summer waiting for the next season to start, but when it did come round it was certainly worth waiting for as, inspired by Peter Reid and magnificently captained by Kevin Ball, Sunderland amassed 105 points – more than any team had ever done in any division.

That glorious 1998–99 season saw Sunderland bid farewell to the 20th century by playing football of the quality the club's finest sides of the century would have been proud of. The team was based on partnerships. First and foremost was the partnership between players and supporters, a partnership that the team's talisman Niall Quinn insisted he had come back to find when he returned to the club as chairman in 2006.

The Mighty Quinn, of course, was partnered by 'SuperKev', Kevin Phillips, the pair notching 41 goals in 78 appearances between them. Both missed games through injury, but stand-ins Michael Bridges and Danny Dichio carried the torch in their absence. Strikers cannot score without ammunition, and on the left flank Micky Gray and Allan 'Magic' Johnston were sheer brilliance. Bally locked down central-midfield, dovetailing immaculately with either Lee Clark or the incisive Alex Rae, while in central-defence Paul Butler and Andy Melville were solid in front of first-class new 'keeper Thomas Sorensen, and whenever a gap appeared utility man Darren Williams would slot in so you could not see the join.

That leaves the right wing, which was the preserve of Makin and his fellow Mancunian Nicky Summerbee. They were every bit as effective as the Gray/Johnston combo on the left but contrasting in style. Makin was tougher in the tackle than his fellow full-back Gray, Summerbee was in no way as tricky on the ball as 'Magic' Johnston but did his job every bit as well. Just as Dick Malone describes how his partnership with Bobby Kerr meant they were on the same wavelength and automatically knew where to find their partner without looking, Summerbee would track back to cover Chris just as Makin would bomb forward to take defenders away from his winger. The beauty

Chris Makin in 1999.

of Summerbee was that while 'Magic' was tying defenders in knots, leaving them on their backsides on the left, Nicky didn't need to bother to beat them. All he was interested in was finding half a yard of space to whip in his cross. That he succeeded in doing consistently, to the delight of the men on the end of his usually immaculate crosses. Without doubt he was one of the best wingers Sunderland have had in living memory, so does Chris believe his partnership with Summerbee was the best he ever experienced? 'Yes, definitely. There's no doubt about that. The season after the Play-off Final we had a great squad. Reidy had put a bit of experience back into the team, but we still had a good average age and we proved what a good side we were. If we'd beaten Charlton on penalties at Wembley promotion might have come too soon for us and we could have struggled in the Premiership, but by the time we went up a year later we knew we were a Premiership side. We'd changed into a different animal, we were mentally stronger.'

That side achieved the club's highest League placing in half a century and Chris was right at the heart of the game that set that season up. A heavy opening-day hammering at Chelsea was followed up by a hard-fought victory over Play-off winners Watford, a goalless home draw with Arsenal and defeat at Leeds. Going into the first derby of the season at St James' Park, Sunderland sat 16th in a table of 20 having scored just one goal that was not a penalty.

Defeat at Newcastle is always unthinkable for a Sunderland supporter, but defeat on this occasion would officially stamp 'bad start' on Sunderland's season report as they looked to avoid a fourth first season relegation in five promotions. A thunderstorm of biblical proportions greeted the gladiators, and within half an hour the Magpies had a lead they took into the break. Sunderland have had many great victories on Tyneside, but this was one of the best. Nicky Summerbee did what he did best and found Niall Quinn's head, with Quinny finishing it off to bring the red-and-whites level.

Much was made of Magpie manager Ruud Gullitt leaving Alan Shearer on the bench, but he was on the pitch by the time Kevin Phillips scored Sunderland's brilliant winner. Much of Makin's popularity stemmed from his Joe Bolton/John Kay like willingness to flatten any opponent in possession. When that opponent is your local rivals' main man the fans love it even more. Phillips' brilliant chip to win the game came from another great Summerbee pass, but the attacking players can only win games if someone has won the ball first, and that goal stemmed from Makin knocking Shearer into next week, as he relates: 'It was a cracking tackle. It was wet on top, and Paul Butler had got right up his backside so when the ball came to him he took a bad touch and I was into him. It was a belter! He got me back two minutes later and whacked my head into the post, but we'd scored by then!'

That victory, and the manner of it, gave the club and its supporters great belief. It was the first in a run of 10 wins in 14 Premiership games. The next two away games were won 5–0 and 4–0, with a 5–0 away Cup win thrown in for good measure. These were dream times for Sunderland coming on the back of the 105-point season, with Makin an essential part of the team, missing just four games all season.

The final day of the season took Sunderland to Tottenham where, although defeated 3–1 having had Alex Rae sent off, there was still cause for celebration as 'Shoot!' finally got a goal. 'I went on an overlap, and all of a sudden Kevin Phillips slotted me in. I just thought, "Bollocks, I'll have a go." I remember seeing Mark Hughes score one like it with the outside of his right foot, and so I tried it. Even I'll admit it was a good goal!'

Makin is not exaggerating. It was a cracker. Like his predecessor Dick Malone, who only ever scored twice for the Lads but made them both superb, Chris's goal was a beauty. It was a reward fans wanted to see him get. John Kay, for instance, never ever managed a first-team goal. Getting on the score sheet only added to the shouts of 'Shoot' every time Makin got the ball, but although he never scored another it is worth recalling his Wembley penalty and also a 'goal' he claimed but was not awarded on only his fifth appearance for the club, when a shot of his against Oxford found the back of the net but was finally attributed to Oxford's Joey Beauchamp who had deflected it.

Sunderland's second season after promotion contained a certain symmetry with the first, seventh again and another 2–1 win away to Newcastle: 'They got an early goal again in the second game, but we took over and deserved the win. They had no excuses left then because we were the top dogs. They always used to get off to a good start against us. There was the time they went two up at Sunderland before we came back at them. Kev got a couple to draw the match, and we should have won. We probably would have if the game had gone on a little bit longer.

'Those wins at Newcastle showed just how strong we were mentally. Newcastle went 1–0 up early on in both games and both times we came back and beat them. We didn't get lucky and score a couple of lucky goals, we dominated those games. There were a few noises that we'd won the first game because the weather hadn't let Newcastle play, but we went back the following season when the weather was perfect and beat them again. You don't dominate and win two away games against the same team if you're not better than them.'

However, even in a season that saw 11 debutants and 14 departures Makin's exit shocked and disappointed the crowd. Ever present until the end of November, Chris was then in and out of the side until March, when he was surprisingly sold following a home draw with Aston Villa, Sunderland raking in almost three times the half-million pounds they had paid for him. In 'soap opera Sunderland' there are always rumours – and that's exactly what rumours are, just rumours. One that persisted was that Chris had had more away fixtures than were on the fixture list but manager Peter Reid decided to make changes and so Chris went to Ipswich: 'I'd heard a couple of whispers a week or two before that Sunderland were going to sell me, and when you hear whispers like that in football you know your time is up. I wasn't happy about it and I didn't want to go, but it happens in football and I'd had a week or two to get my head around it when the transfer came about. The funny thing was my last game for Sunderland was against Aston Villa, and a week later I played against them again when I was making my debut for Ipswich.

'At the time, Sunderland and Ipswich were both going for European spots. I think Ipswich were about third in the League at the time and they were a good club that I liked, but I was still disappointed to be leaving Sunderland.'

Indeed the Tractor Boys finished two places above Sunderland and qualified for the UEFA Cup, but now following his retirement in 2008 Chris looks back on his career and knows that the time when he had the most success 'Makin whoopee' was at Sunderland: 'There were big wins at Newcastle because they were derby games. The other ones that stand out for me were the Birmingham game when we won the Division One trophy because it was such a party, and we won the game which was the most important thing, and then there was the Chelsea game. We got hammered by them 4–0 at Stamford Bridge in our first match after promotion. They should have had 10 that day because they wasted a load of chances. It was men against boys, but when they came to our place we were 4–0 up against them by half-time. The difference in class between them and us when they beat us was massive, but the gap was the other way round at the Stadium of Light, and it was awesome. We just sat in the dressing room at half-time and were speechless. It was an incredible feeling, absolutely unbelievable.'

Chris's boss at Ipswich was someone who had also impressed in the number-two shirt for Sunderland, George Burley. In years to come Burley would sign Chris twice more: 'Obviously he rated me, and the feeling was mutual. I know that he'd been highly thought of as a player at Sunderland at the end of his career, but he was a legend in Ipswich. I played for him at Ipswich, Derby and Southampton, but although we both played the same position in different ways I don't think he altered my game at all. He knew what he was getting when he signed me. I was always an old fashioned full-back who understood that my first job was to defend. I always thought if I get forward and get some crosses in that's great, but first and foremost I'm there to stop any crosses going in to my own box.'

While Sunderland got close to European qualification a couple of times in the first few years of the 21st century, Ipswich gave Makin the opportunity to play in European competition for the first time. His year at Marseille had been restricted to domestic French football, but the men from Portman Road knocked out Torpedo Moscow and Helsingborg of Sweden thanks to second-leg away wins before a glamour tie with Inter Milan. Chris's side took a 1–0 advantage to the San Siro only to be well beaten with a Christian Vieri hat-trick signalling the end of Ipswich's hopes of a second UEFA Cup triumph.

It was not just in Europe that Ipswich dreams ended. A mid-season run of seven wins in eight games that included a 5–0 hammering of Sunderland looked to have rekindled the Suffolk side's form of the year before, but a disastrous late-season run that began with a 6–0 home reverse to Liverpool sent them spinning back to the second tier. How much of that was due to the effects of a European campaign with a relatively small squad is open to question, certainly Makin missed the last seven games having only previously missed one. Sunderland needed Ipswich to lose on the last day to be sure of staying up. Liverpool duly finished what they had started by sticking five past them without reply at Anfield, while Sunderland took a point from Derby who were already relegated to ensure a four-point gap.

It was Millwall rather than Moscow and Milan on Makin's fixture list in his second full season at Portman Road, and yet astonishingly despite relegation Ipswich had another season of UEFA Cup football ahead of them courtesy of qualification through the 'Fair Play League'. Chris Makin as a regular member of a team that won a 'Fair Play League' may surprise some, but while Makin was a physical player who got stuck in and certainly 'liked a tackle' he was not the type of defender to simply foul people and hope to get away with it. He was a quality player, able to stay on his feet, and while he took his defensive duties to the boundaries of the laws he rarely went beyond them, being sent off just once in a Sunderland shirt.

As in Chris's 1998 Wembley Play-off with Sunderland, it was a penalty shoot-out that did for Ipswich's European campaign. Having eased past a couple of minor sides Ipswich were two minutes away from further progress when a late aggregate equaliser resulted in their tie at Slovan Liberec in the Czech Republic going to spot-kicks. Having missed two of their first four, Ipswich were eliminated before Chris could be called upon. As with Sunderland, Ipswich are one of those clubs with a desperate record on penalty shoot-outs – this was the ninth they had taken part in and the eighth they had lost.

Ipswich's rise from 20th in what is now the Championship at the point they returned from that tie to an end-of-season finish of seventh is evidence of the toll a European campaign takes on a League season, but despite the Tractor Boys ploughing on relentlessly for the rest of the season they had left themselves too much to do.

By this point Makin was playing once again for his former Oldham manager Joe Royle who had succeeded Burley, but an injury five games into the 2003–04 season signalled the end of his time in East Anglia. As with his move from Sunderland to Ipswich that saw Chris debut for his new club against his final opponents at the club he had left, his debut for his new side Leicester proved to be against his final opponents at Ipswich, namely West Ham.

In signing for Micky Adams's Leicester in the Championship Makin joined a squad of well-known players including David Connolly and Dion Dublin, and alongside him in the back four was ex-Arsenal man Martin Keown. Whereas there had been some exciting times at Ipswich, Chris's year at Leicester proved to be a lean one. In and out of a side that finished 15th, he played in just under half the games, missing both matches against Sunderland who took the title that season. Even in the FA Cup, where the Foxes reached the quarter-final, Chris did not play beyond the third round.

Indeed by the time of the quarter-final he had rejoined George Burley on loan at Derby. Having made what proved to be his last Leicester appearance back at Ipswich in mid-February, he completed the season as part of Derby's promotion push, even playing against Leicester but having already missed the Rams' fixtures with Sunderland.

Come the summer and Makin was on the move again, this time to Reading where he was part of their record-breaking team that broke Sunderland's 105-point record. Dislodging full-backs Graeme Murty and Nicky Shorey – one the club captain and the other a future England international – was a tough job and Makin was restricted to a dozen League appearances, but it did place him in a unique position as the only man to play in the two highest-ever points winning teams (ex-Sunderland man John Oster was also in that Reading side but had not joined Sunderland until after the 105-point haul).

'They were very, very similar' reckons Chris in assessing the 105 and 106-point winning teams he played in. 'Both were very strong teams. At Reading as the season wore on they would grind down teams and take over games. When that happens confidence comes and the football comes through as you know you are a good side. If I was to put the two sides together I'd say Sunderland's 105-point side were the better team, even though Reading achieved one more point, but there wasn't much between them whichever way you look at it except that at Sunderland they expected to get promotion, whereas at Reading they wanted promotion – but given the size of the club they couldn't expect it. It's a good, well-run club though Reading, it just doesn't have the sort of fan base Sunderland has.'

Chris Makin on his final appearance at the Stadium of Light, playing for Southampton in November 2006.

Meanwhile, having become manager of Southampton, George Burley signed Chris for the third time in August 2006. The move gave Chris a final game at the Stadium of Light when the Saints earned a draw in November of that year, but Makin was out injured when Sunderland hit the top of the League when winning the return game at Easter. Nonetheless, he was back in action come the end of the season when he ended up back at Derby County in a Play-off semi-final that went to penalties. Chris did not need to face the dilemma of whether to take one as he had been subbed late on, but yet again his side lost a shoot-out, leaving him to countenance another season in the Championship.

That proved to be short-lived as a routine home draw with Colchester in September 2007 turned out to be the final game of his career. Although it was several months until time was officially called on his playing days, as every avenue was explored to see if Chris could continue, the end came as no surprise: 'I knew straight away. I'd had a similar injury at Ipswich, but this one was much more severe, and so as the day approached when it was confirmed that I was finished I'd had the time to mentally prepare myself for it.'

Of the other cult heroes featured here, those that have hung their boots up include one in social work, two in haulage, one supplying parts to the motor trade and a postman, but what the future will hold for Chris is as yet unknown. 'That's a big question for me. I've moved back to Manchester and sorting the insurance out for my hip injury takes a long time. It was a good time to move back to Manchester because my son Cameron is five so it was the right time to get him settled into a local school. The future possibilities I don't know about yet, other than I know I'm going to take a break from football.'

As always, time moves inexorably on. Chris played in the first game at the Stadium of Light, and no doubt in the decades to come there will be many more cult heroes, and in all likelihood a fair few of them will continue to be full-backs. Already history looks like it might be repeating itself as a young Manchester-born right-back builds a reputation as a solid, no nonsense defender. Many supporters have drawn comparisons between Phil Bardsley and Chris Makin, with Chris observing: 'I saw Phil play for Sunderland against Manchester City when I came up to the Stadium of Light to see a game towards the end of Sunderland's first season back in the Premier League under Roy Keane. He played well that day, and while he's not a straightforward full-back you can tell straight away that he loves a tackle. I don't know if you can play like I did when I was at Sunderland in today's game. Looking at Phil Bardsley you can see that he wants to rattle the winger, but in the modern game you have to stay on your feet. He's done well so far, and I hope he can go on to do well at the club. I rate him, but you have to look at the top full-backs now. People like Patrice Evra and Gael Clichy are more or less wingers, and that's what you have to aim for.'

Julio Arca talks about it being his destiny to play for Sunderland. Chris Makin was born on the night Sunderland's triumphant team of 1973 brought the FA Cup back to Wearside, so it seems appropriate that Sunderland should have been the club where the fans took to him the most. A strong, dependable player, good enough to be an integral part of a record-breaking team but not a world beater even in his own imagination, Chris Makin was a typical Sunderland cult hero and like every one of them will always be guaranteed the warmest of welcomes whenever he steps foot back in Sunderland.

WHO NEEDS CANTONA?

RICHARD ORD

Defender

Born: 3 March 1970, Murton, County Durham.
Signed for Sunderland: Associate schoolboy 1 March 1984
Apprentice 1 July 1986
Professional 4 July 1987
Transferred: 24 July 1998 to QPR £675,000

Sunderland: 223+20 League appearances, 7 goals
256+28 total appearances, 8 goals
York City: (Loan) 2 February 1990, 3 League appearances, 0 goals
QPR: 24 July 1998, 0 League appearances

There have been many cult heroes at Sunderland in addition to the favourites interviewed in *Sunderland Cult Heroes*. Perhaps you have a player who to you summed up why you support Sunderland, there would be something about him that you especially liked. He might even have been your hero and no one else's. Possibly it was a player you felt was not appreciated by the crowd, so you would stick by him. Maybe out there there is a dedicated follower of Denis Longhorn, Milton 'Tyson' Nunez, or Wayne Entwistle.

This chapter looks at some of the players who, like Vic Halom, Joe Bolton, Nyron Nosworthy and so on, undoubtedly had their cult followings. Chief among these is the player whose chant spawned this chapter heading: Richard Ord, after all as the song goes: 'Who needs Cantona when we've got Dickie Ord?'

Richard Ord in 1993.

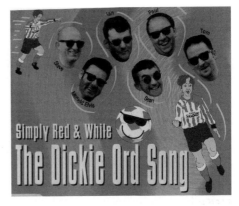

The answer, of course, is that Sunderland did indeed need Eric Cantona, one of the most skilful players of his generation – unless, of course, Sunderland had Howard Wilkinson as a manager; it was Wilko who sold Cantona from Leeds to Manchester United for a bargain £1 million! As it was, Sunderland supporters made the most of their home-grown defender Dickie Ord. Like Dick Malone, Ordy was a tall defender capable of showing deft control that belied his lanky stature.

A group of fans even released a CD: *Who Needs Cantona When We've Got Dickie Ord?* in his honour. Beginning: 'Robbie Fowler, Collymore, Vialli & Gullit/Dickie Ord's the boy we've got to bite the Premier bullet.' The most significant lines though were: 'The great thing is and it makes us proud/If he wasn't on the pitch he'd be with us in the crowd.' Supporters like to know that the shirt worn by players is as important to them as it is to the fan who has not only paid good money to watch but will spend the rest of the week dwelling on last week's performance, wondering about next week's, and often defending the team's record after yet another disappointment.

> *'Who needs Cantona when we've got Dickie Ord?' was a chant of some irony at the time of its terrace invention, but as his SAFC career progressed Dickie did develop into a decent centre-back whose cultured left foot was often a joy to behold. An avid Sunderland fan as a youngster, he came from a family who all had red-and-white blood in their veins and who followed the club all over the country. Ord was also the recipient of one of the finest pop writing lines of all-time when the world-renowned Simply Red and White recorded their follow up to Cheer Up Peter Reid, Who Needs Cantona When We've got Dickie Ord?. The immortal line of: 'He's from Murton One thing's certain, he's not scared of these' could never have been penned by Lennon or McCartney, Jagger or Richards or the Gallagher brothers. Nope, never!*
> Tom Lynn, Sunderland supporter, Sunderland and member of Simply Red and White.

Being a local lad and ardent Sunderland supporter, Ordy was onto a winner from the start. His debut coinciding with the club's biggest win in over three decades did him no harm either.

> *Richard Ord would have the cheesiest grin you'd ever seen when he scored and would just run around celebrating like crazy, but who could blame him? He was just a local kid that suddenly found himself playing for his boyhood idols. Could any of us claim we'd behave any different?*
> Andrew Smithson, Sunderland supporter, Sunderland.

Eric Gates scored four goals in a 7–0 win over Southend in November 1987, but that match is mainly remembered for 17-year-old Ord's assured and composed performance in central-defence. Here, it was felt, was perhaps the best home-grown defender since Colin Todd, whose own debut at the same age as Ord had come 21 years earlier.

Establishing himself in the side the following season and going mental when he scored his first-ever goal cemented Richard's place in supporters' affections, but these plummeted at the first home game of his second full season, 1989–90, when, standing in for Gary Bennett, Ord was deemed to have been at fault as four goals were leaked in a home defeat to Ipswich. It proved to be a promotion season despite Play-off defeat due to Sunderland benefiting from the punishment meted out to Play-off winners Swindon, however Ord featured in a mere handful of games, the last being in early December, ironically in the return match with Ipswich.

Winning the fans over in the way that fellow cult hero Dick Malone had begun for Ordy when he stepped in to fill what was then a problematic left-back slot for Sunderland. Drafted in for a top-flight debut away to that most physical of teams, Wimbledon's 'Crazy Gang', Ordy stepped up to the plate and gradually began to re-establish the reputation people had jumped to heap onto his young shoulders when barely out of school. Despite good runs in the team, though, it was not until 1994–95 that Ordy managed to equal the achievement of his first full season and reach 30 League appearances in a season, but when he did play people warmed to his performances. Mixed in with the determination that was evident, the crowd began to notice little flashes of skill in tight situations.

By the time of the 1996 Championship win, which was firmly based on the Division's meanest defence, Ordy was a player who hardly missed a game and was by now a firm favourite, not least

Champions, 1996: Ord is second from the right, on the front row.

indicated by the CD in his honour as Sunderland prepared for their first-ever attempt at Premier League football. Although the team struggled, Ordy was a success, other than for a pair of red cards within a month.

Awarded a testimonial, Richard was unfortunate to miss his own match against Steau Bucharest through injury. That bad luck continued when, after fully recovering from injury, he ended his Sunderland career in a 1998 Play-off defeat at Sheffield United after which he was transferred to QPR only to suffer a career-ending injury within the first few minutes of his first appearance.

Returning to the North East, Richard Ord tried his hand at being a publican and became a leading light in the establishment of the first-class indoor footballing 'Soccarena' at Durham. Fittingly, as the song said, 'If he wasn't on the pitch he'd be with us in the crowd' and indeed Ordy is now a familiar face among the fans at the Stadium of Light.

> *Murton's finest was not only a superb defender but a real heart-on-your sleeve character who epitomised the dream of a Sunderland fan playing for his home-town club. His fearless approach and astute reading of the match was interespersed with some barnstorming charges forward which inspired the 'Cantona chant'. His efforts to lift the waning spirits after the Play-off Final defeat were testimony to his devotion to 'his' team and 'his' cause.*
> Mike Love, Sunderland supporter, SENSSA.

REUBEN AGBOOLA

Defender

Born:	Camden, London, 30 May 1962.
Signed for Sunderland:	9 January 1985 from Southampton, £150,000
Transferred:	9 November 1991 to Swansea City

Southampton:	July 1978, 89+1 League appearances, 0 goals
Sunderland:	9 January 1985, 129+11 League appearances, 0 goals
	156+14 total appearances, 0 goals
Charlton Athletic:	(Loan) April 1986, 1 League appearance, 0 goals
Port Vale:	(Loan) 22 November 1990, 9 League appearances, 0 goals
Swansea City:	November 1991, 26+ 2 League appearances, 0 goals
Woking:	August 1993
Gosport Borough:	November 1994

A teammate of Richard Ord's during his early years with the club was Londoner Reuben Agboola. Reuben was a typically tough Sunderland full-back and attracted his own group of fans who afforded him cult-hero status, the cry of 'Reubennn, Ruebennn' accompanying a good tackle or pass, but never a goal, as like John Kay he was a full-back who never found the net. Like several Sunderland cult heroes, Reuben was a tough customer. Although London born, he was also the first Sunderland player to be capped by an African country when he twice represented Nigeria in 1991.

Reuben Abboola in 1989.

Indeed, playing for Nigeria made Agboola the first Sunderland player to be capped by any country outside the UK and Republic of Ireland. However, while Ord's debut caused statisticians to rifle through the record books looking for as big a win as Ordy was initially involved in, Agboola's first appearance failed to make it into the records at all.

Signed by Len Ashurst, a manager who should know a left-back when he sees one given his stature as Sunderland's record outfield appearance maker, having made the left-back berth his own for over a decade, Agboola did well in the opening half of his debut against Liverpool only to find the match abandoned at half-time due to the frosty conditions. With that game duly expunged from the records, Reuben's official bow came back at the club he had just left, Southampton.

Reuben had become a sinner not a saint when he had fallen out with Southampton manager Lawrie

Team coach card game with Stan Cummins.

Sliding in on Leeds United's David Batty.

McMenemy, so imagine how thrilled he was during his first close season as a Sunderland player. His new club had been relegated, but at least they had reached a Cup Final...although he had not been involved as he was Cup tied and the manager who bought him was sacked. Oh well, there is always the opportunity for a new start...except that your new club's new manager is the old manager you had fallen out with, resulting in you moving from one end of the country to the other!

Agboola played just 19 of the 82 League matches Lawrie McMenemy took charge of for Sunderland, during which he left them doomed to drop to the lowest point in the club's history. Recalled to the team immediately after McMenemy resorted to his notorious midnight flit, Reuben became a regular in the following season's promotion triumph.

Over the next couple of campaigns Reuben nailed down the left-back spot for long periods, playing in the 1990 Play-off triumph over Newcastle, and the Wembley game with Swindon that resulted in promotion by default.

Quick across the ground, Reuben Omojola Folasanje Agboola is, alphabetically at least, the very first in the list of over 900 players who have represented Sunderland. Playing the first five top-flight fixtures after the fortuitous 1990 promotion, he spent time on loan to Port Vale, returning for a farewell with one more Sunderland appearance in September 1991 before moving on to Swansea and later into non-League with Woking and Gosport Borough.

> *Reuben's child went to the same school as us, meaning ours was probably the only playground in Sunderland where most kids were fighting to 'be' Agboola and not Gabbiadini at playtime. The doting father would often be waiting at the gate come home time – another reason for us to long for the bell to ring. Malcolm Crosby's children attended the school at the same time; how we got any work done I'll never know.*
> Andrew Smithson, Sunderland supporter, Sunderland.

ALEX RAE

Midfield

Born: Glasgow, 30 September 1969.
Signed for Sunderland: 1 June 1996, £1 million
Transferred: 19 September 2001 to Wolves, £1.2 million

Bishopbriggs FC
Glasgow Rangers: (Three-month trial)
Falkirk: 1986, 71+12 League appearances, 20 goals
Millwall: August 1990, 205+13 League appearances, 63 goals
Sunderland: 1 June 1996, 90 + 24 League appearances, 12 goals
                         109 + 27 total appearances, 15 goals
Wolves: 9 September 2001, 88+19 League appearances, 15 goals
Glasgow Rangers: 22+12 League appearances, 1 goal
Dundee: 24+2 League appearances, 3 goals
                         Manager from 224 May 2006

Alex Rae was just as tigerish in the tackle as Reuben Agboola. The Scottish midfielder became hugely popular at Sunderland despite a mixture of injuries, suspensions and personal problems meaning he never managed to make as many as 20 consecutive appearances for the Lads.

When he did play, though, Rae was a terrific midfielder. Sunderland have had loads of midfielders who can get it and give it, and a handful who, like Kevin Arnott, could use it once in possession, but Rae had a bit of everything. He certainly had a touch of devilment about him on the pitch, and the fans loved that. Nippy and incisive, Rae certainly had the committed approach that so endeared the likes of Joe Bolton and John Kay to the crowd. He could provide the killer pass and chipped in with his fair share of goals from midfield. He had plenty of courage,

Alex Rae in 1997.

as evidenced by his successful penalty in the 1998 Play-off Final shoot out, and he had a touch of Vic Halom's ability to play to the crowd – such as when twice bouncing the ball off the head of an unimpressed Roy Keane in a heated exchange with Manchester United.

Alex was certainly one for winding up the opposition – unfortunately he also got wound up himself. Only Kevin Ball and Gary Bennett (each with five dismissals) have been sent off more in Sunderland colours than Rae, who saw red four times, yet Bennett and Ball each played comfortably more than twice as many games for the club. Dismissed at Charlton a couple of months before the Play-off game between the clubs, Alex got an early bath at Leeds just over a year later and at Spurs the same season for treating David Ginola to a 'Glasgow Kiss'. To cap off his rap sheet, Rae got involved in a dust up in a crucial and controversial game at home to Manchester United in 2001 being sent off along with Sunderland's Michael Gray and United's future Sunderland player Andy Cole.

Nonetheless, the fans loved the bundle of hyper-energy that was Alex Rae, who added to his popularity by being great crack off the pitch too. Having later satisfied his ambitions to play for Rangers, Alex surprised many by moving into management with Dundee and hugely impressed the footballing public by achieving what so many footballers try to do and fail, namely to overcome drink and personal problems.

> *Loved the club, loved the fans, who loved him. Personally, Alex Rae was one of my all-time favourites to have donned the red-and-white stripes. Committed, talented with no little skill, Rae was a key figure of the side that raced to the Premier League in the late 1990s. Also suffered well-documented off-the-field problems, but it was how he fought back from that which gained an awful lot of respect from Sunderland supporters.*
> Keith Chapman, Sunderland supporter, Jarrow.

> *His fiery character, mischievous antics and exciting talents provided a heady cocktail that was both explosive and exhilarating. His partnership with Lee Clark was one of the most exciting in recent Sunderland history. Bouncing the ball off Roy Keane's head (twice!) bordered on reckless bravado and the cupped ear celebration at Charlton after a superb goal, live long in the memory.*
> Mike Love, Sunderland supporter, SENSSA.

LIONEL PEREZ

Goalkeeper
Born: 24 April 1967, Bagnois Ceze, France.
Signed for Sunderland: 1 August 1996, £200,000
Transferred: 30 June 1998 to Newcastle United, free

Nimes Olympique: 1990
Girondins de Bordeaux: 1993
Nimes Olympique: (Loan) 1994–95

Stade Lavallois:	(Loan) 1995–96
Sunderland:	1 August 1996, 74+1 League appearances
	83+1 total appearances
Newcastle United:	June 1998, 0 League appearances
Olympique Lyonnais:	(Loan) March 1999
Scunthorpe United:	(Loan) October 1999, 9 League appearances
Cambridge United:	March 2000, 78 League appearances
Enfield	
Stevenage Borough	

While Alex Rae and Chris Makin were tucking penalties away in the 1998 Play-off Final against Charlton at Wembley, the goalkeeper getting nowhere near any of the Addick's spot-kicks was Frenchman Lionel Perez. The game had only gone to extra-time after 'Lee-onel' had come unnecessarily charging off his line for a late corner and got nowhere near the ball, leaving Charlton's Richard Rufus to easily score his first goal in 165 games for the Londoners and deny Sunderland victory, and with it promotion.

While Perez could frustrate, he could also thrill. Supporters knew that despite his Wembley abberations, had it not been for him Sunderland would not even be in the Final. His double-save to deny Paul Devlin and Dean Saunders in the pulsating semi-final against Sheffield United was by common consent the best double-save fans had seen since Monty's back at Wembley in 1973.

> *An eccentric in the way he wore his goalkeeper's strip, his general appearance, and his style of goalkeeping in his penalty box. However, he became a fans' modern day Jimmy Montgomery by making his double save in the Play-off semi-finals against Sheffield United.*
>
> Barbara Cromar, Sunderland supporter, Chopwell.

Like Nyron Nosworthy, Perez originally came to the club as a squad player only to quickly be jettisoned into the first team when the man he was understudying was injured. In Lionel's case a career-ending broken leg to Tony Coton soon after he arrived thrust him into the action. Having impressed in a trial match at Gateshead, Perez was taken on only to gift a goal to Aston Villa reserves in the last minute of his first home appearance. Boasting long flowing locks and playing with his sleeves rolled up, he looked a dashing figure. Returning from his single close-season break as a Sunderland player, he returned from the continent with locks shorn and a lovely new blond rinse, but those trademark rolled up sleeves were still in evidence and indeed were symbolic of his commitment, Lionel always looked ready for action.

Despite his eccentricity during his spell as number one, Sunderland signed four other goalkeepers who failed to dislodge him. Lionel did not inspire confidence in his defence because they were always unsure whether he was going to come storming off his line or stay rooted to it. Nonetheless, he endeared himself to the crowd with a string of spectacular saves, a penchant for looking the part and developing a tremendous rapport with the red-and-white army.

Lionel with the long-haired look.

Lionel after his close-season makeover.

> *Eccentricity is a 'keeper's prerogative. When you add Gallic flair and a potency for changing hair styles (and colour) and being the first 'keeper in Sunderland's living memory to play in short sleeves, Lionel's cult status was inevitable. However, such frivolities were only part of a relatively short career which will be remembered for some amazing shot-stopping and lightening quick distribution.*
> Mike Love, Sunderland supporter, SENSSA.

On one occasion at Leicester after Perez had had a blinder, Peter Reid came out of the press room having waxed lyrical about 'Lee-onel's' performance only to go ballistic in the way only Reidy could with his goalkeeper who he discovered had missed the team bus home. The manager had travelled by car and was intending to head off to the North West afterwards, but no amount of offers from press or other club staff to give the hero of the night a lift home would dissuade the manager from changing his plans and taking Perez back to the North East himself. It was a journey Perez desperately wanted to avoid but had to contend with.

On another occasion, after defying Arsenal at Highbury, Perez's compatriot, Gunners manager Arsene Wenger raved about 'Lee-onel's' performance, pointing out the importance of professionalism. Minutes later as the assembled press left the ground, there was Perez hidden behind a burger van smoking a sneaky ciggy before joining his teammates for the homeward journey.

> *Having been rested for the game, Lionel Perez sat with the away fans at the Riverside when we played Middlesbrough in the League Cup one season. Sunderland lost, and as most fans contemplated how they would get to their coach in one piece Lionel came striding past unflinchingly, gave a Gallic shrug to the police as they held back congregating hoards of Boro fans and forced his way through off into the night; all with the sleeves of his denim jacket rolled up of course.*
> Andrew Smithson, Sunderland supporter, Sunderland.

Perez was without doubt a firm cult hero with the fans. He was not the greatest goalkeeper in the world, but at times he looked as if he might be. Perez played with Dickie Ord and might well have had an affirmative answer to the question, 'Who Needs Cantona?' as he had played alongside him in their youth at Nimes, not to mention being a teammate of Zinedine Zidane at Bordeaux. As with all cult heroes, though, the feeling the fans had for Perez was mirrored by his love for them: 'I had a very good rapport with the public in France, but not like I have at Sunderland with 42,000 people. It was something very emotional and very special. I play with my heart, I give everything and people know and feel that. People in Sunderland are very proud, and I am very proud as well,' he said, adding after his final sensational performance at the Stadium of Light: 'It is hard to describe the strength the fans give me. What an atmosphere. At the beginning of the game I thought, "Nothing can happen to me here. You don't have to be afraid of anything in front of these people. They are with you."'

THE ARCHDEACON

L.R. ROOSE

Goalkeeper

Born: 27 November 1877, Holt, near Wrexham.
Signed for Sunderland: 14 January 1908 from Stoke
Transferred: 4 April 1911 to Huddersfield

Aberystwyth University
Aberystwyth Town: 1895–1900
Druids: 1900
London Welsh: 1900–01
Stoke City: 1901–04, 81 League appearances
Everton: 1904–05, 18 League appearances
Stoke City: 1905–07, 66 League appearances
Sunderland: 1908–11, 92 League appearances
                                      99 total appearances
Celtic: 1910, 1 Cup semi-final appearance
Port Vale Reserves: 1910, 1 reserve team appearance
Huddersfield Town: 1911, 5 League appearances
Aston Villa: 1911, 10 League appearances
Woolwich Arsenal: 1911–12, 13 League appearances
Aberystwyth Town
Llandudno

The modern-day fan can feel alienated by the antics of playboy players. Lurid stories of hotel room liaisons with two women at a time, lavish lifestyles and hob-nobbing with the nation's biggest celebrities can leave some supporters lamenting the loss of decorum associated with times gone by. What would people from a century ago have made of the behaviour of some so called modern-day stars who do not always take things seriously, and whose every move is documented in tabloid 'kiss and tells'?

Early portrait of L.R. Roose.

A century ago it was exactly such behaviour that helped make goalkeeper L.R. Roose a massive cult hero on Wearside. Such was his reputation that he was given a rapturous reception when he returned to Roker in the colours of Arsenal, after his departure from the club was commemorated by a gala dinner in his honour and the presentation of an illuminated manuscript handed over on behalf of the people of Sunderland in recognition of what Roose had done for the club. This was in marked contrast to a return Roose made to Stoke, the club he spent longest at, where the crowd invaded the pitch to literally chase him out of town!

This was a man who thought nothing of sitting on the crossbar and chatting to supporters while play was at the other end, a man who once conceded a goal in a full international match because he had turned his back on the play to tell jokes, a man who courted the country's most notorious sexually charged personality, music hall star Marie Lloyd, and who was known to have a woman or two lined up in almost every town he played. On one occasion he bedded a beauty queen in a competition he had judged, only to be caught in the act by his girlfriend.

Leigh Richmond Roose claimed to be a doctor, although he was not qualified, signed himself 'The Archdeacon' because of the religious family he came from, and numbered the author of *The War of the Worlds* – H.G. Wells – among his schoolteachers. Roose played as an amateur, although his 'expenses' must have made him the club's costliest player – he occasionally chartered his own personal train to get him to the match and charged it to the club. In addition, his regular habit of bouncing the ball right up to the halfway line when it was still within the laws for a goalkeeper to handle the ball that far away from goal, resulted in the laws of the game being changed.

Sunderland fans loved him…even though on a visit to Wearside as a Stoke player a couple of years before he signed for Sunderland he had punched a Sunderland supporter unconscious!

Roose kept goal for Sunderland on the day they won 9–1 away to Newcastle in 1908. A century on from that historic occasion no team have ever surpassed Sunderland's achievement in registering a record top-flight away win. Newcastle would be the opposition again in 1910 when Roose was injured, never to play for Sunderland again. Six years later he was dead, slain on the battlefields of World War One.

Debate in contemporary football constantly rages over 4–5–1, 4–4–2, the wisdom or otherwise of playing one up front, someone 'in the hole' or a midfield diamond. It used to be a simple game, football. Way back in Roose's Edwardian era players had a position and they stayed in it. The emphasis may well have been largely on attack compared to the modern game, but positions were set in stone. If you were a full-back you stayed back, none of those Dick Malone-esque marauding runs thank you very much. If you were centre-forward you could damn well stay on the halfway line if your team were defending a corner, never mind coming back to defend the 'front stick'.

Dick Roose dared to be different. In fact he dared do just about anything. In his day the laws of the game allowed goalkeepers to handle the ball anywhere inside their own half. For other goalkeepers this barely mattered because coming off their line was not something many were keen on, let alone bouncing the ball halfway up the pitch. Roose, though, revelled in it. A game did not go by without him bringing the ball halfway up the pitch and then launching it to a teammate in a position to strike. Roose's teammate George Holley, still Sunderland's fourth-highest ever goalscorer, benefitted more than most from Roose's raids and reckoned, 'He was the only one who did it because he was the only one who could kick or throw a ball that accurately over long distances, giving himself time to return to his goal without fear of conceding.'*

L.R. Roose.

L.R. Roose was larger than life. He was the kind of chap who would fill a room through his sheer presence. Goalkeepers then and now have thrived on being perceived as a bit different, even crazy at times, and Roose set standards in that direction that no amount of South American goalkeepers – Paraguay's Chilavert and his free-kicks on the edge of the opposition box, Colombia's Higuita with his scorpion kick, imprisonment for kidnapping and dribbling to the halfway line, or Campos of Mexico and his vomit-inducing personally designed goalkeeper kits – can even dream of getting near to!

'He was always something of an exhibitionist. It didn't matter whether he was playing in front of thousands of spectators or just a couple of people in his back garden. He would always play to a crowd. He saw himself as an entertainer,'* according to his nephew Dick Jenkins.

Roose marked his international debut for Wales in 1900 by bowing to the crowd behind his goal before leaving the pitch at half-time, he had a pre-match ritual that bordered on the obsessive, not to say affected, reportedly pacing around his goal talking away to himself, and he would wave to the crowd in a manner taken for granted now but unheard of then. On the occasion of his Football League debut for Stoke in 1901 he announced his arrival by racing onto the pitch and bowing to all four sides of the ground, before swinging on the crossbar before the game even kicked-off.

Sometimes modern goalkeepers will make a save that looks a bit flashier than it needs to be, some like the photographers to capture a shot as well as them. Roose made sure people knew when he had made a good save, as from time to time he was wont to follow a save by climbing on to the crossbar to acknowledge the applause. Just imagine Roy Keane's reaction if Craig Gordon tried that! On Roose's second home appearance for Sunderland, on New Year's Day 1908 against Woolwich Arsenal, he is reported to have saved a shot with his chest, caught the rebound on his foot and then indulged in a bit of 'keepy-uppy'.

If he had been useless the supporters would have tortured him. Walter Scott, the goalkeeper brought in by Sunderland the season after Roose left, was sacked by the club, with the *Sunderland Echo* of 21 September 1912 reporting his complaint that, 'some spectators had not given him a chance, as at every match a certain clique gathered round the goal and throughout the game made use of offensive epithets towards him. This was enough to make him downhearted and put him off his play.'

Roose would not be so easily put off. Football fans have always included their fickle element, and Sunderland have had their share. Dick Malone referred to his 'six favourite fans' who gave him stick 60-odd years later, but the wise-cracking know alls, who of course could always do better than the player they had paid to watch, were unlikely to take on the powerful Wales international goalkeeper. In 1906 Roose played at Roker Park for Stoke. Games between the two clubs have rarely been classics and this one was no different, a single goal settling matters for the home side, but the post match excitement made up for it. Players, officials and guests met afterwards for a meal and a drink but one Sunderland supporter, evidently somewhat the worse for wear, had some less than pleasant things to say about the visitors. It all became too much for Roose when he overheard his team being described as, 'Ten cads and a goalkeeper.' Not restricted by the penalty area during games, he similarly burst beyond accepted bounds here, marching over to the loudmouth and delivered a haymaker, knocking the chap out.

Leigh received a two-week suspension from the FA for his troubles, but when he began playing for Sunderland just under two years later supporters already knew that they tangled with this man at their peril. The crowd loved him though. At Sunderland Roose found fans as passionate as him, people who would not take any rubbish at all but people who, once you earned their respect, you had it forever. When it was time for Roose to leave Roker one of the things the club gave him from the proceeds of a collection was a silver box containing a piece of grass from the pitch at Roker Park, and inscribed, 'From 10 cads to a goalkeeper.'

He arrived at the right time to become a hero. Almost four years had passed since Sunderland's first great goalkeeper Ted Doig had departed after over 450 appearances. Doig was a top goalkeeper, and in the century since Sunderland supporters have simply expected to have a class custodian. Eight had been tried but none had matched the standards set by Doig until Roose's arrival. It is not as if Roose did not concede many, in the season he arrived Sunderland let in more goals then any team in the country, 15 more than bottom of the table Birmingham. On the other hand, only champions Manchester United outscored them.

Supporters lapped up his antics, be it the pre-match warm up, the chatting and joking with the crowd, his habit of dishing out the sort of robust challenges that goalkeepers normally were on the receiving end of, or the way in which despite being the 'keeper he was very much the first line of attack as well as the last line of defence. Beyond the showmanship, L.R. Roose was a top-class goalkeeper, perhaps not just the best in the country. Commonly known as 'The Prince of Goalkeepers' before he joined Sunderland, Roose had been named in a 'World XI' selected by *The Daily Mail*.

In his first full season he helped Sunderland to third place, their highest for six seasons after some indifferent mid-table finishes. The highlight came in December 1908 when he was part of the team that triumphed 9–1 away to Newcastle. The match turned on the one goal Newcastle scored, Roose only being beaten by a most controversial penalty on the stroke of half-time that meant the sides went in level. Goodness knows how furious the Sunderland players were in that interval, and no doubt Roose had as much to say as anyone, but just 28 minutes after the re-start Sunderland had produced their best-ever display by scoring a further eight times without reply.

Roose was to have only one more full season before a return trip to Tyneside brought his days as Sunderland 'keeper to an end. He was making his 99th appearance for the Lads on 19 November 1910. Sunderland went into the derby as League leaders, unbeaten in the opening dozen games. Always capable of handing knocks out, Roose was not about to whinge when he was on the receiving end and sportingly refused to attach any blame to his opponent for the injury in what was a phenomenally more physical game then than it is now. 'I got the ball in my hands when Rutherford came at me with his two knees. My left arm made a sort of lever for him, but it could not stand the strain and broke.'

Caricature of L.R. Roose in his Sunderland days.

After two months in plaster, Roose attempted a comeback but was never considered fit enough to play for Sunderland, although he returned to international action with Wales by early March. Despite living and working in London he still travelled to Sunderland games, standing on the terraces alongside supporters to cheer the team on and further endear himself to the crowd.

Unable to regain his place, Roose decided to leave. As an amateur he could not be bound by contracts, but there was no bad feeling, and his departure from Wearside was on the best of terms. Not for the first time Sunderland applied to the FA for permission to stage a benefit match in his honour, but also not for the first time the FA – constantly frustrated by what they viewed as Roose's abuse of his amateur status due to outrageous expenses claims – refused to sanction such a game.

Instead a gala dinner was organised in Sunderland to show appreciation for him. It was the second such occasion he had been honoured in this way. After a mere 14 games with the club, his role in helping stave off a first-ever relegation (that would continue to be staved off for a further half century) was marked by a dinner where he was presented with an 'Illuminated Address' which remains in the possession of the Roose family to this day. This four-page leather-bound document paid tribute to the contribution L.R. Roose had made: 'On the behalf of the inhabitants of Sunderland and District, we the members of the Testimonial Committee, ask your acceptance of this address as an expression of our appreciation of the very valuable services you rendered to Sunderland Football Club during the 1907/08 season. We feel that the satisfactory position obtained by the club in the League table at the end of the season was largely due to the splendid and masterly exposition of goal defence shown by you at the most critical period of the club's history. Nor can we forget the services you so generously gave to the club, or overlook the confidence you inspired among the other members of the team. We trust that your connection with the club will, as hitherto, be harmonious and pleasant, and in the name of a very large and representative body of subscribers, we offer our most hearty good wishes for your future welfare.'

What a magnificent tribute. After such a beginning, no wonder that the supporters took the Welshman to their hearts. If the Sunderland crowd like you they will forgive you just about anything. All of the cult heroes in this book made mistakes from time to time, they are only human after all. In Roose's case, probably his most embarrassing moment for Sunderland came at Bramall Lane in 1909 when Sheffield United's 'keeper Ernest Needham got on the score sheet with a kick from one end to the other that caught Roose out of position having gone walkabout. Later the same season he missed Sunderland's home match with Bolton to represent Wales against Scotland at Kilmarnock, only to concede the game's only goal four minutes from time because he was preoccupied with chatting to a spectator when beaten from 40 yards.

Being seen to drop a clanger did not dissuade the Scots of Roose's reputation for being probably the best goalkeeper in Britain. As Celtic were in the middle of a goalkeeping injury crisis they asked him to play for them the following weekend when they had a Scottish Cup semi-final against Clyde. Being an amateur player not under professional contract to any club, Roose was at liberty to accept, which he did, and so instead of playing for Sunderland at Chelsea he could not resist the opportunity of playing in the semi-final north of the border. As he did throughout his time with Sunderland, Leigh lived in London because of his job at Kings College Hospital in Holborn. He sometimes claimed to be a doctor, but he never qualified. He did pass preliminary exams but kept withdrawing from the degree course he always said he intended to take, as more and more football offers – and the love of the high life – came his way.

An appearance at Stamford Bridge would have been a nice easy trip for him…but also a not very profitable one on the expenses front, whereas a trip all the way to Glasgow…well that was a different proposition.

Having blundered when not concentrating against Scotland a week earlier, the outing for Celtic proved to be another disaster as two of his mistakes cost Celtic the game and the chance of the double, as they went on to clinch the title. Roose may have been a hero to Sunderland supporters, but he was a villain in the eyes of Celtic's followers and argued vehemently with them as he left the pitch.

Restored to the Sunderland line up despite saying 'I don't want to go to Chelsea' three quarters of a century before Elvis Costello, Roose was to miss one more Sunderland game that season, again preferring to play for someone else. This time, though, it was not the glamour of a Scottish Cup semi-final appearance for Celtic that lured him away, it was the magnetic pull of the opportunity to turn out for Port Vale reserves that made him forgo Sunderland's final home First Division match of the season against Bradford City!

The son of a Presbyterian Minister, 'He who would Valiant be' did so because it afforded him the chance to return to his former club Stoke City. It was an unmissable opportunity to return to the club for whom he had made 146 of his career total of 284 League games and twice left in acrimonious circumstances over expense payments. Stoke at this time were not even members of the two-tier Football League. They had resigned because of financial reasons in 1907 – probably due in some part to the outlandish expense claims of Roose, who at his most lavish allegedly once presented the Potters with the bill for chartering his own private train from London to get him to their game! Stoke remained out of the Football League until 1919, three years after Roose's death.

Like Sunderland, Stoke have not been short of their share of great goalkeepers, Gordon Banks and Peter Shilton are among those to have given great service to the club. L.R. Roose takes his place alongside goalkeepers of that calibre. Stoke first attracted him with the offer of an unlimited expense account in 1901. His lavish London lifestyle could not be funded on his salary working at Kings College hospital. Only the best restaurants, the best West End shows and an assortment of women would suffice for football's first playboy, and Stoke's treasurer must have shuddered every time an expenses claim arrived. Stoke put up with this while they had the money to pay their star man and key player, but when their finances became strained so did their relationship with Leigh, who felt that his performances meant he was keeping his side of the bargain.

After helping save Stoke from relegation at the end of that 1904–05 season Roose left the club, planning to ignore football and concentrate on his medical studies. Imagine Craig Gordon retiring in his mid-20s (Roose was 26 at this stage). If he was out of contract there would be a queue a mile long trying to get his signature. As an amateur, Roose was not bound by a contract and was available to anyone, probably the club best able to bankroll extravagant expenses, but he rejected the long list of clubs who pursued him.

A bit like a supporter who does not renew their season ticket after a bad season and then is fed up being dragged around the shops every Saturday afternoon and cannot wait to start going to the match again, Roose began to miss the game and accepted an offer from Everton in November. Oddly enough, he debuted against Sunderland and cost the Toffees the only goal of the game when a cross did not stick and he dropped it at the feet of Arthur Bridgett. Bridgett had been his teammate at Stoke, would be in the future, and replaced Leigh in goal when injured on his final Sunderland appearance.

Despite the bad start, Roose did well for Everton, helping them to runners'-up spot in the League and the semi-final of the FA Cup. Twice the Cup run took him back to Stoke, Everton dismissing Stoke and later meeting Aston Villa there in the semi-final. On both occasions he was afforded a hero's welcome. That may well have contributed to Leigh returning for a second spell with Stoke after he had fallen out with Everton.

If anything Roose did better in his second spell in the Potteries. Mid-table in the top flight in his first year back everything was going well, but when Stoke slumped to relegation in his second season economies began to bite again resulting in the most acrimonious departure. With the club in dire financial straits someone leaked information about payments being made to an unnamed player, who everyone knew was Roose. Livid at being cast as a villain, Leigh left the club for Sunderland early the following season.

In the contemporary game there are a handful of high-profile individuals who have had their names besmirched by rumoured financial wrongdoings. Even when unproven, such people have had to live with the whiff of suspicion that follows them. This was the scenario that surrounded Leigh Richmond Roose when he came to Sunderland. It was the reason the FA twice refused to sanction benefit matches Sunderland wanted to give him, and why instead Sunderland tried to at least show its appreciation by way of the 'Illuminated Address.'

Thus, it was that on St George's Day 1910 a meaningless end-of-season game between Sunderland and Bradford was no place for a man with a point to prove who could be playing against Stoke on their own patch for their local rivals Port Vale, reserve match or not!

Given a hero's welcome as a visitor with Everton after his first departure, there was to be no warm welcome for Roose on this occasion. He appeared to know as much, choosing to wear an old Stoke top to keep goal for Vale and refusing to change out of it when asked to. The outcome of the game would seal the destination of the local reserve League title, but evidently Roose wanted to show Stoke what they were missing and played out of his skin. Leigh had made his point and two thirds of the way through the game his former fans had seen enough and invaded the pitch to make a point of their own. Once their hero, the stories of what Roose had cost the ailing club combined with his provocative appearance for their local rivals in an old Stoke shirt resulted in City fans literally chasing him off the pitch and out of the ground.

Unruffled, Roose was back in goal for Sunderland at Hillsborough a week later, but there was to be just 13 more appearances for the Wearsiders the following season before injury struck.

If Carlsberg did comic book football characters, surely it would have to be L.R. Roose. In so many ways he was years and years ahead of his time. In the last 30 years or so several 'keepers have been renowned for being prepared to race out of their box to clear danger; David James, Bruce Grobbelaar and Ray Clemence have all been alert to the need to sometimes dash out and effectively act as a sweeper, but Roose made this into an art form long before any of their fathers were born.

L.R. Roose's nephew Dick Jenkins with the Illuminated Address presented to L.R. Roose on behalf of Sunderland supporters.

Moreover, players now are increasingly aware of the money to be made from memorabilia, but despite two players netting hat-tricks when Sunderland hammered the Magpies 9–1 it was goalkeeper Roose who took the match ball home!

Showing the same contempt for authority as Len Shackleton would do half a century on, Roose responded to a request to itemise his expenses, which were subject to close inspection, with such items as a charge for a pistol to ward off the opposition!

Whether such opposition where the pistol may be required meant onrushing forwards or irate husbands and boyfriends is open to conjecture. While tabloid sex scandals involving footballers are 10 a penny nowadays, they were the source of sensation in Roose's day. Most notoriously he enjoyed a hugely public relationship with the top music hall star of the day Marie Lloyd, possibly the first 'Posh and Becks' in the game, not that Marie Lloyd was posh! Known for living close to the edge and for being sexually flirtatious in an age where decorum was the done thing, Lloyd made the perfect partner in terms of putting Leigh on the news pages before the word 'celebrity' had even entered the language.

Roose became one of the game's most recognisable faces in an age when faces of famous people were not generally known, because there were few photographs in newspapers or early match programmes, while TV, let alone the internet, simply did not exist. During this era, footballers were so unrecognisable outside their home area that players selected for international matches were issued with an admittance card so they could get into stadiums where they were meant to be playing.

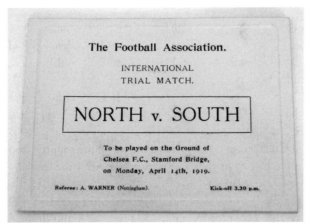

The Football Association.

INTERNATIONAL
TRIAL MATCH.

NORTH v. SOUTH

To be played on the Ground of
Chelsea F.C., Stamford Bridge,
on Monday, April 14th, 1919.

Referee: A. WARNER (Nottingham).   Kick-off 3.30 p.m.

Player's admittance card so players could gain admittance to grounds for internationals. Roose was one of the few not to need these as his face was so well known.

This, of course, only added to his reputation as a larger-than-life character. So too did his fondness of being less than serious at times. Roose was known as a practical joker. His captain at Sunderland, Charlie Thomson, used to say, 'You wouldn't know if he was serious' when commenting on whether Roose meant it when asking people in crowds if they would like to buy him dinner that night. Most famously he turned up for an international match in Ireland in March 1909 with his hand bandaged and claiming to have broken two bones. Saying he was determined to play, he waited until the game had kicked-off before removing the bandage to reveal there was no injury after all.

Playing that international meant he missed Sunderland's defeat at the hands of bottom of the table Leicester Fosse. Altogether Leigh played 24 times for his country, winning his last nine caps while with Sunderland. Until Thomas Sorensen came on the scene 90 years later those nine caps were more than the combined total won by every other goalkeeper while on Sunderland's books.

Roose's international debut had come before his Football League debut as he was playing for Aberystwyth Town when he first represented Wales in February 1900, keeping a clean sheet as Ireland were beaten at Llandudno. It was a great month for Leigh as Aberystwyth Town also won the Welsh Cup, Leigh being carried shoulder high by the club's supporters at the Final.

Roose had made his name playing for Aberystwyth University initially and later played for Druids before representing London Welsh. His career path had then been Stoke, Everton and Stoke again before he joined Sunderland. Subsequent to his Sunderland career and not withstanding 'guest' appearances for teams as diverse as Celtic to Port Vale Reserves, L.R. Roose went on to play for Huddersfield, Aston Villa, Woolwich Arsenal, Aberystwyth Town again and finally Llandudno. Regardless of which team he was playing for, however, Roose always wore his unwashed Aberystwyth Town shirt he had worn when winning the Welsh Cup for luck.

Sixteen months after his final game for Sunderland he was afforded a 'homecoming', reserved for crowd favourites, when supporters greeted his arrival at the railway station. After playing well for Woolwich Arsenal, who were beaten 1–0, he threw his Woolwich Arsenal shirt to supporters as a token of his appreciation of their support.

Leigh's trademark bouncing of the ball to the halfway line was still firmly in evidence, but in that summer of 1912 the Football Association – still evidently not fans of Roose – amended the Laws of the game so that from that day to this the goalkeeper may only handle the ball within his penalty area. Few goalkeepers were affected by this and none so much as Roose, but it is strange to think that when a goalkeeper is sent off for handling marginally outside the box what Leigh Richmond Roose would make of it.

Such trivialities as the amending of the laws of a game soon paled into insignificance, as Roose and a generation of young men would be sacrificed in the Great War. Enlisting in the Royal Army

Medical Corps in 1914, Leigh was in France by October, while back at home the Football League continued in full until the end of that season. Before the football season was over Leigh had reached one of the killing fields of the World War One, Gallipoli. In 1916 Roose joined the Royal Fusiliers, going on to be awarded the Military Medal for bravery.

On 7 October 1912, 28,000 people saw two goals from George Holley – who Roose corresponded with during the war – help Sunderland turn a half-time deficit into a 3–1 win away to Aston Villa. Exactly four years later L. R. Roose was sent 'over the top' and into battle as a Royal Fusilier, somewhere near the French town of Gueudecourt. Roose had been one of the country's top sportsmen, one of the greatest characters in the history of the game and a figure who, though long forgotten now, was perhaps the only Sunderland player to have enough stories about him to outshine even Len Shackleton. He had lived the high life that London could offer, he had by all accounts bedded more women than your average 21st-century rapper, and here he found himself, facing machine-gun fire and seeing his friends killed in front of him. The son of a pacifist, his father's case would be strengthened by the senseless waste of millions of people who died in World War One, that figure including Leigh Richmond Roose, who was killed just four years to the day since a carefree afternoon as Sunderland's goalkeeper at Villa Park. Sunderland's left-back that day, Albert Milton, would also lose his life to the war. Lance Corporal L.R. Roose (or Rouse as the army accidentally recorded his name) was last seen alive by the former England amateur international Gordon Hoare.

Only 38, Leigh Richmond Roose had led a life and a half when he became one of the tragic victims of the Great War. He played fewer games for Sunderland than there have been years since his first, and yet the impression he made on Sunderland supporters is such that he rivals even the greatest of modern-day cult heroes for the accolade of the greatest ever. What is certain is that Leigh Richmond Roose proved that even 100 years ago Sunderland supporters would take a player to their hearts and keep him there forever. The players featured in this book have all since earned their place in this most special of clubs.

* Quotes marked with an asterisk are used with permission and are taken from Spencer Vignes's excellent book: *Lost in France, 2007.*

ROLL OF HONOUR

Bruce Anderson
Gary Anderson
J Anderson
Ian Bainbridge
A G Barber
Jim Barker
Michael Baron
Matthew Gordon Bell
Stephen Birkett
Chris Broadhurst
Colin Brown
Gordon Brown
Graeme Brown
Norman Brown
James Bundred
Jimmy Cairns
Russell Carter
Niamh Finlay Chadwick
Philip Chater
George Collingwood
David Coombe
The Crooks Family -
Bishop Auckland
Robert David Crosby
Robert Thomas Darbyshire
Colin Dart
Chris Davis
Tom Davis
Diane Dimmock
Alan Dodds
Keith Douglas
David Dowell

Andrew Dunn
Norman Ede
Mark Fawcett
George Fenwick
Phillip J Goodwin
Chris Groves
Scott John Hagan
Chris Harvey
Aoibheann Heaney
John Hellens
Gillian Hill
Dean Hudspith
Chris Lacey
Mike Love
Leonard Lumsden
Joe Marley
Derek (Jack) Mason
Lindsey Mcluckie
Michael McNally
Roy Mills
Alastair Morrison
Sam Mountain
Steven O'Connor
Derek Parker
Brian Patterson
Elliott Carr Patterson
David Plunkett
Carl.J.A.Pritchard
Kevin Ramsey
Eamonn Ratton
Gerard Cairan Ratton
Tony Ratton

Geoff Riseborough
Marshall Ritchie
Norman Robson-Smith
Andrew J Russell
Trevor Selvey
Matthew Peter Sharp
Maurice Sheehan
Andrew Shuttleworth
Clifford Simpson
Pete Sixsmith
Malcolm Slator
Darren Smith
George Smith
Gordon L Smith
Gregory G Smith
David Soulsby
Judith Stanford nee Gurney
M.L.D.D Stook
Joe Syer
Adam David Theaker
Neil Philip Thornton
Cecil Trotter
Steven Tweddle
Matthew Joseph Walker
Ian Webster
Douglas White
Dave Wilding
Paul Wilkinson
Paul Wilkinson
Billy Wilkinson
Thomas Woodward